THE OAKWOOD PRESS

IRELA... NARROW GAUGE RAILWAYS

A Reference Handbook

by
Joe Begley & Steve Flanders

Lartigue Railway, Ballybunion, Co. Kerry

THE OAKWOOD PRESS

© Oakwood Press & Joe Begley & Steve Flanders 2012

British Library Cataloguing in Publication Data
A Record for this book is available from the British Library
ISBN 978 0 85361 710 5

Typeset by Oakwood Graphics.
Repro by PKmediaworks, Cranborne, Dorset.
Printed by Information Press Ltd, Eynsham, Oxford.

Bessbrook & Newry Tramway power car, 4th June, 1932.
H.C. Casserley, courtesy R.M. Casserley

Front cover : Londonderry & Lough Swilly Railway Hudswell, Clarke 4-8-0 No. 12 makes a fine sight in July 1937 as she passes the back gardens of Old Town and over the level crossing into Letterkenny station with the afternoon passenger working from Burtonport, Co. Donegal. *R.W. Kidner/Oakwood Collection*
Rear cover, top: Two Tralee & Dingle Railway locomotives haul a typical mixed train comprising general freight, cattle empties and passenger carriages towards Dingle near Ballinsteenig station in deepest Co. Kerry on 4th September, 1938. *R.W. Kidner/Oakwood Collection*
Rear cover, bottom: Apart from its innovative railcar, the Clogher Valley Railway also used this freight version. Known as the 'Unit' she is seen here bringing a mixed train into Brookborough station in July 1937. After a subsequent accident which damaged the cab of railcar No. 10, the Unit's cab replaced that of the railcar and can still be seen today in the railway gallery of the Ulster Folk and Transport Museum, Cultra, Co. Down.
Title page: Postcard depicting the remarkable twin-boilered monorail locomotive No. 2 of the Listowel & Ballybunnion Railway. Note the trestle-style track and the curved pointwork - shunting was always a complicated process. *John Langford Collection*

Published by The Oakwood Press (Usk), P.O. Box 13, Usk, Mon., NP15 1YS.
E-mail: sales@oakwoodpress.co.uk
Website: www.oakwoodpress.co.uk

Contents

Introduction 4

Chapter One   A Short History of the

Irish Narrow Gauge Railways 5

Chapter Two   The Ballymena, Cushendall & Red Bay Railway 15

Chapter Three   The Ballymena & Larne Railway 19

Chapter Four   The Ballycastle Railway 27

Chapter Five   The Giant's Causeway Tramway 33

Chapter Six   The Portstewart Tramway 37

Chapter Seven   The Londonderry & Lough Swilly Railway 41

Chapter Eight   The County Donegal Railways Joint Committee 51

Chapter Nine   The Castlederg & Victoria Bridge Tramway 65

Chapter Ten   The Bessbrook & Newry Tramway 69

Chapter Eleven   The Dublin & Lucan Steam Tramway 73

Chapter Twelve   The Clogher Valley Railway 77

Chapter Thirteen   The Cavan & Leitrim Railway 83

Chapter Fourteen   The West Clare Railway 93

Chapter Fifteen   The Listowel & Ballybunion Railway 103

Chapter Sixteen   The Tralee & Dingle Railway 107

Chapter Seventeen   The Schull & Skibbereen Railway 115

Chapter Eighteen   The Cork, Blackrock & Passage Railway 121

Chapter Nineteen   The Cork & Muskerry Light Railway 127

Chapter Twenty   Irish Narrow Gauge Today 132

Appendix One   Irish Narrow Gauge Mileage 1875-1961 134

Appendix Two   Railway Locomotives 136

Appendix Three   Narrow Gauge Coupling Heights 139

Appendix Four   Rolling Stock Drawings 139

Bibliography 151

Introduction

Like most students of the Irish narrow gauge, we came to know of these little railways only after they had gone. Thankfully there was a band of enthusiasts attracted to these lines who committed their memories to print and picture, saving a flavour for those unable to have witnessed the railways at first hand. Transport museums and, more recently, preservation bodies, have also helped by salvaging some of the rolling stock. In recent years, there has been increasing interest in the Irish narrow gauge among railway modellers, with an expansion in the number of commercial kits and products now available.

The factual information contained in this booklet has been gleaned over the years from diverse sources including the many books and journals listed and discussion with many like-minded individuals. In compiling the various tables we have attempted to represent what we feel is the most reliable information. We are more than aware that differences of opinion exist and the passage of time makes access to original records more difficult. This work is not intended as a substitute for the many excellent books and articles on the subject and the reader is referred to the Bibliography for a list of those available for the various railways.

We are indebted to Richard Casserley, John Langford and the Stephenson Locomotive Society for the use of their photographs, and to the many friends and associates with whom we have enjoyed discussions on the subject of Ireland's railways over the years.

All royalties from the sale of this book are being donated to Irish narrow gauge preservation.

Joe Begley, Steve Flanders
2012

Tralee & Dingle Railway 2-6-2T No. 5 near Lispole on 4th September, 1938.
R.W. Kidner/Oakwood Collection

Chapter One

A Short History of the
Irish Narrow Gauge Railways

The narrow gauge railways of Ireland were a fascinating collection of lines built, often in the wildest and most impoverished parts of the land, each with its own individual character and tales of struggle for survival. Though narrow gauge, the 3 ft gauge adopted resulted in rolling stock of a size not too distant from that of the 5 ft 3 in. standard gauge and some engines, such as the magnificent Lough Swilly 4-8-4 tanks, were as heavy and as powerful as their standard gauge counterparts.

The Irish narrow gauge systems were born out of the developing Irish railway network of the mid-1850s. Having settled on a standard gauge of 5 ft 3 in., numerous lines snaked out across the landscape to eventually connect large centres and ports, each sponsored by independent concerns, though amalgamations and takeovers soon occurred. The desire to capitalize on this expanding network led to a number of proposals for branch lines to ever more remote parts of the country and it was generally in these more remote parts that the narrower gauge of 3 ft was adopted.

But the very nature of the countryside they served often meant they were doomed to struggle from the outset. The majority of lines were to be found on the western seaboard where the land is poor and the weather often severe. The potato blight that produced famine conditions for the Irish peasant in the 1840s spawned an emigration culture that was to continue through the 19th and well into the 20th century. Over their lifetime, narrow gauge lines were to witness a diminishing catchment population as the younger people left to find a better life in the growing cities, or further afield. Falling earning potential, accompanied by ever rising costs, would contribute to their ultimate downfall.

The 3 ft gauge lines had their origin in the hills of County Antrim, to the east of Ballymena, where rich iron ore deposits had been identified in the 1840s, though mining did not begin in earnest until the late 1860s. Lack of local coal deposits meant the ore could not be smelted in Ireland but had to be shipped to industrial Britain and, as the nearest railway was the Belfast & Northern Counties in Ballymena, this required ore to be transported overland and then taken by train to the ports of Belfast or Larne for shipment. The nature of the roads in Antrim and the anticipated volume of ore made this an impractical option so an alternative was to construct a railway line to the Antrim coast. Proposals were first advanced for a line from Ballymena to Cushendall with an extension on to the relatively sheltered harbour at Red Bay. Parliamentary approval for the Ballymena, Cushendall & Red Bay Railway (BC&RBR), to be built to a gauge not exceeding 3 ft, was granted on the 18th July, 1872.

But the mantle of the first Irish 3 ft gauge line to open went to the nearby Glenariff Railway, an independent line built to convey iron ore from the Antrim Hills to the coast, four miles away and 610 ft below. It was built by the Glenariff Iron Ore and Harbour Company and as it was built entirely on private land with the aim only to carry ore and not passengers, it did not require

Parliamentary approval. The line opened for traffic in 1872 and continued in operation until 1882, being fatally affected by the downturn in the iron trade during the 1870s. Though some attempts were made to reopen the line and to connect with the nearby BC&RBR, these proved unsuccessful and the company was liquidated in 1885. Its assets were auctioned to discharge its debts, primarily unpaid ground rent. At auction, the company's two engines and some 40 wagons were bought by the Londonderry & Lough Swilly Railway (L&LSR), which was then undergoing a process of re-gauging to 3 ft.

Meanwhile, the BC&RBR had opened as far as Cargan in May 1875 and Retreat in October 1876. Further progress from here to Red Bay would have resulted in a descent of 1,000 ft in some 5½ miles and the prospect of such severe grades resulted in a rethink, which meant the line was extended no further and the company had the distinction of not serving one of the destinations in its title. But the positive experience gained was to influence the adoption of the 3 ft gauge widely in Ireland, first, locally with the Ballymena & Larne and Ballycastle lines, opened in 1877 and 1880 respectively, but also further afield, and the 1880s were to witness a rapid expansion of such railways.

Northern Counties Committee locomotive No. 42 at Ballycastle. *John Langford Collection*

Private finance resulted in eight new narrow gauge railways during this decade. The Letterkenny Railway Company was originally incorporated in July 1860, though 23 years, several route alterations and several further Acts were to pass before the line eventually opened. The final Act of 1880 included the proposal to construct a line from Letterkenny to link to the Londonderry & Lough Swilly Railway to the 3 ft gauge, based on the experience of the Antrim lines. The standard gauge L&LSR had opened in 1863 to Farland Point, and to Buncrana the year later. The Farland branch was soon abandoned and the Letterkenny line was to link to this abandoned section and join the L&LSR at Tooban Junction. The 1880 Act also authorized the L&LSR to regauge its line and this was achieved in 1885.

Earlier, in April 1882, the West Donegal Railway (WDR) opened, following many years agitation by the traders and people of Donegal to have a westward extension of the Finn Valley Railway (FVR) from Stranorlar to their town. The standard gauge FVR had opened in 1863, linking Stranorlar to Strabane on what was to become the Great Northern Railway of Ireland (GNR(I)) network. The WDR only went ahead after the decision was made to build to the 3 ft gauge based on the emerging experience of this gauge in Antrim. However, funds ran out resulting in the line terminating in a field at Druminnin, four miles east of Donegal. It was to be another seven years before Donegal was reached.

In June of the same year, 1882, Ireland's first roadside tramway opened linking the coastal village of Portstewart with the nearby GNR(I) with a line of just over one mile. In July the following year, the Castlederg & Victoria Bridge Tramway connected the village of Castlederg in County Tyrone to the GNR(I) at Victoria Bridge, while the Dublin & Lucan Tramway began services between the village of Lucan on the River Liffey to the Dublin United Tramways terminus at Conyngham Road, next to the Phoenix Park. Two electric tramways were also opened, both using hydro-electric power. The first, the Giant's Causeway Tramway opened from Portrush to Bushmills in January 1883, extending the final two miles to the Giant's Causeway in 1887. The second, the Bessbrook & Newry Tramway, followed in October 1885, linking the flax mill town of Bessbrook to Newry, just over three miles distant. Additionally, a unique little railway was built between Listowel and the seaside town of Ballybunion, the only example of the Lartigue monorail system in the British Isles.

The Tramways & Public Companies (Ireland) Act of August 1883 replaced earlier acts of the same name which, since 1862, had allowed the construction of tramways along public roads, though at first only animal power was permitted and even when mechanical power was authorized, speed restrictions of 6 mph persisted. The 1883 Act removed speed restrictions for lines constructed more than 30 feet from the centre of the road. The Act also offered State assistance in the shape of a guarantee to the Baronies, whereby the Government would repay half of the Baronies' liability under the Baronial Guarantee arrangements, provided it did not exceed 2 per cent of capital and the line was operational.

Under the terms of this Act, six lines were incorporated, the first being the Cavan, Leitrim & Roscommon Light Railway & Tramway Co., later abbreviated to the more familiar Cavan & Leitrim Railway (C&LR) when proposed extensions into Co. Roscommon never materialized. Approval was granted for construction of three sequential light railways totaling 33¾ miles from Dromod on the Midland Great Western Railway through central Leitrim to Belturbet on the Great Northern Railway, in County Cavan. In addition, a 14¾ mile tramway was authorized from Ballinamore to Arigna. Further to the north, the Clogher Valley Tramway began life in December 1883 and secured permission for construction of a roadside tramway, 37 miles in length, through the counties of Tyrone and Fermanagh and linking the Great Northern Railway stations of Maguiresbridge and Tynan. In West Cork, the West Carbery Tramways & Light Railways Co. Ltd was incorporated to construct two tramways: the Schull & Skibbereen Tramways & Light Railways and the Skibbereen, Glandore and Union Hall Tramways & Light Railways, though strong local opposition led to the cancellation of the latter proposal. The Schull & Skibbereen linked the broad gauge Cork, Bandon & South Coast Railway station at Skibbereen with the small fishing village of Schull, 15½ miles westward around Roaring Water Bay.

In suburban Cork, the Cork & Muskerry Light Railway (C&MLR) provided a 15½ mile route from Western Road in Cork to Coachford, with a 2¼ mile branch to Blarney. A separate company, the Donoughmore Extension Light Railway, was subsequently formed to construct an 8½ mile branch to Donoughmore from St Anne's on the Blarney line, though this was always worked by the C&MLR. The West Clare Railway Co. Ltd (WCR) was incorporated in December 1883 to construct 27 miles of railway of 3 ft gauge from Ennis to Miltown Malbay. The South Clare Railway Co. Ltd (SCR) was registered as a public limited liability company on the 9th June the following year and their proposal, to construct a line from Cappa Pier, on the Shannon Estuary, to Kilrush and Kilkee and extending northwards to join the West Clare at Miltown Malbay, achieved the necessary approval on 6th July, 1884. Although nominally a separate company, the SCR shared a number of Directors and other major posts with the WCR and the line was operated by the WCR throughout. The sixth and perhaps the most spectacular of these new lines was the Tralee & Dingle Light Railway (T&DR), whose 31½-mile main line from Tralee to Dingle, crossed the Dingle peninsula's Slieve Mish mountains on some of the steepest gradients of the Irish narrow gauge. In addition, a predominantly flat branch line from Castlegregory Junction near Camp largely followed the road to Castlegregory, six miles distant. The Act also allowed the West Donegal to complete its line from its unsatisfactory temporary terminus at Druminnin to Donegal town.

Through the 1890s there followed a series of mergers, re-gauging and extension. Within a few short years of opening, the WDR was beset with financial difficulties and in 1892 it formally merged with the FVR to become the Donegal Railway Company, with the FVR converting to the narrow gauge the following year. A Royal Commission, headed by Sir John Allport, had been appointed to examine the efficiency of the railways and recommended the construction of light railways. Consequently, the Government passed the Light Railways (Ireland) Act of 1889 authorizing further state assistance. The Donegal Railway benefited from this funding with the construction of a further 43 miles of permanent way, comprising extensions from Donegal to Killybegs and from Stranorlar to Glenties, opened in 1893 and 1895 respectively.

In 1891, the Government formed the Congested Districts Board, aimed at improving the lot of residents of those areas, mainly in the west of Ireland, where the land was too poor to support the local population. Following the recommendations of the Board, the Government passed further legislation in the form of the Railways (Ireland) Act of 1896, under which, if it could be proven that a railway was necessary for development of a district and if an existing company would develop and maintain the line, the Treasury would make free grants towards the construction of the line. Two lines were built under this act - the Buncrana to Carndonagh and the Letterkenny to Burtonport extensions, both operated by the L&LSR. Government involvement was something of a mixed blessing as the L&LSR was to discover - often there were differences of opinion in construction between the company and the Government agencies who were anxious to contain cost.

The birth of the 20th century brought further expansion, mainly in Donegal, with the opening of the Government-funded Carndonagh (1901) and Burtonport (1903) extensions and the County Donegal Railway's (CDR) independently-financed extensions to Derry (1900) and Ballyshannon (1905). The latter weakened the finances of the CDR considerably and in 1906 the company was acquired jointly by the Midland Railway of Britain and the GNR(I), and was subsequently administered by a committee representing both concerns, the County Donegal Railways Joint Committee (CDRJC). The last addition to the CDRJC's network was the line from Strabane to Letterkenny, opened in 1909 by the nominally-independent Strabane & Letterkenny Railway Company but operated throughout by the CDRJC. This was the last passenger-carrying, narrow gauge line to open in Ireland and brought the CDRJC's mileage to 124½.

In the south, the Cork, Blackrock & Passage Railway (CB&PR), which had opened in 1850 as a suburban, 5 ft 3 in. gauge line, was facing stiff competition from the city's urban tramways and sought to extend further south to Crosshaven. Financial considerations led to a decision to build the extension to 3 ft gauge, with conversion of the existing system. This was achieved in October 1900, with the extension to Crosshaven opening in 1904.

The last narrow gauge line to open was a 4¼ mile extension from Arigna on the Cavan & Leitrim Railway to serve the coal pits of Derreenavoggy and Aughabehy. Such extensions had been opposed by Leitrim County Council for many years but during World War I, when Irish railways were under Government control, land was acquired, the necessary powers granted, and the line opened in June 1920. Within 10 years, it was closed beyond Derreenavoggy, 1½ miles from Arigna.

The 20th century was also to witness the rise of the motor car and the rapid increase of road transport, which was ultimately to bring about the demise of much of the narrow gauge railway system. However, the poor lands of the west of Ireland in particular and the resulting poor condition of the roads meant a lengthy stay of execution for some lines. Typically, the narrow gauge lines had a hand-to-mouth existence until the onset of World War I, when the first real threat to their survival occurred. Defence of the Realm legislation resulted in Irish railways coming under obligatory Government control, which lasted from January 1917 until August 1921, by which time wages had risen steeply and working costs had increased considerably. Though some compensation was available through Government payouts, this was insufficient to offset working costs, and fares increased as a result. An increasing number of private road transport operators appeared offering competition to the railway companies, who, for a number of years, were prevented by legislation from offering their own road services.

The political climate of Ireland was also to create difficulties. The Easter rebellion of 1916 was followed by a protracted war of independence in many of the more rural parts of Ireland. This was to lead to disruption of services, mainly when crews refused to operate trains if British troops were aboard. Such trains that did operate in these circumstances often came under insurgent attack, resulting in cessation of many services. With the ending of hostilities and the creation of the Irish Free State, further unrest followed with the Civil War, when many of the rural lines suffered widespread damage and services were again halted. Such cessations only gave competing road operators further advantage as the local population was forced to seek alternative transport. The creation of the Free State border caused particular problems for the two Donegal lines, where the need for customs inspection was to result in considerable delay and disruption to traffic. The cross-border operation of these two concerns meant they were excluded from the amalgamation of all Irish railway companies, under the Great Southern Railways (GSR) banner, which came into effect on 1st January, 1925.

The post-war economic downturn and subsequent recession resulted in much industrial unrest. Strikes in the mining industry impacted on the railways by disrupting supply and the consequent increases in the cost of coal were a further blow to operating profits. A railway strike of 1933 particularly affected the narrow gauge lines of Northern Ireland. Although many were not directly involved, the GNR(I) was and the dependence of the narrow gauge lines on their broad gauge links resulted in severe curtailment of services, from which some never recovered.

First to close was the unique Listowel & Ballybunion monorail on 14th October, 1924. Never profitable from the outset, it suffered extensive rolling stock damage during the 'Troubles'. Attempts were made for its inclusion in the GSR merger of 1924, but when these proved unsuccessful, a High Court writ for its closure was obtained

The Dublin & Lucan was altered, somewhat surprisingly, to 3 ft 6 in. gauge, and electrified in 1896 but succumbed to bus competition in 1924. It was subsequently reopened and again regauged, on this occasion to 5 ft 3 in., by Dublin United Tramways and survived until 1940.

In Northern Ireland, the little Portstewart Tramway had struggled financially from the outset and after only 15 years went into liquidation in 1897, whereupon it was taken over by the Belfast & Northern Counties Railway which, in turn, subsequently became part of the Northern Counties Committee (NCC) of the Midland Railway (later London, Midland & Scottish Railway (LMS)). Its short roadside route left it particularly vulnerable to road competition and Ireland's first narrow gauge tramway also became the first to close, in January 1926.

The post-war economic climate badly affected the independent Ballycastle Railway Company and when it failed to find any concern willing to take on the operation, it closed to all traffic in April 1924. Eventually, the NCC agreed to take it over and it reopened as the Ballycastle section of the NCC in August 1924, remaining in operation until 1950. The Ballymena, Cushendall & Red Bay section of the NCC fared less well. Traffic from the mines soon diminished and passenger services were withdrawn by the NCC in 1930. The line beyond Rathkenny was closed in 1937, with complete closure three years later.

In Tyrone, the Castlederg & Victoria Bridge Tramway's roadside location also left it vulnerable to the threat of road competition, which rapidly escalated in the 1920s, when a number of operators from Omagh and Derry began to provide services in the Tramway's territory. In response, the company introduced a paraffin-fuelled railcar which briefly provided a competitive mode of passenger traffic. The struggle for financial survival was constant, however, and the death knell was sounded with the withdrawal of labour as part of the 1933 rail strike that affected much of Northern Ireland's railways for 10 weeks early in the year. Operations were never resumed.

The Clogher Valley Railway had also struggled. The Baronial Guarantees in its Act of Incorporation were a constant thorn in the side of the ratepayers and ultimately led to a Government enquiry in 1927. As a result, the company was placed under control of a committee of management, one of whom, Henry Forbes, manager of the CDRJC, recommended the introduction of diesel railcars. These offered a temporary respite but rising road competition took their toll and closure occurred on 31st December, 1941.

The Ballymena & Larne section of the NCC also suffered badly as a consequence of the 1933 strike and passenger services did not resume when it ended. Bit by bit the line closed and was lifted, though occasional goods services operated to the Ballyclare paper mill until July 1950.

The two electrically-operated tramways in Northern Ireland were less affected by some of the factors affecting the coal burning, steam-operated services. Nevertheless they also suffered at the hands of the road operators. The Bessbrook & Newry Tramway, a little-known concern off the tourist trails, had adopted a unique approach to dealing with road competition by using flangeless goods vehicles which could also operate along the roadway but the end ultimately came in January 1948. The Giant's Causeway & Portrush Tramway was heavily used during the tourist season but little thereafter and inevitably the excellent summer receipts could not sustain the concern year long. The need for renewal of the permanent way, coupled with the lack of interest by the Ulster Transport Authority in taking it on and the unwillingness of the Northern Ireland government to support operation, brought about the end in September 1949.

In the south, matters were little better for the narrow gauge lines incorporated into the GSR in 1925. These included the CB&PR and the C&MLR, both in suburban Cork and both increasingly suffering from the competition offered by the city's tramway and bus services. The CB&PR had the only section of double track on the Irish narrow gauge but this was reduced to a single line in 1927, with the entire line closing in 1933. The C&MLR followed in 1935, though the company at least had the dubious pleasure of outliving the rival electric tramway. The Schull & Skibbereen Railway (S&SR) in West Cork had only survived because statutory income from the county rates in the form of Baronial Guarantees had been included in its Act of Incorporation. It came under GSR control in 1925 but income didn't improve. The outbreak of World War II brought problems, particularly a shortage of locomotive coal, which resulted in the GSR suspending services on the S&SR in April 1944. It was reopened in December 1945 by the new state transport company Córas Iompair Éireann (CIÉ), the result of the merger of the GSR and the Dublin United Transport Co. in January 1945. Road bus services in west Cork had been expanding in the meantime with the extension of the Cork to Skibbereen passenger service to Schull. Consequently, the resumed train services were to last for only a further 13 months.

In Kerry, meanwhile, the T&DR engines battled with the steepest grades on Irish railways in crossing the Slieve Mish mountain range, providing a vital link to Tralee for the little fishing village of Dingle. But through the 1930s, these gradients and the tight curves on the line, coupled with a general deterioration of the permanent way, resulted in train journey times becoming excessive at a time when improvements to roads in the district resulted in the creeping growth of road competition. By 1939, the company would have had to replace the permanent way if it was to remain competitive and the decision was made to suspend passenger services to Dingle, with effect from the 17th April. A single daily goods continued to operate across the mountains but all services on the short Castlegregory tramway branch on the north coast of the Peninsula were terminated. The goods service to Dingle continued until 1944 when, as a result of fuel shortages, it was reduced to an 'as required' service. In 1947, CIÉ reduced this further to a solitary cattle working serving Dingle Fair on the last Saturday of each month. This continued until 1953, by which time the cattle fair trains had become too uneconomic to survive and CIÉ closed the entire section.

The C&LR, meanwhile, had in many ways benefited from being under the GSR banner as, with the run down of other lines, locomotives and rolling stock were transferred to the C&LR to support its own ageing stock. Engines from the CB&PR and the T&DR ran alongside its vintage Stephenson's 4-4-0T engines, but proposals to transfer West Clare and Schull & Skibbereen Railway engines were never followed through. The coaching and wagon stock were supplemented by vehicles from the T&DR, CB&PR, the C&MLR and the Clogher Valley Railway (CVR). The C&LR was kept afloat largely by coal traffic from the Arigna mines but when a coal-fired station was built locally, and began to absorb the entire output of the mines, this valuable traffic source was lost, leaving the section economically non-viable. Services ceased on the 31st March, 1959.

In Donegal, the two largest narrow gauge railway companies were also finding survival increasingly difficult, operating as they were in remote areas with ever decreasing populations. The introduction of the Free State border and the consequent delays to services didn't help matters. The two companies had different philosophies for dealing with the difficulties they faced, the CDRJC rising to the challenge of road competition with the introduction of petrol and diesel railcars, with a 'stop anywhere' policy, while the L&LSR saw its future in road transport and from the 1930s began to amass a fleet of buses and lorries. Of its railway operations, the first to go was the Buncrana-Carndonagh extension, which closed in 1935 after only 34 years of operation. The follies of construction of the Burtonport Extension had been apparent from the early days. The Board of Works' drive for economy meant a direct approach was adopted, often bypassing towns it nominally served by several miles. This was compounded by the onset of World War II and the Burtonport Extension was closed in August 1940, whereupon track-lifting began. Public protest and the wartime fuel shortages granted a stay of execution as the line was then used to transport considerable quantities of turf. Operations continued as far as Gweedore until 1947 when the entire section from Letterkenny was closed. This reduced the rail route mileage operated by the L&LSR from a peak of 99 to 30¾ miles, with just the Londonderry to Letterkenny section and the link from Tooban Junction to Buncrana remaining. Passenger workings were gradually wound down though they persisted to Buncrana, especially for Bank Holiday traffic. Goods workings, with usually a brake coach for occasional rail passengers continued but, increasingly, the public were carried by road. The deteriorating permanent way could no longer support the heavier locomotives, confining them to the Pennyburn shed, and the final train ran into Graving Dock terminus on 8th August, 1953.

The CDRJC was also experiencing financial strain, despite the railcar economies. Traffic receipts were insufficient to sustain the Glenties branch which closed to passenger traffic in December 1947, occasional goods services continuing for a further two years. The Derry branch was the next to follow. Since 1948 this was under the control of the Ulster Transport Authority (UTA) who were unwilling to support uneconomic lines and brought about closure in December 1954. In Donegal itself, the permanent way was badly in need of replacement but the owning companies were suffering their own financial hardship. Closure applications were made but deferred, due to the poor state of the Donegal roads, but the end was inevitable and all services ceased on the 31st December, 1959. The CDR continued as a road operator until taken over by CIÉ in 1971.

The last of the Irish narrow gauge lines to close was the West Clare section of the GSR. This comprised two railways, the West Clare Railway from Ennis to Miltown-Malbay and the South Clare Railway from Kilrush and Kilkee to join the WCR at Miltown. Though nominally separate concerns, the entire system was operated as a single unit with headquarters and workshops at Ennis. The early days were beset with problems resulting in frequent delays which became immortalized in the songs of Percy French. The company, though, like many of the Irish narrow gauge companies, operated in a harsh environment. The stony lands of County Clare are rarely able to support the growth of trees so there is little to mitigate the strong winds off the Atlantic. In its latter days, CIÉ attempted to prolong the life of the system through the introduction of diesel railcars, similar in design to the latest models to run on the CDRJC. This was followed by the introduction of diesel locomotives to haul the freight services. Nevertheless, these measures were insufficient and the West Clare passed into history on the last day of January 1961, and with it, the Irish narrow gauge.

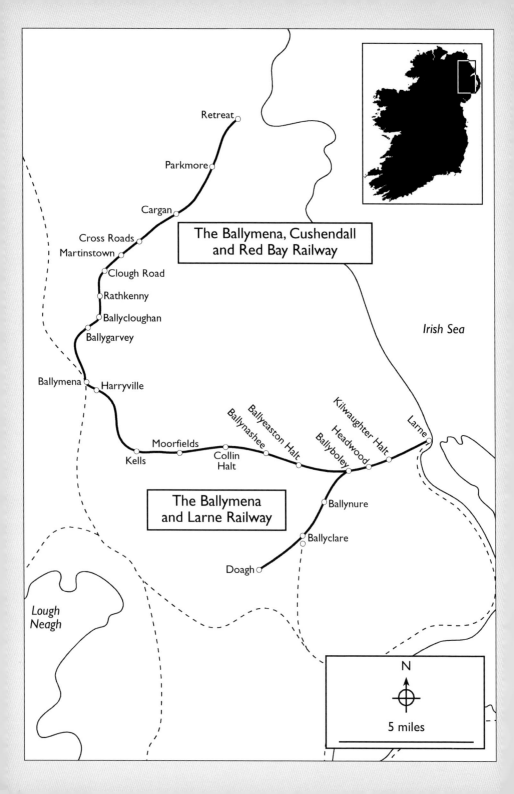

Retreat

Parkmore

Cargan

The Ballymena, Cushendall and Red Bay Railway

Cross Roads
Martinstown
Clough Road
Rathkenny
Ballycloughan
Ballygarvey

Irish Sea

Ballymena   Harryville

Kilwaughter Halt

Ballyeaston Halt   Headwood   Larne

Ballynashee   Ballyboley

Moorfields

Kells   Collin Halt

The Ballymena and Larne Railway

Ballynure

Ballyclare

Doagh

Lough Neagh

N

5 miles

Chapter Two

The Ballymena, Cushendall & Red Bay Railway

In the hills to the north-east of Ballymena, rich iron ore deposits had been discovered and had been mined since the mid-19th century. Lack of a local coal supply meant smelting of the mined ore could not be undertaken locally, leaving the mine owners with the problem of transporting the ore away from the locality. Horse-drawn transport was proving impractical due to the state of the roads and the volume shipped thus leading to discussions around extended rail connections. A rail connection, on the Irish standard gauge, was already established to Ballymena, with the Belfast & County Down Railway (B&CDR). Proposals were advanced for a link from Ballymena through the mining area to the Antrim Coast, to the sheltered harbour at Red Bay, giving options for transport either to the B&CDR at Ballymena or for transport from the Antrim Coast. A Dublin-based engineer, William Lewis, was appointed to survey the proposed line. The main concern identified was the sharp descent to sea level, from the peak near Retreat of 1,045 ft over 4½ miles, which would have resulted in severe grades of up to 1 in 21.

The Act of Incorporation of the Ballymena, Cushendall & Red Bay Railway in July 1872 is of particular interest in that it was the first Irish Railway to be authorized to build a line to a gauge of less than the Irish standard gauge of 5 ft 3 in. The wording of the Act was for a gauge between 2 ft and 3 ft - it's believed the choice of 3 ft may have been influenced by the recent adoption of this gauge in the Isle of Man.

Delays in securing the necessary share capital followed and almost a year passed before the contract for discussion was signed, and that only for 11¼ miles

Ballymena on 9th August, 1930. No. 111 departs with the 5.25 pm service to Parkmore.
H.C. Casserley, courtesy R.M. Casserley

15

The Ballymena, Cushendall & Red Bay Railway

Locomotives

No.	Manufacturer	Type	Year	Works No.	Engine name	Driving wheel dia.	Leading/trailing wheel dia.	Total wheel base	Coupled wheel base	Cyls (in.)	Heating surface (sq. ft)	Grate area (sq. ft)	Water capacity (galls)	Coal capacity (cwt)	Boiler pressure (psi)	Weight (t. cwt.)	Max. axle load (t. cwt.)	Tractive effort at 85% (lb.)	Wdn
1	Black, Hawthorn	0-4-2ST	1874	301	-	3'1"	2'7"	11'10"	6'4"	12x19	457	6.5	500	8	140	25-10	11-5	8,820	1923
2	Black, Hawthorn	0-4-2ST	1875	302	-	3'1"	2'7"	11'10"	6'4"	12x19	457	6.5	500	8	140	25-10	11-5	8,820	1923
3	Black, Hawthorn	0-4-2ST	1875	303	-	3'1"	2'7"	11'10"	6'4"	12x19	457	6.5	500	8	140	25-10	11-5	8,820	1911

Notes
No. 1 – Renumbered 60 by B&NCR, later 101 in 1897. Rebuilt 1907. Renumbered 101A in 1920 and placed in reserve stock.
No. 2 – Renumbered 61 by B&NCR, later 102 in 1897. Rebuilt 1907. Renumbered 102A in 1920.
No. 3 – Renumbered 62 by B&NCR, later 103 in 1897.

Carriages

No. (B&NCR)	Type	Built	Maker	Length	Compts	Seats	Wheel dia.	Wheel centres	Bogie centres	Withdrawn
1	Bogie first	1876	Midland Wagon Co.	22'6"	1	22				1934
2	Tramcar (8 wheel) third	1886	B&NCR Belfast	36'9"*	2	40	2'0"	3'9"	24'0½"	1954
3	Tramcar (8 wheel) third	1886	B&NCR Belfast	36'9"*	2	40	2'0"	3'9"	24'0½"	1932
4	Tramcar (8 wheel) third	1889	B&NCR Belfast	36'9"*	2	40	2'0"	3'9"	24'0½"	1932
5	Tramcar (8 wheel) third	1889	B&NCR Belfast	36'9"*	2	40	2'0"	3'9"	24'0½"	1929
316	Bogie third	1891	B&NCR Belfast	36'9"*	2	40	2'0"	3'9"	24'0½"	1934
317	Bogie third	1891	B&NCR Belfast	36'9"*	2	40	2'0"	3'9"	24'0½"	1930
329	Bogie first/third composite	1898	B&NCR Belfast	40'0"	2	12/32				1932
330	Bogie first/third composite	1898	B&NCR Belfast	40'0"	2	12/32				1932
331	Bogie third	1898	B&NCR Belfast	40'0"	2	44				1929
332	Bogie third	1898	B&NCR Belfast	40'0"	2	44				1929

Notes
* Total length. Body 31 ft 10½ in.
No. 1 – Converted to third. Renumbered 312.
No. 2 – Renumbered 306 (1889/90).
No. 3 – Renumbered 307 (1889/90).
No. 4 – Renumbered 319 (1889/90).
No. 5 – Renumbered 320 (1889/90).

Wagons
At acquisition by B&NCR – 3 covered wagons, 239 open wagons, 2 brake vans.

from Ballymena to Cargan. The countryside through which the line ran offered no particular obstacles and there were no engineering works of note, construction being completed in 15 months. The line opened for transport of ore, at the request of the mining companies, in March 1875 and for general traffic on 1st July - in this it was narrowly beaten to the honour of being the first Irish 3 ft gauge railway to operate by the short-lived line of the Glenariff Iron Ore & Harbour Company who opened their own mineral line to the sea in 1874.

Early returns were good, the iron ore traffic being particularly lucrative and eventually finances allowed extension to Retreat, which opened to traffic in October 1876. The original aim of continuing the line beyond Retreat, down the glenside to Red Bay, could not be realized, due to the severe downward gradient, and Retreat became the accepted terminus. Thus the BC&RBR had the dubious distinction of not serving one of the place names in its title! Instead of transport to the coast for shipment, ore travelled inland to Ballymena where it was either transhipped onto standard gauge wagons for transfer to the ports of Larne or Belfast, or, subsequently continued on the Belfast & Northern Counties Railway (B&NCR)-owned Ballymena & Larne narrow gauge line to the latter port.

But the iron ore market was soon to collapse, due to depression in the cross-channel iron trade, and the company remained independent only until October 1884, when falling mineral traffic together with a need for permanent way replacement led to the passing of a Parliamentary Bill authorizing the acquisition of the BC&RBR by the broad gauge Belfast & Northern Counties Railway. Until now, the great bulk of traffic on the BC&RBR had been from the output of the mines, with no passengers carried. With the decline of mineral traffic, Ballymena was expanding as an industrial centre, attracting workers from the surrounding countryside, and the B&NCR were keen to develop passenger traffic, in an effort to stimulate tourism and day-tripper traffic to this very scenic part of Ireland. This necessitated improvements to the permanent way, with replacement of the rail with 50 lb. steel rail and construction of platforms at stations, and following these changes, with the necessary Board of Trade approval obtained, passenger services began to Knockanally (later known as Martinstown) on 5th April, 1885 and to Parkmore on 1st September, 1888. But improvements were not continued to Retreat and no passenger service was ever introduced over this section.

Acquisition of the Cushendall line proved a poor investment for the B&NCR as, within a few years, iron-ore receipts had rapidly diminished and receipts from passenger and other merchandise traffic fell far short of compensating. The Midland Railway (MR) of England, keen to extend into Ireland, put forward a proposal for purchase which was accepted and formal acquisition of the B&NCR by the MR took place on 1st July, 1903, operation being overseen by a Northern Counties Committee. Although the question of extension to Cushendall again briefly surfaced, the NCC solution was to provide road transport.

During World War I, the NCC, like all other Irish railways, was under the statutory control of the Irish Railways Executive Committee from 1st January, 1917 until August 1921. As with all the railways, finances were affected by sharp increases in wages and the cost of materials but fare increases were delayed by government order. An unexpected boost to income, though, resulted from a revival in iron-ore production, sparked by war needs. The war was followed by political unrest leading up to the creation of the Irish Free State and the subsequent Civil War. Railway lines were targets in these troubled times and the Cushendall section suffered its fair share - the worst being when almost all the station houses were set alight on a single night in March 1921.

The MR was absorbed into the LMS which continued to administer its lines in Ireland through the NCC. Though there was some investment in infrastructure, the rise in road competition had begun and the narrow gauge lines, which also had competition from parallel standard gauge routes, were particularly affected. Passenger services on the Ballymena-Parkmore section were terminated in October 1930. The protracted Railway strike of 1933 was to be the death knell of the Antrim Narrow Gauge, many services not resuming when the strike ended. Goods Services on the Cushendall section continued until 1937, when the Rathkenny-Retreat section was closed, the Rathkenny Creamery only keeping the rest of the line open until 1940, when the traffic transferred to the roads and the line finally closed.

Chronology

18.07.1872	BC&RBR incorporated.
26.03.1875	Opened from Ballymena to Cargan (iron ore only).
01.07.1875	Opened from Ballymena to Cargan (general merchandise).
08.10.1876	Opened to Retreat.
14.10.1884	Acquired by Belfast & Northern Counties Railway.
05.04.1886	Passenger services to Knockanally commenced.
27.08.1888	Passenger services extended to Parkmore.
01.07.1903	B&NCR purchased by Midland Railway. Operation by Northern Counties Committee.
01.10.1930	Passenger services Ballymena to Parkmore withdrawn.
10.04.1937	Goods services Rathkenny to Retreat withdrawn.
02.06.1940	Complete closure.

Route

Distance	Station/Halt/Crossing	Opened	Closed*	Notes
0	Ballymena	1886	1940	
2¾	Ballygarvey	1889	1930	
4	Ballycloughan	1889	1940	
6	Rathkenny	1886	1940	
6¾	Clough Road	1886	1930	
8¼	Knockanally	1886	1937	Later Martinstown - renamed 1920
9¾	Crossing	1875	1937	
9¾	Cross Roads	1888	1937	Originally Carrocowan - renamed 1889
11¼	Cargan	1875	1937	
13½	Parkmore	1888	1937	
16¼	Retreat	1876	1937	

* Complete closure - all stations closed to passengers 1930.

Chapter Three

The Ballymena & Larne Railway

The Ballymena and Larne Railway (B&LR) largely resulted from the development of Larne as a major sea port in the 1860s. James Chaine, the son of a prosperous Co. Antrim linen merchant, who had bought the port and set about developing it, recognised the potential of the mineral ore traffic from the northern hills which, at that time, was being transported to Ballymena and thence to Belfast for shipment to England. He was instrumental in promoting a rail connection from Ballymena to Larne to bring this freight to the port. The first proposal was for a line to Ballyclare for which parliamentary approval was received in August 1873, though this was amended a year later, with the Ballymena & Larne Railway Company replacing the earlier Larne & Ballyclare Railway. The three foot gauge was chosen following the experience of the nearby Ballymena, Cushendall & Red Bay Railway.

The intake of capital after the 1874 Act was slow, and two years passed before the contract for construction was awarded to Thomas Dixon of Celbridge. After initial good progress, leading to optimistic expectations of an early opening, poor weather and lack of finance slowed things down. The section from Larne to Ballyclare opened for goods traffic, in a semi-completed state, in September 1877.

Doagh station on 9th August, 1930. Locomotive No. 109 prepares to leave with the 7.10 pm working to Ballyboley. *H.C. Casserley, courtesy R.M. Casserley*

The Ballymena & Larne Railway

Locomotives

No.	Manufacturer	Type	Year	Works No.	Driving wheel dia.	Leading/trailing wheel dia.	Total wheel-base	Coupled wheel-base	Cyls (in.)	Heating surface (sq. ft)	Grate area (sq. ft)	Water capacity (galls)	Coal capacity (cwt)	Boiler pressure (psi)	Weight (t. cwt.)	Max. axle load (t. cwt.)	Tractive effort at 85% (lb.)	Wdn
1	Beyer, Peacock	2-4-0T	1877	1687	3'9"	2'0"	14'3"	6'3"	11x18	392	6.95	385	20	120	17-12	7-0	7,440	1920
2	Beyer, Peacock	0-6-0T	1877	1700	3'3"	-	10'6"	10'6"	13½x18	508	9.1	450	20	140	21-1	7-7	8,050	1933
3	Beyer, Peacock	0-6-0T	1877	1701	3'3"	-	10'6"	10'6"	13½x18	508	9.1	450	20	140	21-1	7-7	8,050	1931
4	Beyer, Peacock	2-4-0T	1878	1828	3'9"	2'0"	14'3"	6'3"	11x18	392	6.95	450	26	140	19-3¾	7-0	7,440	1933
5	Beyer, Peacock	2-6-0ST	1880	1947	3'3"	2'0"	12'6"	7'0"	14x18	508	10.5	500	24	140	25-14	7-10	10,800	1934
6	Beyer, Peacock	0-6-0T	1883	2304	3'3"	-	10'6"	10'6"	13½x18	695	9.1	450	22	140	22-9	7-7	8,050	1932
69 (S2)	Beyer, Peacock	2-4-4CT	1892		3'9"	2'0"	25'9"	6'3"	14¾/21x20	825	12	570	30	200	42-1	11-8	16,435	1946
70 (S)	Beyer, Peacock	2-4-2CT	1892	3463	3'9"	2'0"	20'3"	6'3"	14¾/21x20	673	11.3	570	20	160	31-17	10-0	13,150	1954
112 (S1) (NCC)	York Rd (NCC)	2-4-2CT	1908	3464	3'9"	2'0"	22'3"	6'3"	14¾/21x 20	673	11.3	570	20	160	33-00	10-0	13,150	1950
113 (S1) (NCC)	York Rd (NCC)	2-4-2CT	1909		3'9"	2'0"	22'3"	6'3"	14¾/21x20	673	11.3	570	20	160	33-00	10-0	13,150	1954
103 (S) (NCC)	York Rd (NCC)	2-4-2CT	1919		3'9"	2'0"	20'3"	6'3"	14¾/21x20	673	11.3	570	20	160	31-17	10-0	13,150	1938
104 (S) (NCC)	York Rd (NCC)	2-4-2CT	1920		3'9"	2'0"	20'3"	6'3"	14¾/21x20	673	11.3	570	20	160	31-17	10-0	13,150	1954

Notes

No. 1 – Rebuilt 1893 (given 12½ in cyls). Renumbered 63 by B&NCR, later 104 by NCC.

No. 2 – Renumbered 65 by NCC, later 106 by NCC. Rebuilt 1897/1908. Transferred to Ballycastle section 1924.

No. 3 – Renumbered 66 by B&NCR, later 107 by NCC. Rebuilt 1898/1912. Transferred to Ballycastle section 1927.

No. 4 – Rebuilt 1889 (given 12½ in. cyls). Renumbered 64 by B&NCR, later 105 by NCC. Transferred to Ballycastle Section as spare in 1926. Sold to the Castlederg & Victoria Bridge Tramway 1928.

No. 5 – Renumbered 68 by B&NCR, later 109 by NCC.

No. 6 – Renumbered 67 by B&NCR, later 108 by NCC. Rebuilt 1898/1906. Transferred to Ballycastle section 1924.

No. 69 – Originally 2-4-2T, built by B&NCR for B&L section. Renumbered 110. Rebuilt 1931 as 2-4-4T ('S2' class). Poor performer thereafter and little used after 1940.

No. 70 – Built by B&NCR for B&L section. Renumbered 111 (1897). Transferred to Ballycastle section in later years. Renumbered 44 (1948).

No. 112 – Built by NCC for B&L section. Renumbered 102 (1920). Rebuilt 1928 ('S1' class). On Ballycastle section for a time around 1936. Renumbered 42 (1939).

No. 113 – Built by NCC for B&L section. Renumbered 101 (1920). Rebuilt 1930 ('S1' class). Transferred to Ballycastle section c.1932. Renumbered 41 (1940).

No. 103 – Built by NCC for B&L section. ('S' class.)

No. 104 – Built by NCC for B&L section. Renumbered 43 (1940). Transferred to Ballycastle section 1947. ('S' class.)

Carriages

No. (B&NCR)	Type	Built	Weight (tons)	Maker	Length	Compts	Seats	Wheel dia.	Wheel centres	Bogie centres	Withdrawn
301	6w brake/composite	1877		Bristol Wagon Works Co.	29'6"	first(1)/3rd(3)	6(first)/24(3rd)	21¾"	10'0"	-	1927
315	6w brake/composite	1877		Bristol Wagon Works Co.	29'6"	first(1)/3rd(3)	6(first)/24(3rd)	21¾"	10'0"	-	1932
304	Bogie first saloon	1877		Bristol Wagon Works Co.	33'0"	-	20	21¾"			1934
302	Bogie composite	1879		Bristol Wagon Works Co.	34'9"	133133	12(first)/32(3rd)	21¾"	4'9"	24'7"	1929
322	Bogie composite	1879		Bristol Wagon Works Co.	34'9"	first(1)/3rd(5)	6(first)/40(3rd)	21¾"	4'9"	24'7"	1930
321	Bogie brake composite	1879		Bristol Wagon Works Co.	34'9"	33133	6(first)/32(3rd)	21¾"	4'9"	24'7"	1934
303	Bogie composite	1879		Bristol Wagon Works Co.	35'6"	133133	12(first)/32(3rd)	21¾"	4'9"	24'7"	1932
314	Bogie brake composite	1879		Bristol Wagon Works Co.	35'6"	first(1)/3rd(4)	12(first)/16(3rd)	21¾"	4'9"	24'7"	1934
318	Bogie composite	1879		Bristol Wagon Works Co.	41'3"	first(3)/3rd(4)	18(first)/32(3rd)	21¾"	4'9"	24'7"	1928
305	Bogie brake composite	1879		Bristol Wagon Works Co.	41'3"	first(2)/3rd(4)	12(first)/32(3rd)	21¾"	4'9"	24'7"	1927
308	4w third	1881/2		B&L Works	14'1"	-	16				1934
309	4w third	1881/2		B&L Works	14'1"	-	16				1929
310	4w third	1881/2		B&L Works	14'1"	-	16				1954
311	4w third	1881/2		B&L Works	14'1"	-	16				1954
313	4w third	1881/2		B&L Works	14'1"	-	16				1929
327	Bogie third	1895		B&NCR	40'0"	2	42				
328	Bogie third	1895		B&NCR		2	42				
318	Bogie third	1928	13¾	NCC	41'3"	2	22/30	21¾"	4'9"	31'3½"	1952
350	Bogie composite first/third	1928	16	NCC	50'0"	2(first)/2(3rd)	12(first)/31(3rd)	21¾"	5'6"	38'0"	1954
351	Bogie composite first/third	1928	16	NCC	50'0"	2(first)/2(3rd)	12(first)/31(3rd)	21¾"	5'6"	38'0"	1954
352	Brake/third	1928	16	NCC	50'0"	2	24	21¾"	5'6"	38'0"	1952
353	Brake/composite	1928	16	NCC	50'0"	2(first)/2(3rd)	12(first)/31(3rd)	21¾"	5'6"	38'0"	1954

Notes

No. 327 – Converted to caravan coach No. 16 1937.
No. 328 – Converted to caravan coach No. 21 1938.
No. 318 – New body built on underframe by NCC 1928.
No. 308 – Wagon conversion. Converted back to wagon 1926. Renumbered 5308 Dec. 1934.
No. 309 – Wagon conversion. Converted back to wagon 1929. Renumbered 5309 Dec. 1934.
No. 310 – Wagon conversion. Converted back to wagon 1919. Renumbered 5310 Dec. 1934.
No. 311 – Wagon conversion. Converted back to wagon 1919. Renumbered 5311 Dec. 1934.
No. 313 – Wagon conversion. Converted back to wagon 1929. Renumbered 5313 Dec. 1934.
No. 318 – (Rebuilt): New body on 1879 underframe. Transferred to Ballycastle 1933. Sold to CDRJC 1952 (CDR No. 58).
No. 350 – Transferred to Ballycastle 1933.
No. 351 – Transferred to Ballycastle 1933. Sold to CDRJC 1952 (CDR No 59).
No. 352 – Transferred to Ballycastle 1930. Rebuilt as 3rd 1936. Sold to CDRJC 1952 (CDR No. 57).
No. 353 – Transferred to Ballycastle 1933.

Wagons

Quantity	Type	Built	Maker
20	Covered goods	1877/1878	Bristol Wagon Works
17	Cattle wagons	1877/1878	Bristol Wagon Works
190	Open goods	1877/1878	Bristol Wagon Works
10	Timber trucks	1877	Bristol Wagon Works
3	Goods brake vans	1877	Bristol Wagon Works
12	Ballast wagons	1880	Bristol Wagon Works
100	Mineral wagons	1880/1882	Bristol Wagon Works

Notes

Five covered goods converted to carriages, one to brake van 1880; one other converted to brake van 1883.

Wagons as classified under the NCC

NCC Class	Type	Length	Width	Wheelbase	Tare weight
1	End-tip wagons	12'6"	6'6"	7'0"	2t 8cwt
2	End-tip wagons	12'6"	6'6"	7'0"	2t 10cwt
3	End-tip wagons	11'4"	5'10½"	5'4"	2t 8cwt
4	End-tip wagons	11'4"	5'10½"	5'4"	2t 8cwt
5	End-tip wagons	11'4"	6'6"	5'4"	2t 8cwt
6	End-tip wagons	12'6"	6'10"	7'0"	2t 12cwt
7	End-tip wagons	12'6"	6'10"	7'0"	2t 13cwt
8	End-tip wagons	12'5"	6'10"	7'0"	3t 2cwt
9	End-tip wagons	14'0"	7'0"	8'0"	3t 7cwt
10	8-ton open	14'0"	7'0"	8'0"	3t 7cwt
11	Timber truck	12'6"	6'6"	7'0"	2t 11cwt
12	4-ton hopper	9'0"	5'9"	5'3½"	2t 7½cwt
13	8-ton hopper	9'8"	5'9"	6'2"	2t 19cwt
14	6-ton ballast wagon	12'6"	6'6"	7'0"	2t 7cwt
15	8-ton ballast wagon	14'0"	7'0"	8'0"	3t 7cwt
16	Covered wagons (6 ton)	14'0"	6'6"	8'0"	3t 14cwt
17	Covered wagons (6 ton)	14'5"	6'8"	8'0"	3t 11cwt
18	Covered wagons (6 ton)	14'5"	6'8"	8'0"	3t 16cwt
19	Cattle wagon (short)	12'6"	6'6"	7'0"	3t 11cwt
20	Cattle wagon (6 ton)	14'0"	6'6"	8'0"	3t 13cwt
21	Cattle wagon (6 ton)	14'0"	7'0"	8'0"	3t 15cwt
22	Brake van (ex-B&LR)	16'6"	6'7¾"	7'0"	–
23	Brake vans	16'6"	8'4"	9'0"	5t 4cwt
24	Brake vans	14'6"	6'7½"	8'0"	5t 3cwt
25	Covered wagons				

By the end of June the following year, the company considered the entire route from Larne to Ballymena to be complete. The Board of Trade inspection finally took place on the 28th July and was damning, with many inadequacies pointed out. These were speedily addressed and services commenced on 24th August, 1878.

Under the original Parliamentary Act of 1874, the B&LR terminus in Ballymena was at Harryville, comewhat isolated from other companies. A new Act of 1878 allowed for an extension to link with the Ballymena, Cushendall & Red Bay Railway and at the same time authorized an extension from Ballyclare to Doagh. The former opened in September 1880 while work on the latter was delayed, finally opening in May 1884. Other extensions towards Derry and to Belfast were proposed but never progressed. Arrangements were made with the mining companies for the transport of ore but tonnage carried never reached expectations and very soon suffered as a result of depression of the cross-channel iron trade, to which the company responded with reduced rates, further reducing income. Despite the introduction of economies, it became apparent that the B&LR could not survive as an independent concern and the company passed into B&NCR ownership in 1889.

The B&NCR set about making improvements to the permanent way, rolling stock and station buildings and built a coal storage siding at Harryville. Investment increased traffic numbers but the section was never profitable. The B&NCR was in turn taken over by the Midland Railway of England in 1903, after which affairs were under the control of a committee of management styled the Northern Counties Committee.

For the B&LR, the mail trains, connecting with the cross-channel Stranraer boats, were an important source of income. Many passengers elected to change from the broad gauge at Ballymena and travel to Larne by the shorter narrow gauge route, despite the narrow gauge trains being less comfortable to travel in, a fact supported by a number of complaints of rough running. This was ultimately addressed in 1928 by the NCC (by now under the control of the LMS, successor to the Midland) with the introduction of four new corridor coaches with improved comforts. They came at a time when passenger numbers were already declining and their time on the B&L section was to be short.

Government control of the railways in Ireland, administered by the Irish Railways Executive Committee, came into effect on 1st January, 1917, lasting until August 1921. This period saw running costs, both wages and material, rise steeply, while the Goverment initially put a cap on fares, before ultimately allowing an increase of 50 per cent. There were, in addition, no payments made for transport of military personnel or supplies. With the ending of control in 1921, the NCC received its share of compensation payments made under the Irish Railways (Settlement of Claims) Act of 1921. The war, though, did provide some respite in that local iron-ore production was revived by the needs of war and disused mines were reopened with a resulting increase in traffic.

Following World War I, the civil unrest in Ireland that followed the 1916 uprising had less impact on the railways in the north than was the case elsewhere in the country. With the creation of the Irish Free State in 1921, County Antrim became a part of Northern Ireland and was little affected by the Civil War that resulted from the partition of the country.

NCC locomotive No. 42 works the Ballyclare goods at Larne on 10th May, 1950.
John Langford Collection

But the increased costs of the war years and the rise of the motor car in the 1920s took their toll. On 1st October, 1930, passenger services were withdrawn on the Ballyclare-Doagh sections, but continued to run between Ballymena and Larne, and to Ballyclare from Ballyboley Junction. Goods traffic continued between Ballyclare and Doagh.

In early 1933, the NCC, like the majority of railways in Northern Ireland, was affected by a lengthy strike from 31st January until 10th April, resulting from a proposed 10 per cent wage reduction. Officials and the few train crews who had turned up for work maintained a skeleton service, supplemented by buses and lorries. The LMS (NCC) responded by announcing the ending of narrow gauge passenger train services with, in addition, the closure of the Ballyclare to Doagh goods service.

The advent of World War II brought further closure when, on 2nd June, 1940, the Ballymena-Ballyboley portion of the old B&L track was also closed, with the rails being lifted soon afterwards and the scrap being used for the war effort. This left 11½ miles of track from Larne to Ballyclare surviving on the traffic mainly generated by the paper mill at Ballyclare.

A further change in ownership occurred after the war. Railways in Britain were nationalized leading to the LMS becoming part of the new British Railways, which quickly disposed of its Irish possessions. Consequently, the NCC was sold to the government of Northern Ireland. The Ulster Transport Authority took over and set about closing unprofitable lines. With the closure of the Ballyclare Paper Mill in 1950 the writing was truly on the wall for the the B&L section and the UTA duly announced closure with effect from Monday 3rd July, 1950.

Chronology

07.07.1874	Ballymena & Larne Railway Company incorporated.
01.09.1877	Opened from Larne Harbour to Ballyclare (freight only).
24.08.1878	Opened to Ballymena (passengers and freight).
22.09.1880	Short line connection to BC&RBR.
01.05.1884	Doagh extension opened.
July 1889	Amalgamated with B&NCR.
1903	B&NCR acquired by NCC(MR).
1923	LMS acquires MR.
1933	Passenger services from Ballymena to Larne and from Ballyboley Jn to Ballyclare and freight service from Ballyclare to Doagh not resumed following 1933 railway strike.
1940	Ballyboley Jn to Ballymena closed (freight).
03.07.1950	Complete closure.

Route

Distance	Station/Halt/Crossing	Opened	Closed	Notes
0	Larne Harbour	1878	1950	Closed to passengers 1933.
1	Larne	1878	1950	Closed to passengers 1933.
4	Kilwaughter	1878	1933	Opened for passengers 1885.
6¼	Headwood	1882	1940	Originally Ballygowan. Closed to passengers 1933.
7¾	Ballyboley Junction	1878	1940	Originally Ballyclare Junction. Closed to passengers 1933.
10	Ballyeaston	1880	1933	Passenger only, closed 1881-1911.
12	Ballynashee	1879	1940	Closed to passengers 1933.
15½	Collin	1887	1933	
17½	Moorfields	1878	1940	Closed to passengers 1933.
20½	Kells	1878	1940	Closed to passengers 1933.
24¾	Harryville	1878	1940	Closed to passengers 1881.
25¼	Ballymena	1880	1940	Closed to passengers 1933.
7¾	Ballyboley Junction	1878	1940	
9½	Ballynure	1878	1933	Closed to passengers 1930.
11½	Ballyclare	1878	1933	Closed to passengers 1930.
13½	Doagh	1884	1933	Closed to passengers 1930.

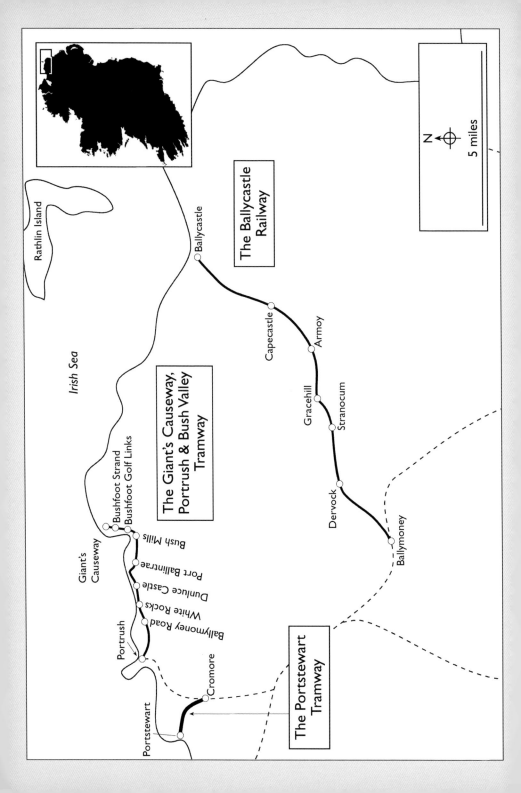

Rathlin Island

Irish Sea

Giant's Causeway

Bushfoot Strand
Bushfoot Golf Links
Bush Mills
Port Ballintrae
Dunluce Castle
White Rocks
Ballymoney Road
Portrush

The Giant's Causeway, Portrush & Bush Valley Tramway

Portstewart
Cromore

The Portstewart Tramway

Ballycastle

Capecastle

Armoy

Gracehill

Stranocum

Dervock

Ballymoney

The Ballycastle Railway

N

5 miles

Chapter Four

The Ballycastle Railway

Proposals for a rail connection to the town of Ballycastle were first advanced soon after the Ballymena, Ballymoney, Coleraine & Portrush Junction Railway (later acquired by the Belfast & Northern Counties Railway) opened in 1855. But it was not until 1878 that the Ballycastle Railway Act was passed, authorizing a 16½ mile extension from Ballymoney. Though initial proposals were to build to the Irish standard gauge, the 3 ft gauge was adopted following the experience of the nearby Ballymena & Larne and Ballymena, Cushendall & Red Bay railways. Construction commenced early in 1879 and was completed by September 1880, the line opening to traffic on 19th October of that year.

From Ballymoney, the line followed a progressive, fairly gentle upward climb to reach a peak, at 319 ft, between Armoy and Capecastle, while beyond Capecastle there was a steep three-mile descent at an average gradient of about 1 in 50 to Ballycastle. There were just two engineering works of any note - a short tunnel near Capecastle and a four-arch stone viaduct at Ballycastle.

From early days, plans were advanced for a link from the Ballycastle Railway (BR) at Dervock to a proposed railway from Portrush to Bushmills, and though the latter was built (as the Giants Causeway Tramway) the extension to Dervock never materialized. The company did, though supply a four-horse carriage to a local haulier who in turn operated a service from Ballycastle to the Causeway during the summer months. Proposals were also advanced for construction of a tramway from the terminus in Ballycastle to the seafront at Shore Road but again never came to anything.

Much of the line ran through bogland and the track proved to be insufficiently ballasted and subject to waterlogging. As a consequence, within

On 18th April, 1948 locomotive No. 43 stands at Ballycastle with coaches numbered 352 and 353 in the platform.   *H.C. Casserley, courtesy R.M. Casserley*

The Ballycastle Railway

Locomotives

No.	Manufacturer	Type	Year	Works No.	Name	Driving wheel dia.	Leading/ trailing wheel dia.	Total wheel-base	Coupled wheel-base	Cyls (in.)	Heating surface (sq. ft)	Grate area (sq. ft)	Water capacity (galls)	Coal capacity (cwt)	Boiler pressure (psi)	Weight (t. cwt)	Max. axle load (t. cwt.)	Tractive effort at 85% (lb.)	Wdn
1	Black, Hawthorn	0-6-0ST	1879	554	Dalriada	3'3"	-	11'9"	11'9"	13x19	574	7	450	25	150	24-0	8-10	10,500	1924
2	Black, Hawthorn	0-6-0ST	1879	555	Countess of Antrim	3'3"	-	11'9"	11'9"	13x19	574	7	450	25	150	24-0	8-10	10,500	1924
3 (first)	Black Hawthorn	0-6-0ST	1877	513	Lady Boyd	3'3"	-	11'0"	11'0"	12x19	574	7	400	25	150	22-0	8-7	8,900	1908
3 (2nd)	Kitson & Co	4-4-2T	1908	4665		3'7"	2'6"	22'5"	6'6"	14½"x21"	852	12.0	800	35	165	39-11	10-15	15,000	1946
4	Kitson & Co.	4-4-2T	1908	4666		3'7"	2'6"	22'5"	6'6"	14½"x21"	852	12.0	800	35	165	39-11	10-15	15,000	1946
105	Beyer, Peacock	2-4-0T	1878	1828		3'9"	2'0"	14'3"	6'3"	11"x18"	392	6.85	360	20	140	19-3	7-0	7,440	1933
106	Beyer, Peacock	0-6-0T	1877	1700		3'3"	-	10'6"	10'6"	13½"x18"	508	9	450	20	140	21-1	7-7	8,050	1937
107	Beyer, Peacock	0-6-0T	1877	1701		3'3"	-	10'6"	10'6"	13½"x18"	508	9	450	20	140	21-1	7-7	8,050	1931
108	Beyer, Peacock	0-6-0T	1883	2304		3'3"	-	10'6"	10'6"	13½"x18"	529	9	450	20	140	22-9	7-7	8,050	1932
44	Beyer, Peacock	2-4-2CT	1892	3464		3'9"	2'0"	20'3"	6'3"	14¾"/21"x20"	673	11.3	570	20	160	31-17	10-0	13,150	1954
102	York Rd (NCC)	2-4-2CT	1908	-		3'9"	2'0"	22'3"	6'3"	14¾"/21"x20"	673	11.3	570	20	160	33-0	10-0	13,150	1954
41	York Rd (NCC)	2-4-2CT	1909	-		3'9"	2'0"	22'3"	6'3"	14¾"/21"x20"	673	11.3	570	20	160	33-0	10-0	13,150	1954
43	York Rd (NCC)	2-4-2CT	1920	-		3'9"	2'0"	20'3"	6'3"	14¾"/21"x20"	673	11.3	570	20	160	31-17	10-0	13,150	1954

Notes

Nos. 1 & 2 – Rebuilt 1895.

No. 3 – (first) rebuilt 1896 to same spec. as Nos 1 & 2. Withdrawn 1908, eventually sold 1912.

No. 3 (2nd) renumbered 113 by NCC; rebuilt Belfast and transferred to B&L section - height of cab and boiler mountings reduced; back to Ballycastle section in February 1943.

No. 4 – renumbered 114 by NCC; rebuilt Belfast and transferred to B&L section - height of cab and boiler mountings reduced.

No. 105 – Ex-B&LR No. 4. Renumbered 64 by B&NCR, later 105 by NCC. Rebuilt 1889 (spec. as rebuilt). Transferred to Ballycastle Section as spare in 1926. Sold to Castlederg & Victoria Bridge Tramway in 1928.

No. 106 – Ex-B&LR No. 2. Renumbered 65 by B&NCR, later 106 by NCC. Rebuilt 1897/1908. Transferred to Ballycastle section for reopening 1924.

No. 107 – Ex-B&LR No. 3. Renumbered 66 by B&NCR, later 107 by NCC. Rebuilt 1898/1912. Transferred to Ballycastle section 1927.

No. 108 – Ex-B&LR No. 6. Renumbered 67 by B&NCR, later 108 by NCC. Rebuilt 1898/1906. Transferred to Ballycastle section for reopening 1924.

No. 44 – Ex-B&LR No. 70. Renumbered 111 (1897). Transferred to Ballycastle section in later years. Renumbered 44 (1948).

No. 102 – Built by NCC for B&L section as No 112. Renumbered 102 (1920). Rebuilt 1930 (S1). On Ballycastle section for a time around 1936 (as No. 102); back to B&L. Renumbered 42 (1939).

No. 41 – Built by NCC for B&L section as 113. Renumbered 101 (1920). Rebuilt 1928 (S1). Transferred to Ballycastle section c.1932. Renumbered 41 (1940).

No. 43 – Built by NCC for B&L section as 104. Renumbered 43 (1940). Transferred to Ballycastle section 1947.

Carriages

No.	Type	Built	Weight (tons)	Maker	Length	Compts	Seats	Wheel dia.	Wheel centres	Bogie centres	Withdrawn
1	Composite 6w	1880	-	Railway Carriage Co.	31'3"	3/1/1/3/3		2'6"	10'3"	-	1924
2	Composite 6w	1880	-	Railway Carriage Co.	31'3"	3/1/1/3/3		2'6"	10'3"		1924
3	Composite 6w	1880	-	Railway Carriage Co.	31'3"	3/1/1/3/3		2'6"	10'3"	-	1924
4	Third 6w	1880	-	Railway Carriage Co.	31'3"	5		2'6"	10'3"		1924
5	Third 6w	1880	-	Railway Carriage Co.	31'3"	5		2'6"	10'3"		1924
6	Third 6w	1880	-	Railway Carriage Co.	31'3"	5		2'6"	10'3"		1924
7	Third 6w	1880	-	Railway Carriage Co.	31'3"	5		2'6"	10'3"		1924
	Brake 4w	1880	-	Railway Carriage Co.	18'0"	-		2'6"	10'6"	-	1924
	Brake 4w*	1892	-	BR, Ballymoney							1924
	Bogie 3rd	1896	-	Metropolitan Carriage &Wagon Co.	38'0"	8	80	2'6"	4'0"	26'8"	1924
	Bogie 3rd	1898	-	Metropolitan Carriage &Wagon Co.	38'0"	8	80	2'6"	4'0"	26'8"	1924
14	Bogie 3rd	1900	-	Metropolitan Carriage &Wagon Co.	38'0"	8	80	2'6"	4'0"	26'8"	1924
	Brake 3rd	1900	-	Metropolitan Carriage &Wagon Co.	38'0"	4	40	2'6"	4'0"	26'8"	1924
306	Tramcar (8 wheel) third	1886	-	B&NCR Belfast	36'9"			2'0"	3'9"	24'0½"	1950
329	Bogie composite first/third	1898	-	B&NCR Belfast	40'0"			2'0"	3'9"	24'0½"	1932
330	Bogie composite first/third	1898	-	B&NCR Belfast	40'0"			2'0"	3'9"	24'0½"	1932
318	Bogie 3rd	1928	13¾	NCC	41'3"	2	22/30	2'1¾"	4'9"	31'3½"	1952
350	Bogie composite first/third	1928	16	NCC	50'0"	2(first)/2(3rd)	12(first)/31(3rd)	2'1¾"	5'6"	38'0"	1954
351	Bogie composite first/third	1928	16	NCC	50'0"	2(first)/2(3rd)	12(first)/31(3rd)	2'1¾"	5'6"	38'0"	1952
352	Brake/third	1928	16	NCC	50'0"	2	24	2'1¾"	5'6"	38'0"	1952
353	Brake/composite	1928	16	NCC	50'0"	2(first)/2(3rd)	12(first)/31(3rd)	2'1¾"	5'6"	38'0"	1954

Notes

No. 1 Became 2/1/1/2/3 in 1885

* Converted from flat wagon. Little used 1914-1924.

No. 306 Ex-Ballymena, Cushendall & Red Bay Railway (BC&RBR). Verandah ends - 31'10½" saloon body.

No. 329 Ex-BC&RBR.

No. 330 Ex-BC&RBR.

No. 318 Built for B&L section - new body on 1879 frame. Transferred to Ballycastle 1933. Sold to CDRJC 1952 (CDR No. 58).

No. 351 Built for B&L section. Transferred to Ballycastle 1933. Sold to CDRJC 1952 (CDR No 59).

No. 352 Built for B&L section. Transferred to Ballycastle 1930. Rebuilt as third 1936. Sold to CDRJC 1952 (CDR No. 57).

Wagons (original order)

Quantity	Type	Built	Maker	Length	Width	Wheelbase	Wheel dia.	Capacity
40	Open	1880	Railway Carriage Co.	14'0"	7'0"	8'0"	2'6"	6 tons
15	Covered wagons	1880	Railway Carriage Co.	14'0"	7'0"	8'0"	2'6"	
5	Cattle wagons	1880	Railway Carriage Co.	14'0"	7'0"	8'0"	2'6"	
2	Guard's vans	1880	Railway Carriage Co.	14'0"	7'0"	8'0"	2'6"	

Wagons at closure

Quantity	Type	Built	Maker	Length	Width	Wheelbase	Wheel dia.	Capacity (cu. in.)	Tare weight
1	End tipping open	1880	Railway Carriage Co.	12'6"	6'6"	7'0"	?	100	2t 8cwt
8	End tipping open	1880	Railway Carriage Co.	14'0"	7'0"	8'0"	2'6"	280	3t 7cwt
25	Centre door open			14'0"	7'0"	8'0"	2'6"	280	3t 7cwt
4	Dropside/ballast			12'6"	6'6"	7'0"	?	99	2t 7cwt
2	Timber truck			12'6"	6'6"	7'0"	?		2t 11cwt
1	Travelling crane						?		
5	Flat roofed covered			14'5"	6'8"	8'0"	?	484	3t 11cwt
1	Flat roofed covered			14'5"	6'8"	8'0"	2'6"	522	3t 16cwt
4	Flat roofed covered			14'1"	6'7"	8'0"	?		
3	Cattle	1880	Railway Carriage Co.	14'0"	7'0"	8'0"	2'6"	535	3t 15cwt
7	Centre canvas covered	1880	Railway Carriage Co.	14'0"	6'6"	8'0"	2'6"	466	3t 14cwt
3	Brake vans	1880	Railway Carriage Co.	14'0"	6'7½"	8'0"	2'6"	539	5t 3cwt
2	Brake vans			16'0"	8'4"	8'0"	?	483	5t 3cwt

three years a number of the sleepers showed signs of decay, though an added factor was that they were found to be of inferior quality and below the specification originally ordered. The trackbed was in need of repair and further ballasting and through the life of the railway was to require constant attention and prove a drain on funds.

Passenger traffic was steady, though the vast majority was third class. Market days and 12th July resulted in surges in passenger numbers, which the company catered for through use of open goods wagons. Despite this, the company struggled financially, mainly due to a lack of local support - one-third of issued shares were not taken up resulting in the company having to borrow heavily and arrange a deferred payment agreement for the rolling stock. By 1885, the company was effectively bankrupt and unable to pay interest owing on Board of Trade loans resulting in seizure and attempted sale of rolling stock, but as the cost of the stock remained unpaid, the sale could not proceed. Integration with the B&NCR - in 1887 - resulted in improvements in traffic and some easing of the financial situation and this was further helped in 1896 when the Commissioners of Public Works sold off their interest in the railway - a £20,000 loan plus outstanding interest of over £4,000 - which the Directors acquired for £12,000, thus providing a slender positive balance and permitting a rare share dividend.

Like all other Irish railways, the company was affected by the outbreak of World War I, during which it came under Government control in the form of the Irish Railway Executive Committee (IREC) from 1917 until 1921. During this time, wages and the cost of coals rose steeply and weren't matched by fare rises. The company's perilous finances were further threatened and only bailed out by further emergency loans. The IREC settlement in 1921 provided a lump sum, but this was immediately offset against accrued losses. At least the troubles which affected much of Ireland with the post-1916 independence struggle had little impact in north Antrim. But there was a rise in motor traffic, which threatened the company's independent survival, and as the Northern Ireland Government was unwilling to offer support, application for closure was made in January 1924, with operations to cease on the 24th March of that year. Before that date, negotiations had started with the Northern Counties Committee with a view to selling the line as a going concern. Though these negotiations stalled and the line closed for some of the summer, the NCC did reopen the line in August 1924, though formal approval of transfer of ownership was to take another year. The period of closure only afforded the opportunity for competitor motor vehicle services to gain a foothold in the local transport service.

Following transfer, the NCC looked to reconfigure the Ballycastle operation to make it more economical. Staff were reduced and some replaced by NCC personnel. The BR's generous allocation of rolling stock was critically examined and, as the entire passenger fleet lacked continuous braking, it was withdrawn and auctioned, the majority finding a new lease of life as seaside homes along the nearby coast. Two of the engines were scrapped, the others underwent repair and were transferred to the Ballymena & Larne section, while NCC engines appeared on the Ballycastle section. Workshop tasks were transferred to Belfast with the closure and demolition of the BR's shops and engine shed at Ballymoney. The line was made single throughout, stations were downgraded and buildings demolished. However, the NCC did upgrade the track by replacing rails and strengthening ballast, as well as provided new carriages. Once established, services on the Ballycastle section continued uneventfully for a number of years.

Unlike other parts of Ireland, the north of Antrim was little affected by World War II. Some small increase in passenger traffic resulted from the occasional military transport or the movement of troops to a rest camp in Ballycastle, while the Ministry of Food's policy for decentralization of essential foodstuffs resulted in lucrative extra freight traffic.

With the ending of the war, however, this extra traffic disappeared and the rise of road transport further drained services. The Northern Ireland government passed legislation to permit unified control of road and rail services and this led to the creation of the Ulster Transport Authority. This came into being in October 1948 and assumed control of NCC operations from April 1949. From the outset, the UTA was unwilling to subsidize unprofitable lines and though consideration was given to conversion of the Ballycastle section to broad gauge, this never materialized and when the UTA applied for closure, little opposition was offered. The last trains ran on the 2nd July, 1950 with few turning out to bid farewell to the trains. Three of the corridor carriages transferred to the line following the closure of passenger services on the Ballymena & Larne section were acquired by the County Donegal Railways Joint Committee and served on that line until closure on the last day of 1959. The line lay unused until the necessary abandonment order was made in August 1953 when the rails were lifted and the proceeds sold. Thus the Ballycastle Railway, one of the pioneers of the Irish narrow gauge, passed into history, after 70 years of service.

Chronology

22.07.1878	Ballycastle Railway Company incorporated.
18.10.1880	Line opened from Ballycastle to Ballymoney.
04.04.1924	Ballycastle Railway closed.
11.08.1924	Line reopened following takeover by LMS (NCC).
03.07.1950	Line closed (under UTA).

Route

Distance	Station/Halt/Crossing	Opened	Closed
0	Ballymoney	1880	1950
4½	Dervock	1880	1950
6¾	Stranocum	1880	1950
8¼	Gracehill	1890	1950
10¼	Armoy	1881	1895
11	Balleny Siding	1881	1895
13	Capecastle	1882	1950
15	Ballast Pit Siding	1897	1950
16	Tow Viaduct	1880	1950
16¼	Ballycastle	1880	1950

Chapter Five

The Giant's Causeway Tramway

The origins of the Giant's Causeway, Portrush and Bush Valley Railway and Tramway Company Ltd (GCT) lay in the desire to provide a rail link for the town of Bushmills, either a coastal link to the Portrush terminus of the Belfast & Northern Counties Railway (later Northern Counties Committee of the MR/LMS) or through a connection to the Ballycastle Railway at Dervock. Leading the proposals were two local brothers, Dr Anthony Traill and William Traill, both of whom had connections with Trinity College in Dublin. Both options were initially supported, the Ballycastle option probably resulting in the 3 ft gauge being adopted for the tramway, although in the end, the connection to Dervock was never taken further. Though initially proposed as a steam tramway between Portrush and Bushmills, when Parliamentary approval was received in August 1880, authority was also granted for the use of electric power.

The use of hydro-electric power was championed by the Traill brothers, who had academic connections with pioneers in the development of electricity as a practical power source. They proposed to use the power of a 24 ft waterfall on the River Bush, a mile from Bushmills, to drive two water turbines, which together could develop 104 hp (later upgraded to 160 hp). Until this could be made available, power was provided by a steam driven generator located at Portrush, which was subsequently used to supplement the hydro-electric source. A diesel plant later replaced the original steam engine, and supplied current for the Portrush - Dunluce section. Power was conducted to the trams via a thin conductor rail, carried on wooden posts 17 in. above the ground alongside the inner rail and away from the public road, which the tramway followed.

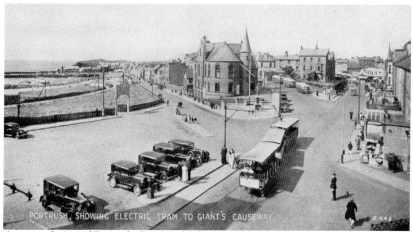

A postcard view of Portrush showing the Giant's Causeway tramway.
John Langford Collection

The Giant's Causeway Tramway

Locomotives

No.	Manufacturer	Type	Year	Name	Driving wheel dia.	Wheelbase	Cyls	Boiler pressure	Weight	Wdn
1	Wilkinson	0-4-0	1883		2'0"	5'10½"	7½"x12"	120 psi	7 t 0 cwt	1908
2	Wilkinson	0-4-0	1883		2'0"	5'10½"	7½"x12"	120 psi	7 t 0 cwt	1898
3	Wilkinson	0-4-0	1886	Dunluce Castle	2'0"	5'10½"	8"x12"	160 psi		1931
4	Wilkinson	0-4-0	1896	Brian Boroimhe	2'0"	5'10½"	8"x12"	160 psi		1931

Notes

No. 1 – Body of goods wagon added to frame and wheels to form ballast wagon 1910.

Nos. 3 & 4 – Mainly on standby from 1915. Sold to local contractor 1931.

Electric cars & trailers

No.	Source	Type	Year	Remarks	Class	Length	Wheelbase	Seats	Withdrawn
1		4 wheel	1883		Closed first	15'0"*	6'6"	18	1949
2		4 wheel	1883		Closed first	15'0"*	6'6"	18	1949
3		4 wheel	1883	Siemens 4 hp engine	Open first	15'0"*	6'6"	18	1945
4		4 wheel	1883	Siemens 4 hp engine	Open first	15'0"*	6'6"	18	1949
5		4 wheel	1883		Open third	18'6"	6'6"	24	1949
6		4 wheel	1883		Open third	18'6"	6'6"	24	1949
7		4 wheel	1883	Siemens 4 hp engine	Open third	18'6"	6'6"	24	1949
8		4 wheel	1887		Open third	18'6"	6'6"	24	1920s
9		4 wheel	1888		Composite	15'6"***	6'6"	6(first)/16 (ordinary)	1949
10		4 wheel	1888		Open third	15'6"***	6'6"	24	1949
11	Local conversion	4 wheel	1888	Trailer - converted from goods wagon			6'6"	20	
12	Local conversion	4 wheel	1888	Trailer - converted from goods wagon			6'6"	20	
13	Local conversion	4 wheel	1888	Trailer - converted from goods wagon			6'6"	20	1949
14	Local conversion	4 wheel	1888	Trailer - converted from goods wagon			6'6"	20	
15	Local conversion	4 wheel	1888	Trailer - converted from goods wagon			6'6"	20	1949
16	Local conversion	4 wheel	1891	Trailer - converted from goods wagon			6'6"	20	1949
17	Local conversion	4 wheel	1891	Trailer - converted from goods wagon			6'6"	20	
18	Local conversion	4 wheel	1897					28	
19	Local conversion	4 wheel	1897					28	1949
20		4 wheel	1899	For overhead operation, 2 x 19.5 hp motors		22'0"	7'0"	28	1949
21		4 wheel	1899	For overhead operation, 2 x 19.5 hp motors		22'0"	7'0"	28	1949
22		4 wheel	1902	For overhead operation, 2 x 19.5 hp motors		22'0"	7'0"	28	1949
23		4 wheel	1908	For overhead operation, 2 x 19.5 hp motors		22'0"	7'0"	28	1949
24		4 wheel	1937	2 x 25 hp motors				28	1949

Notes

* Length over body. End platforms extra 3 ft either end giving overall length of 21 ft.

** Length over body. End platforms extra 2ft 4½in either end giving overall length of 20 ft 3 in.

No. 4 – Converted for overhead power operation 1899. Motor removed 1902.

Nos. 3 & 7 – Motor removed when overhead power operation commenced 1899.

No. 9 – Placed on new truck and motorized 1909, 2 x 19.5 hp motors. New wheelbase 7 ft 0 in.

No. 24 – Purchased 1937 following closure of the Dunfermline & District Traction Company. Regauged from 3 ft 6 in.

Following the ceremonial cutting of the first sod on 21st September, 1881, construction proceeded rapidly. William Traill was the company's Engineer responsible for both construction of the permanent way and establishing electric power. The line was laid on an elevation on the seaward side of the road, which required widening to accommodate, and was single track throughout. Five passing loops were initially provided, subsequently increased to eight. Construction of the line itself was completed within a year, though problems with the installation of electric power delayed full completion.

Board of Trade inspection was carried out in January 1883 and was approved with the exception that use of the conductor rail was not permitted through the streets of Portrush and Bushmills. This resulted in two enclosed steam tramway locomotives being purchased from Wilkinson & Co. Ltd of Wigan, both to haul trains over these sections and also for freight workings. Formal opening of the line was in September 1883, though it was stated that the line had been operational since February 1883, probably operated by the steam locomotives.

The potential of the Giant's Causeway tourist traffic was soon recognized and an extension of the tramway to the famous tourist attraction opened to the public in July 1887.

In early days, many problems were experienced with electric operation, mainly due to inconsistency in supply from the generator. As a result, two further, slightly larger engines were delivered from Wilkinson in 1886 and steam operated mileage was to exceed electric for some years to come. Following an early fatality, a Board of Trade investigation found dangerous fluctuations in the voltage and the conductor rail was replaced with power provided through overhead wiring from July 1899. This proved a more efficient way of delivering power and electric train mileage steadily increased, eventually overtaking steam mileage. By 1915 only electric mileage was recorded with very little steam haulage thereafter, though not finally dispensed with until the 1920s.

The Tramway was to prove a valuable asset to the local tourist trade, carrying many visitors to the Giant's Causeway in its time, which in turn was a major source of the company's income as anticipated goods traffic never materialized.

Causeway terminus of the Giant's Causeway tramway on 10th August, 1930.
H.C. Casserley, courtesy R.M. Casserley

It was, though, subject to the vagaries of the Irish weather, with a wet summer creating a serious shortfall in finances, and suffered from roadside competition from the early days. This fragility of the company's finances led to the Directors offering the line for sale to the MR, as early as 1903, and, subsequently, many times in the 1920s to its successor the LMS, though without success.

American servicemen based in Northern Ireland provided a welcome boost in traffic during World War II but upkeep of the track and overhead wiring was poor and lack of finance for replacement coupled with falling receipts and an unwillingness on the part of the government of Northern Ireland to offer subsidy, led to closure on 30th September, 1949.

Chronology

28.08.1880	Royal Assent granted.
29.01.1883	Open to traffic.
28.09.1883	Official opening.
06.08.1885	Extension authorized.
01.07.1887	Extension opened.
26.07.1899	Change from conductor rail to overhead supply.
01.01.1917	Under control of the Irish Railway Executive Committee.
01.08.1921	End of Government control.
30.09.1949	Closure.

Route

Distance	Station/Halt/Crossing	Opened	Closed	Notes
0	Portrush	1883	1949	Run-round loop and siding adjacent to B&NCR station.
½	Portrush Tram Depot	1883	1949	Passing loop.
1¾	Royal Portrush Golf Club	1883	1949	Passing loop.
2½	Ballymoney Road	1883	1949	Crossing, passing loop.
3¼	White Rocks	1883	1949	Passing loop.
3½	Clooney Hill	1883	1949	Summit of line 193 ft.
3¾	Giant's Head	1883	1949	Passing loop.
4¼	Dunluce Castle	1883	1949	Passing loop.
5	Port Ballintrae	1883	1949	Passing loop.
5½	Gortnee	1888	1949	Passing loop.
6¼	Stanalane	1883	1949	Passing loop.
6¾	Bushmills	1883	1949	Passing loop.
7	Bushmills Market Yard	1883	1890	
6¾	Bushmills	1883	1949	Passing loop.
7¼	Bushfoot Golf Links	1887	1949	Passing loop.
7¾	Sandhills	1887	1949	Passing loop.
8	Victoria Jubilee Bridge	1887	1949	
8¼	Bushfoot Strand	1887	1949	Passing loop.
8½	Runkerry	1887	1949	Passing loop.
9¼	Giant's Causeway	1887	1949	

Chapter Six

The Portstewart Tramway

When railways extended from Ballymena to Coleraine and Portrush in the 1850s, the north Antrim coast town of Portstewart was bypassed, being served by a station some two miles from the town, due to the refusal of a local landowner to grant access. As a result, Portstewart was left behind as the improved access afforded by the railways improved the lot of the surrounding towns, and the local traders began to agitate for a branch line or tramway connection.

A number of proposals were advanced but no progress resulted for a number of years until the provisions of the Tramways Act permitted steam traction on roadside tramways and removed the requirement to obtain the authority of an Act of Parliament, an application to the Lord Lieutenant for an Order in Council sufficing. Following this, the Portstewart Tramway Co. (PT) was promoted to construct a line on the 3 ft gauge between the station and the town and the Order in Council was granted in April 1880.

A substantial portion of the required capital was provided by the Belfast & Northern Counties Railway, who had subsequently acquired the initially-independent Portrush line. As a result the service was organized to link with the B&NCR service, largely dictated by the arrival and departure of trains at the station. Laying of the 1¾ miles of track had been completed by April 1882 and, following inspection, was passed and opened to traffic in June 1882. The tramway ran entirely on the public road and was single track with two passing loops.

Apart from an initial few years of moderate success, the undertaking was not very prosperous and, when heavy repair of the line became necessary, lack of funds put them under control of a receiver in 1892. Although the company battled on until 1897, it was eventually offered for sale and was purchased by the B&NCR, who

A sunny day in Portstewart with the tramway facing little competition from road vehicles.
John Langford Collection

The Portstewart Tramway

Locomotives

No.	Manufacturer	Type	Year	Works No.	Driving wheel dia.	Wheelbase	Cylinders	Heating surface (sq. ft)	Grate area (sq. ft)	Boiler pressure (psi)	Weight	Tractive effort at 85% (lb.)	Withdrawn
1	Kitson	0-4-0	1882	T56	2'4½"	5'0"	8"x12"	116	5.17	150	9 t 0 cwt	3,680	1926
2	Kitson	0-4-0	1883	T84	2'4½"	5'0"	8"x12"	116	5.17	150	9 t 0 cwt	3,680	1926
3	Kitson	0-4-0	1901	T302	2'2¾"	4'6"	9½"x12"	133.4	5.72	160	11 t 0 cwt	5,320	1926

Notes
No. 1 – Cylinder diam. later reduced to 7½ in., boiler pressure red to 140 psi. Preserved in Hull Transport Museum.
No. 2 – Cylinder diam. later reduced to 7½ in., boiler pressure red to 140 psi. Preserved in Belfast Transport Museum.
No. 3 – Sold to contractor.

Carriages

No.	Type	Maker	Built	Length	Compts	Wheel dia.	Wheel centres	Withdrawn
1	4 wheel, double deck	Metropolitan-Cammell	1882	12 ft 7½ in.*	first down/third up		4'9"	1899
2	4 wheel, single deck	Metropolitan-Cammell	1882	16 ft 7½ in.			6'0"	1926
3	4 wheel luggage van	Metropolitan-Cammell	1882					1926
4	Bogie, double deck	Milnes (Birkenhead)	1897		third	2'6"		1926
1 (2nd)	Bogie, double deck	Milnes (Birkenhead)	1899		third	2'6"		1926

Notes
* Length over body. End platforms extra 4 ft 6 in. either end.
No. 2 – Largely used as spare after arrival of Nos. 4 and second No. 1.
No. 3 – Luggage van with some provision for passengers. For smokers.

invested heavily to raise standards on the line with the purchase of new rolling stock and relaying much of the track. They also built a new depot building on the Parade in Portstewart, replacing the original, inadequate structure. Following these improvements, passenger numbers and consequent revenue increased.

But the days of the B&NCR itself were numbered and it was taken over by the Midland Railway in 1903, operations being overseen by its Northern Counties Committee. Under the NCC there was little further investment in the tramway during the following decade and as the equipment aged and breakdowns occurred more frequently, traffic and revenue declined. As replacement of the infrastructure became necessary, World War I intervened and investment was suspended.

Emerging from the war years and ultimately from Government control, which ended in 1921, the tramway faced a different economic climate - costs had escalated in the war years and road transport offered a realistic alternative to rail transport. The lack of investment deferred by the war years had left the track and motive power in serious need of repair. The NCC briefly proposed rerouting its main line to take it nearer the centre of Portstewart but opposition from the urban council prevented such a move. Then, in 1923, the NCC became part of the LMS as part of the Grouping of Britain's railways.

The tramway track continued to deteriorate, but the LMS (NCC) was reluctant to invest in replacement and in September 1925 served notice of closure. In 1926 the steam tramway was replaced by a road omnibus service provided by a local contractor under contract to the NCC. The last tram ran on 30th January, 1926 from the station to the depot where it was met by a large crowd in a party mood. The Portstewart tramway had the distinction of being the first Irish narrow gauge tramway to open but also enjoyed the dubious distinction of being the first to close. Two of its three locomotives survive in museums in Belfast and Hull.

Chronology

26.04.1880	Order-in-Council granted to the Portstewart Tramway Company.
26.06.1882	Tramway opened.
15.10.1892	Company placed in receivership.
01.06.1897	Ownership transferred to B&NCR.
01.07.1903	Midland Railway (NCC) takes control.
01.01.1923	MR becomes part of LMS.
22.09.1925	Application for closure.
30.01.1926	Closure.

Route

Distance	Station/Halt/Crossing	Opened	Closed	Notes
0	Portstewart B&NCR	1882	1926	Locally known as Cromore.
	Mill Road Crossing	1882	1926	
	Millbank	1882	1926	Request stop.
½	Golf Links Halt	1882	1926	Request stop.
	Victoria Terrace	1882	1926	Passing loop.
1¾	Portstewart Depot	1882	1926	New building erected by NCC in 1899.

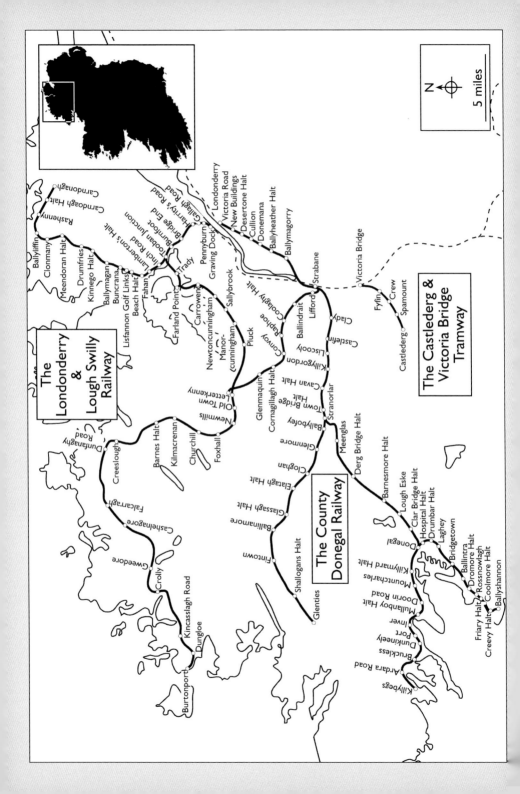

5 miles

N

The Londonderry & Lough Swilly Railway

The Castlederg & Victoria Bridge Tramway

The County Donegal Railway

Cardonagh
Cardonagh Halt
Rashenny
Ballyliffin
Clonmany
Meendoran Halt
Drumfries
Kinnego Halt
Ballymagan
Buncrana
Listannon Golf Links
Beach Halt
Fahan
Lamberton's Halt
Inch Road
Tooban Junction
Burnfoot
Bridge End
Harry's Road
Gallagh Road
Trady
Farland Point
Carrowen
Newtoncunningham
Manorcunningham
Sallybrook
Pennyburn
Graving Dock
Londonderry
Victoria Road
New Buildings
Desertone Halt
Cullion
Donemana
Ballyheather Halt
Ballymagorry
Strabane
Lifford
Coolaghy Halt
Pluck
Convoy
Raphoe
Ballindrait
Liscooly
Clady
Castlefin
Killygordon
Victoria Bridge
Fyfin
Crew
Spamount
Castlederg
Glenmaquin
Cornagillagh Halt
Old Town
Letterkenny
Newmills
Foxhall
Churchill
Kilmacrenan
Barnes Halt
Creeslough
Dunfanaghy Road
Falcarragh
Cashelnagore
Gweedore
Crolly
Kincasslagh Road
Dungloe
Burtonport
Glenties
Shallogans Halt
Fintown
Ballinamore
Glassagh Halt
Elatagh Halt
Cloghan
Glenmore
Ballybofey
Town Bridge Halt
Cavan Halt
Stranorlar
Meenglas
Derg Bridge Halt
Barnesmore Halt
Lough Eske
Clar Bridge Halt
Hospital Halt
Drumbar Halt
Donegal
Laghey
Bridgetown
Ballintra
Dromore Halt
Rossnowlagh
Coolmore Halt
Ballyshannon
Mountcharles
Killymard Halt
Doorin Road
Mullanboy Halt
Inver
Dunkineely
Bruckless
Ardara Road
Port
Killybegs
Friary Halt
Creevy Halt

Chapter Seven

The Londonderry &
Lough Swilly Railway

The Londonderry & Lough Swilly Railway began life in the early 1860s as an Irish standard gauge line, built to improve communication between the important trade centre and port of Derry and the land and villages along the banks of Lough Swilly. Its route utilized a number of large embankments built to reclaim land subject to tidal flooding in Lough Swilly. The initial line, opened on the very last day of 1863, was from the quayside at Derry, via Burnfoot, then along the top of the Trady embankment to Farland Point to connect with a steamer serving the villages and towns along the shores of Lough Swilly. While under construction, powers were obtained to extend northwards to the seaside resort of Buncrana, from a junction just west of Burnfoot, which opened in 1864. Within three years, though, the Farland branch was abandoned, being little used.

Long term demands from the traders of Letterkenny, for a rail connection to the town, were eventually satisfied in 1883, when the Letterkenny Railway Co. opened its 3 ft narrow gauge line from Letterkenny to link with the L&LSR at Tooban Junction. The line was operated by the L&LSR who regauged the line to Buncrana to 3 ft in 1885 giving a unified narrow gauge network of 37 miles. The nominally-independent Letterkenny Railway Co. was wound up after only four years of operation, due to failure to repay interest on Government loans, and the line was taken over by the Board of Works. The L&LSR agreed to continue to work the line and so began the company's chequered association with the Board.

In the furthest north-west of Donegal, L&LSR 4-8-0 No. 12 pulls a typical mixed train out of Burtonport yard on 24th June, 1937.   *H.C. Casserley, courtesy R.M. Casserley*

The Londonderry & Lough Swilly Railway

Locomotives

No.	Manufacturer	Type	Year	Works No.	Name	Driving wheel dia.	Leading/trailing wheel dia.	Total wheel-base	Coupled wheel-base	Cyls (in.)	Heating surface (sq. ft)	Grate area (sq. ft)	Water capacity (galls)	Coal capacity (cwt)	Boiler pressure (psi)	Weight (t. cwt.)	Max. axle load (t. cwt.)	Tractive effort at 85% (lb.)	Wdn
1	Black, Hawthorn	0-6-2T	1882	684	J.T. Macky	3'6"	2'4½"	16'10"	9'3"	13"x19"	592	8¾	500	25	140	24-0		9,100	1911
2	Black, Hawthorn	0-6-2T	1883	742	Londonderry	3'6"	2'4½"	16'10"	9'3"	13"x19"	592	8¾	600	25	140	24-0		9,100	1912
3	Black, Hawthorn	0-6-2T	1883	743	Donegal	3'6"	2'4½"	16'10"	9'3"	13"x19"	592	8¾	600	25	140	24-3		9,100	1913
4 (17)	Black, Hawthorn	0-6-0T	1885	834	Inishowen	3'6"	-	11'0"	11'0"	14"x20"	592	8¾	650	25	140	26-0	8-6		1940
5 (5A)	R. Stephenson & Co.	2-4-0T	1873	2088	-	3'9"	2'6"	12'0"	6'6"	15"x20"	696½	10½	600			26-10			1900
6 (6A)	R. Stephenson & Co.	2-4-0T	1873	2089	-	3'9"	2'6"	12'0"	6'6"	15"x20"	696½	10½	600			26-10			1900
5 (15)	Hudswell, Clarke	4-6-2T	1899	518	-	3'9"	2'2"/2'6"	22'4½"	9'0"	15"x22"	832	12½	900	30	150	40-10	8-0	14,050	1954
6 (16)	Hudswell, Clarke	4-6-2T	1899	519	-	3'9"	2'2"/2'6"	22'4½"	9'0"	15"x22"	832	12½	900	30	150	40-10	8-0	14,050	1953
7	Hudswell, Clarke	4-6-2T	1901	577	Edward VII	3'9"	2'2"/2'6"	22'4½"	9'0"	15"x22"	777¼	12½	850	25	150	41-0	8-0	14,050	1940
8	Hudswell, Clarke	4-6-2T	1901	562	-	3'9"	2'2"/2'6"	22'4½"	9'0"	15"x22"	777¼	12½	850	25	150	41-0	8-0	14,050	1954
1	A. Barclay, Sons & Co.	4-6-0T	1902	933	-	3'6"	2'1"	17'4½"	9'6"	14"x20"	628	9½	750	25	150	30-0	8-0	12,000	1940
2	A. Barclay, Sons & Co.	4-6-0T	1902	934	-	3'6"	2'1"	17'4½"	9'6"	14"x20"	628	9½	750	25	150	30-0	8-0	12,000	1954
3	A. Barclay, Sons & Co.	4-6-0T	1902	935	-	3'6"	2'1"	17'4½"	9'6"	14"x20"	628	9½	750	25	150	30-0	8-0	12,000	1954
4	A. Barclay, Sons & Co.	4-6-0T	1902	936	-	3'6"	2'1"	17'4½"	9'6"	14"x20"	628	9½	750	25	150	30-0	8-0	12,000	1953
9	Kerr, Stuart	4-6-2T	1904	845	Aberfoyle	3'9"	2'0"/2'3"	21'8½"	9'0"	14"x20"	650	11	700	20	150	35-0	7-0	12,000	1928
10	Kerr, Stuart	4-6-2T	1904	846	Richmond	3'9"	2'0"/2'3"	21'8½"	9'0"	14"x20"	650	11	700	20	150	35-0	7-0	12,000	1954
11	Hudswell, Clarke	4-8-0	1905	746	-	3'9"	2'1"	21'8½"	13'6"	15½"x22"	1,005½	15	1,500	80	170	37-0	6-12	17,000	1933
12	Hudswell, Clarke	4-8-0	1905	747	-	3'9"	2'1"	21'8½"	13'6"	15½"x22"	1,005½	15	1,500	80	170	37-0	6-12	17,000	1954
13	Hawthorn, Leslie	4-6-2T	1910	2801	-	3'9"	2'3"/2'9"	23'6"	9'0"	14½"x22"	803	11½	1,300	35	175	41-11	8-7	15,250	1940
14	Hawthorn, Leslie	4-6-2T	1910	2802	-	3'9"	2'3"/2'9"	23'6"	9'0"	14½"x22"	803	11½	1,300	35	175	41-11	8-7	15,250	1943
5	Hudswell, Clarke	4-8-4T	1912	985	-	3'9"	2'1"/2'1"	31'0"	13'6"	16"x20"	1,063	17	1,500	50	180	58-15	8-10	17,350	1954
6	Hudswell, Clarke	4-8-4T	1912	986	-	3'9"	2'1"/2'1"	31'0"	13'6"	16"x20"	1,063	17	1,500	50	180	58-15	8-10	17,350	1954

Notes

No. 4 (17) – Renumbered 1913 and name removed. Out of use for several years before scrapped in 1940.

No. 5 (5A) – Ex-Glenariff Iron Ore & Harbour Co. Built 1873. Purchased by L&LSR 1885.

No. 6 (6A) – Ex-Glenariff Iron Ore & Harbour Co. Built 1873. Purchased by L&LSR 1885. Out of use for some years before scrapped in 1904.

No. 5 (15) – Renumbered 1913.

No. 6 (16) – Renumbered 1913. Out of use for several years and cannibalized before scrapped in 1953.

No. 7 – Named for Royal train 1903.

No. 9 – Name removed c.1916. Derelict 1920, scrapped 1927.

No. 10 – Name removed c.1916

No. 11 – Out of use from 1928 and cannabalized to keep No. 12 running. Tender weight 21 tons 10 cwt.

No. 12 – Confined to Letterkenny shed after lifting of Burtonport extension completed 1949. Tender weight 21 tons 10 cwt.

No. 14 – Train engine Owencarrow viaduct derailment 1925.

The company was unwilling to consider extensions into north-west Donegal in view of shortage of finance and the sparse population, despite the passing of the Tramways & Public Companies (Ireland) Act 1883 and the Light Railways (Ireland) Act 1889, both providing financial support for construction of light railways. But the creation of a Congested Districts Board, following the Congested Districts Act of 1891, encouraged an expansion of railways and the passing of a further piece of railway legislation, the Railways (Ireland) Act 1896, provided the wherewithal to the L&LSR for the construction of two lines - an extension north to Carndonagh from Buncrana and the long extension to Burtonport, to take advantage of improvements to the port's harbour.

Both extensions were jointly planned by the Board of Works and the L&LSR with the former, as the paymaster, insisting on a number of economies and relationships between the two were never easy. Nevertheless, the Carndonagh line proceeded relatively smoothly, opening in July 1901. The longer extension to Burtonport crossed some of the most remote land in Ireland. For the Board, Burtonport and its fisheries were the target, the sole objective being to link the fishing port with the rest of Ireland's railway network by the shortest route possible, and, despite traversing almost 50 miles of the county, the railway managed to avoid most of the coastal settlements - at best they were served by stations two or three miles distant. From the outset, therefore, the company lacked an adequate catchment area generating passengers from amongst the local population and was reliant on whatever freight traffic it could win - a significant factor in the line's subsequent demise. With completion of the Burtonport extension, the L&LSR was at its most developed with some 99 miles of narrow gauge line.

Service on the Burtonport extension was poor from the beginning with each party blaming the other for the problems, the ongoing dispute leading to two investigations by Joseph Tatlow, then manager of the Midland Great Western Railway in Dublin, and a further investigation by the Vice-regal Commission on Irish Railways as a result of which some improvements in infrastructure and rolling stock did result. For their part, to overcome deficiencies in the motive power provided for the extension, the L&LSR purchased two 4-8-0 tender engines in 1905, both with the capacity to travel the length of the extension without the need for refuelling, and followed this up with the purchase of two massive 4-8-4T engines in 1912.

But the company continued to struggle and matters were made worse with the outbreak of World War I and the subsequent escalation in running and wage costs. Ireland's struggle for independence after World War I also left its mark with the railway being a target for attack to prevent troop trains from running. Following partition, the war of independence continued as a civil war between those who supported the Free State and those who continued the fight for independence of the whole island of Ireland, and further incidents involved the railway until hostilities largely ended in 1925. An added complication of Partition was the introduction of customs checks on every train passing along the line to Derry and, because four of the Swilly's 99 miles of rail were in Northern Ireland, the company was not incorporated into the Great Southern Railway.

The 1920s and 1930s proved to be the crunch period for the Swilly. The company elected not to follow the example of the County Donegal Railways Joint

Committee, which successfully introduced railcar operations, but instead saw its future in road transport and began the purchase of suitable road vehicles.

Competition from road transport resulted in the demise of the Carndonagh extension north of Buncrana, closed after only 34 years of service. Retrenchment of rail services continued as the road transport fleet rapidly expanded and with it, the company became financially stronger, paying healthy dividends. As World War II was breaking out on Europe, closure of the Burtonport extension was sanctioned and the lifting of rails began in June 1940, despite local protests. However, wartime fuel rationing led to a serious curtailment of road transport and the L&LSR reopened services between Letterkenny and Gweedore at their own financial risk on 3rd February, 1941. Goods trains to Gweedore, with an added passenger coach or two as required, operated throughout the war, carrying much-needed turf. There was, though, little in the way of repair or replacement of the permanent way and by 1946, the line was deemed to be in a dangerous condition and closure was recommended. Regular goods services ceased on the 6th January, 1947 - thereafter occasional specials ran until the section was closed completely in June 1947.

The buses had won, and it was small wonder as at least they actually went into the little towns and villages rather than giving them a passing nod from a bleak hillside several miles away. Regular passenger services ceased on the Tooban-Letterkenny section and though they continued for a short period to Buncrana, due to a lack of a suitable bus service, these too soon disappeared. These operated as mixed trains, with a passenger brake van at the rear. Passengers could use these trains, if they did not mind the somewhat slow going involved by much shunting of freight wagons and vans at wayside stations. Occasional railway excursions continued on public holidays but numbers dwindled and these ceased in 1951.

One of the four Andrew Barclay 4-6-2T locomotives supplied in 1902 for the opening of the Letterkenny & Burtonport Extension Railway and subsequently found to be under-powered for the line.   *R.W. Rush Collection*

Once an adequate road goods service was available the inevitable closure followed and on 1st July, 1953, the last train crossed Derry's Strand Road into Graving Dock station. Few were present to witness the end of railway operations. The company went over entirely to road transport and has since then continued as a major passenger and freight haulier for the north of the county with its buses still a familiar sight on Donegal's roads.

Chronology

26.06.1853	Londonderry & Lough Swilly Railway incorporated (for construction of 8¾ miles from Londonderry to Farland Point - Broad gauge).
01.08.1859	Additional Act passed (other time expired).
22.07.1861	Powers granted for extension to Buncrana.
31.12.1863	Line opened to Farland Point.
09.09.1864	Line opened to Buncrana.
July 1866	Tooban Jn-Farland branch closed.
1876	Letterkenny Railway Act passed.
29.06.1880	Second Act passed allowing construction to 3 ft 0 in. gauge. Also gave authority to L&LSR to regauge their line.
30.06.1883	Letterkenny Railway opened (3 ft 0 in. gauge).
04.02.1885	L&LSR regauging completed.
01.07.1901	Carndonagh Extension opened.
09.03.1903	Letterkenny & Burtonport Extension Railway (L&BER) opened.
30.11.1935	Carndonagh Extension closed.
03.06.1940	Letterkenny & Burtonport Extension closed.
03.02.1941	L&BER reopened to Gweedore (due to wartime fuel shortage and local protest).
06.01.1947	L&BER closed to all traffic. (Some special trains continued until June 1947.)
01.07.1953	Complete closure.

Route

Distance	Station/Halt	Opened	Closed	Notes
0	Londonderry (Graving Dock)	1863	1953	
0¼	Pennyburn Halt	1863	1953	Not public.
2	No. 1 Gates	1863	1953	
2	Gallagh Road	1880	1924	
2	No. 2 Gates	1863	1953	
2¾	Harrity's Road	1863	1864	
3¾	Bridge End	1863	1953	
3¾	No. 3 Gates	1863	1953	
5¼	Burnfoot	1864	1953	Closed 1866-73.
6¼	Tooban Junction	1864	1953	Closed 1866-83. Reopened as Burnfoot Jn - renamed 1920.
7	Inch Road	1864	1953	
7¾	Lamberton's Halt	1927	1948	
9¼	Fahan	1864	1953	
10½	Beach Halt	1939	1948	
11	Golf Platform	1892	1953	Renamed Lisfannon Links 1922.

(continued on page 49)

Carriages

No.	Type	Built	Maker	Length	Compts	Seats	Wheel Diam	Wheel centres	Bogie centres	Withdrawn
1	Third 6 wheel	1884	Railway Carriage Co., Oldbury	31'9"	5 (3rd)		2'6"	10'0"		
2	Composite 6 wheel	1884	Railway Carriage Co., Oldbury	31'9"	3 3 1 1 3		2'6"	10'0"		
3	Composite 6 wheel	1884	Railway Carriage Co., Oldbury	31'9"	3 3 1 1 3		2'6"	10'0"		
4	Third 6 wheel	1884	Railway Carriage Co., Oldbury	31'9"	5 (3rd)		2'6"	10'0"		
5	Composite 6 wheel	1884	Railway Carriage Co., Oldbury	31'9"	3 3 1 1 3		2'6"	10'0"		
6	Third 6 wheel	1884	Railway Carriage Co., Oldbury	31'9"	5 (3rd)		2'6"	10'0"		
7	Third 6 wheel	1884	Railway Carriage Co., Oldbury	31'9"	5 (3rd)		2'6"	10'0"		
8	Third 6 wheel	1884	Railway Carriage Co., Oldbury	31'9"	5 (3rd)		2'6"	10'0"		
9	Third 6 wheel	1884	Railway Carriage Co., Oldbury	31'9"	5 (3rd)		2'6"	10'0"		Pre-1925
10	Third 6 wheel	1884	Railway Carriage Co., Oldbury	31'9"	5 (3rd)		2'6"	10'0"		
11	Third 6 wheel	1884	Railway Carriage Co., Oldbury	31'9"	5 (3rd)		2'6"	10'0"		
12	Third 6 wheel	1884	Railway Carriage Co., Oldbury	31'9"	5 (3rd)		2'6"	10'0"		
13	Third 6 wheel	1885	Railway Carriage Co., Oldbury	31'9"	5 (3rd)		2'6"	10'0"		
14	Composite 6 wheel	1885	Railway Carriage Co., Oldbury	31'9"	3 3 1 1 3		2'6"	10'0"		Pre-1925
15	Third 6 wheel	1885	Railway Carriage Co., Oldbury	31'9"	5 (3rd)		2'6"	10'0"		Pre-1925
16	Third 6 wheel	1885	Railway Carriage Co., Oldbury	31'9"	5 (3rd)		2'6"	10'0"		Pre-1925
17	Third 6 wheel	1885	Railway Carriage Co., Oldbury	31'9"	5 (3rd)		2'6"	10'0"		
18	Third 6 wheel	1885	Railway Carriage Co., Oldbury	31'9"	5 (3rd)		2'6"	10'0"		
19	Third 6 wheel	1885	Railway Carriage Co., Oldbury	31'9"	5 (3rd)		2'6"	10'0"		
20	Tricomposite 6 wheel	1895	Railway Carriage Co., Oldbury	31'9"	5		2'6"	10'0"		
21	Composite 6 wheel	1895	Railway Carriage Co., Oldbury	31'9"	3 3 1 1 3		2'6"	10'0"		
22	Composite 6 wheel	1899	Railway Carriage Co., Oldbury	31'9"	3 3 1 1 3		2'6"	10'0"		
23	Bogie third	1899	Lancaster Railway Carriage & Wagon Co.	35'9"	6	60	2'6"	4'6"	25'9"	
24	Tricomposite	1901	Lancaster Railway Carriage & Wagon Co.	35'9"	3 3 1 1 2 2*		2'6"	4'6"	25'9"	
25	Bogie brake third	1901	Lancaster Railway Carriage & Wagon Co.	35'9"	2	20	2'6"	4'6"	25'9"	
26	Bogie third	1901	Lancaster Railway Carriage & Wagon Co.	35'9"	6	60	2'6"	4'6"	25'9"	
27	Bogie third	1901	Lancaster Railway Carriage & Wagon Co.	35'9"	6	60	2'6"	4'6"	25'9"	
28	Bogie third	1901	Lancaster Railway Carriage & Wagon Co.	35'9"	6	60	2'6"	4'6"	25'9"	
29	Bogie third	1901	Lancaster Railway Carriage & Wagon Co.	35'9"	6	60	2'6"	4'6"	25'9"	
30	Bogie tricomposite	1901	Lancaster Railway Carriage & Wagon Co.	35'9"	3 3 1 1 2 2*		2'6"	4'6"	25'9"	
31	Bogie tricomposite	1901	Lancaster Railway Carriage & Wagon Co.	35'9"	3 3 1 1 2 2*		2'6"	4'6"	25'9"	
32	Bogie brake third	1901	Lancaster Railway Carriage & Wagon Co.	35'9"	2	20	2'6"	4'6"	25'9"	
33	Bogie brake third	1901	Lancaster Railway Carriage & Wagon Co.	35'9"	3	30	2'6"	4'6"	25'9"	
34	Bogie brake third	1901	Lancaster Railway Carriage & Wagon Co.	35'9"	3	30	2'6"	4'6"	25'9"	
35	Bogie third	1901	Lancaster Railway Carriage & Wagon Co.	35'9"	6	60	2'6"	4'6"	25'9"	

L&BER

No.	Type	Built	Maker	Length	Compts	Seats	Wheel Diam	Wheel centres	Bogie centres	Withdrawn
1B	Bogie third	1903	R.Y. Pickering	35'9"	6		2'6"	4'6"	25'9"	
2B	Bogie third	1903	R.Y. Pickering	35'9"	6		2'6"	4'6"	25'9"	
3B	Bogie third	1903	R.Y. Pickering	35'9"	6		2'6"	4'6"	25'9"	
4B	Bogie third	1903	R.Y. Pickering	35'9"	6		2'6"	4'6"	25'9"	
5B	Bogie third	1903	R.Y. Pickering	35'9"	6		2'6"	4'6"	25'9"	

6B	Bogie brake third	1903	R.Y. Pickering	35'9"		3		2'6"	4'6"	25'9"
7B	Bogie brake third	1903	R.Y. Pickering	35'9"		3		2'6"	4'6"	25'9"
8B	Bogie brake third	1903	R.Y. Pickering	35'9"		3		2'6"	4'6"	25'9"
9B	Bogie brake third	1903	R.Y. Pickering	35'9"		3		2'6"	4'6"	25'9"
10B	Bogie tricomposite	1903	R.Y. Pickering	35'9"	3 2 1 1 2 3*			2'6"	4'6"	25'9"
11B	Bogie tricomposite	1903	R.Y. Pickering	35'9"	3 2 1 1 2 3*			2'6"	4'6"	25'9"
12B	Bogie tricomposite	1903	R.Y. Pickering	35'9"	3 2 1 1 2 3*			2'6"	4'6"	25'9"
13B	Bogie third	1910	R.Y. Pickering	35'9"	6			2'6"	4'6"	25'9"

Notes

* Second replaced by third when second abolished in 1929.

No. 1 – Damaged in collision Jun. 1891. To CB&PR 1918-21.
No. 2 – Damaged in collision Jun. 1891. Rebuilt 1921.
No. 5 – Damaged in collision Jun. 1891. Rebuilt as third. Damaged in ambush Jan. 1921.
No. 6 – Damaged in collision Jun. 1891.
No. 7 – Damaged in collision Jun. 1891. Rebuilt 1929.
No. 8 – Rebuilt 1922.
No. 9 – Damaged in collision Jun. 1891.
No. 10 – Rebuilt 1922.
No. 12 – Damaged malicious derailment 1923 and in Owecarrow accident 1925. Rebuilt 1926.
No. 13 – Burnt Pennyburn Feb. 1923. Rebuilt Oct. 1923.
No. 18 – Rebuilt 1922.
No. 20 – Rebuilt 1925.
No. 22 – Damaged in collision Jun. 1891. Rebuilt ? as composite. Burnt Pennyburn Feb. 1923. Rebuilt as third.
No. 23 – Converted to hut at Pennyburn (post-1937).
No. 25 – Damaged in ambush Jan. 1921.
No. 26 – Rebuilt 1927.
No. 27 – Heavy repairs 1921.
No. 28 – 'Carn coach'. Heavy repairs Nov. 1920.
No. 29 – 'Carn coach'. Rebuilt 1927.
No. 30 – 'Carn coach'. Later 3 3 1 1 3 3.
No. 31 – 'Carn coach'. Later 3 3 1 1 3 3.
No. 32 – 'Carn coach'. Burnt Pennyburn Feb. 1923, rebuilt Oct. 23.
No. 33 – 'Carn coach'. Originally third. Rebuilt as brake third 1923.
No. 34 – 'Carn coach'.
No. 35 – 'Carn coach'. Burnt after derailment Feb. 1923. Rebuilt Oct. 23.
No. 1B – Damaged in ambush Jan. 1921.
No. 3B – Heavy repairs 1918.
No. 4B – Heavy repairs 1918. Damaged in Crolley derailment 1925.
No. 6B – Derailed Crolley 1923.
No. 7B – Converted to covered wagon/brake van.
No. 8B – Slightly damaged Owencarrow accident Jan. 1925.
No. 10B – Burnt Pennyburn Feb. 1923. Rebuilt May 1925.
No. 11B – Damaged Owencarrow accident Jan. 1925.
No. 12B – Damaged in Crolley derailment 1923. Reblt May 25. Heavy repairs 1927.

Wagons

Nos.	Type	Built	Maker	Length	Width	Wheelbase	Capacity	Tare weight	Notes
	Flats, falling sides (90)	1887-1914	Pickering	13'0"	7'0"	8'0"			Nos. 2-5, 7, 8, 11, 12, 14-18, 20-30, 35, 37, 39, 83, 85, 87, 89-91, 93-100, 136-138, 140, 141, 143-146, 148-161, 163-167, 169-178, 186-196.
	Flats, centre door (26)			13'0"	7'0"	8'0"			Nos. 13, 31, 33, 34, 36, 80-82, 101-115, 139, 147.
	Covered (27)			14'0"	7'0"	8'0"			Nos. 43, 47, 49, 52, 54, 62, 64-66, 69, 71, 74, 75, 116-118, 120-128, 134, 135.
	Covered, centre canvas (29)			14'0"	7'0"	8'0"			Nos. 19, 44-46, 48, 50, 51, 53, 55-61, 63, 67, 68, 70, 72, 73, 76, 92, 179-184.
	Cattle Trucks (5)								Nos. 41, 42, 77-79.
	Oil Tanks (2)								Nos. 10, 185.
6	Coal Stage (1)			14'0"	7'0"	8'0"			(Burtonport)
119	Stores Van (1)								
	Flats			13'6"	7'0"	8'0"			Nos. 201, 206, 207 - Purchased 1943 from CVR.
	Covered Wagons (7)								Nos. 198-200, 202-205 - Purchased 1943 from CVR.
197	Bogie Flat								Purchased 1943 from CVR.
208	Bogie Flat								Built Pennyburn - frame of coach 23 plus 3 CVR flat bodies.
	Oil Tanks (4)								Nos. 1537-1540. BP & Co.
	Oil Tanks (2)								Nos. 3007, 3008. Anglo-American Co.

L&BER

Nos.	Type	Built	Maker	Length	Width	Wheelbase	Capacity	Tare weight	Notes
	Flats (35)	1903	Pickering				6 t 0 cwt	3 t 15 cwt	Nos. 1-15, 69-88.
	Covered, centre canvas (36)								Nos. 16-20, 23-25, 28-38, 40-43, 45-51, 53, 54, 56, 58-60.
	Covered (15)								Nos. 21, 22, 26, 27, 39, 44, 52, 55, 57, 63-68.
61	Timber Truck	1903	Pickering	14'0"	7'0"	8'0"		3 t 17 cwt	
62	Horse Box		Pickering						
	Bogie Covered (3)								Nos. 89-91. Bogie ventilated fish vans.

Distance	Station/Halt	Opened	Closed	Notes
12¼	Buncrana	1864	1953	
12¼	Buncrana Station Gates	1901	1935	
13	No. 1 Gates	1901	1935	
13¾	No. 2 Gates	1901	1935	
14	Ballymagan	1901	1935	
15¾	Kinnego Halt (No. 3 Gates)	1901	1935	Halt from *c.* 1930.
17¾	Dumfries	1901	1935	
19¼	No. 4 Gates	1901	1935	
21½	Meendoran Halt (No. 5 Gates)	1901	1935	Halt from *c.* 1930.
22	No. 6 Gates	1901	1935	
22¼	No. 7 Gates	1901	1935	
23	Clonmany	1901	1935	
23½	No. 8 Gates	1901	1935	
23¾	No. 9 Gates	1901	1935	
24½	Ballyliffin	1901	1935	
25½	No. 10 Gates	1901	1935	
26¼	Rashenny	1901	1935	
27½	No 11 Gates	1901	1935	
28	Carndoagh Halt	1930	1935	Also 'Campbell's Halt'.
28	No. 12 Gates	1901	1935	
28¼	No. 13 Gates	1901	1935	
28¾	No. 14 Gates	1901	1935	
29¾	No. 15 Gates	1901	1935	
30½	Carndonagh	1901	1935	
6¼	Tooban Junction	1864	1953	Closed 1866-83. Reopened as Burnfoot Jn - renamed 1920.
9¼	Carrowen	1883	1953	
13	Newtoncunningham	1883	1953	
16¾	Sallybrook Station Gates	1885	1953	
16¾	Sallybrook	1885	1953	
18½	Manorcunningham	1883	1953	
20½	Pluck	1883	1953	
24¾	Letterkenny	1883	1953	
24¾	No. 1 Gates	1903	1947	
25½	Old Town	1903	1947	
28½	Newmills	1903	1947	
30	Foxhall	1903	1947	
30½	No. 2 Gates	1903	1947	
31¾	No. 3 Gates	1903	1947	
33½	Churchhill Station Gates	1903	1947	
33½	Churchhill	1903	1947	
35¼	No. 5 Gates	1903	1947	
37	Kilmacrenan	1903	1947	
38	No. 6 Gates	1903	1947	
38½	No. 7 Gates	1903	1947	
39¾	No 8 Gates	1903	1947	
39¾	Barnes Halt	1927	1940	
42½	Owencarrow Viaduct			
44¼	No. 9 Gates	1903	1947	
44½	No. 10 Gates	1903	1947	

Distance	Station/Halt	Opened	Closed	Notes
45½	Creeslough	1903	1947	
46½	Dunfanaghy Road	1903	1947	
47¾	No. 11 Gates	1903	1947	
48¼	No. 12 Gates	1903	1947	
51½	No. 13 Gates	1903	1947	
53½	Falcarragh	1903	1947	
53½	Falcarragh Station Gates	1903	1947	
55	No. 14 Gates	1903	1947	
56¾	Cashelnagore	1903	1947	
56¾	Cashelnagore Station Gates	1903	1947	
59	No. 15 Gates	1903	1947	
60	No. 16 Gates	1903	1947	
62¾	Gweedore	1903	1947	
64	No. 17 Gates	1903	1940	
64½	No. 18 Gates	1903	1940	
66	Crolly	1903	1940	
66½	No. 19 Gates	1903	1940	
70	No. 20 Gates	1903	1940	
71½	Kincasslagh Road	1913	1940	Known locally as Meenbanid.
71½	No. 21 Gates	1903	1940	
72¼	No. 22 Gates	1903	1940	
73	Dungloe Road	1903	1940	Originally Loughmeala.
73½	No. 23 Gates	1903	1940	
74	No. 24 Gates	1903	1940	
74½	Burtonport	1903	1940	

Pushing on through the Barnes Gap near the Owencarrow viaduct, captured on 24th June, 1937.   *H.C. Casserley, courtesy R.M. Casserley*

Chapter Eight

The County Donegal Railways Joint Committee

The narrow gauge network that was to become the County Donegal Railways Joint Committee began life as the standard gauge Finn Valley Railway Co. which opened in September 1863, connecting the town of Stranorlar to the Irish North Western Railway (INWR) network at Strabane. The INWR subsequently became part of the Great Northern Railway of Ireland. A 3 ft gauge westward extension from Stranorlar towards the town of Donegal was opened by the West Donegal Railway in 1882, initially as far as Druminin, four miles short of Donegal, close to Lough Eske. Donegal itself was eventually reached in September 1889. The FVR and WDR merged in 1892 as the Donegal Railway Company (DR) and the FVR section was regauged to 3 ft in July 1894.

By this time, state aid granted under the provisions of the Light Railways (Ireland) Act 1889, had funded the construction of a 19-mile extension from Donegal westwards to the fishing port of Killybegs, opened in August 1893, and a 24-mile branch from Stranorlar, following the course of the upper Finn and the Shallogan rivers to Glenties, which opened in June 1895.

Two further extensions, for which the company raised its own finance were authorized by the Donegal Railway Act 1896. The first, from Strabane to the important port of Derry, overcame opposition from the GNR(I) and opened to traffic in August 1900. The second, a branch line 15½ miles in length, from Donegal southwards to Ballyshannon, required the passing of a second Act, as, due to difficulties raising the necessary finance, the original powers had lapsed. This eventually opened in September 1905.

On 20th April, 1948 No. 5 *Drumboe* stands at Castlefin with the 12.45 pm working from Stranorlar to Strabane. *H.C. Casserley, courtesy R.M. Casserley*

The County Donegal Railways Joint Committee

Locomotives

No.	Manufacturer	Type	Year	Works No.	Name	Driving wheel dia.	Leading/trailing wheel dia.	Total wheel-base	Coupled wheel-base	Cyls (in.)	Heating surface (sq. ft)	Grate area (sq. ft)	Water capacity (galls)	Coal capacity (cwt)	Boiler pressure (psi)	Weight (t. cwt.)	Max. axle load (t. cwt.)	Tractive effort at 85% (lb.)	Wdn
1	Sharp, Stewart	2-4-0T	1881	3023	Alice	3'6"	2'6"	11'6"	6'0"	13x20	555	9¾	500	20	120	20-0	8-0	8,200	1926
2	Sharp, Stewart	2-4-0T	1881	3021	Blanche	3'6"	2'6"	11'6"	6'0"	13x20	555	9¾	500	20	120	20-0	8-0	8,200	1912
3	Sharp, Stewart	2-4-0T	1881	3022	Lydia	3'6"	2'6"	11'6"	6'0"	13x20	555	9¾	500	20	120	20-0	8-0	8,200	1912
4	Neilson	4-6-0T	1893	4573	Meenglas	3'6"	2'1"	16'7½"	9'0"	14x20	604	9¾	650	20	150	30-12¾	8-14	11,900	1935
5	Neilson	4-6-0T	1893	4574	Drumboe	3'6"	2'1"	16'7½"	9'0"	14x20	604	9¾	650	20	150	30-12¾	8-14	11,900	1931
6	Neilson	4-6-0T	1893	4575	Inver	3'6"	2'1"	16'7½"	9'0"	14x20	604	9¾	650	20	150	30-12¾	8-14	11,900	1931
7	Neilson	4-6-0T	1893	4576	Finn	3'6"	2'1"	16'7½"	9'0"	14x20	604	9¾	650	20	150	30-12¾	8-14	11,900	1931
8	Neilson	4-6-0T	1893	4577	Foyle	3'6"	2'1"	16'7½"	9'0"	14x20	604	9¾	650	20	150	30-12¾	8-14	11,900	1937
9	Neilson	4-6-0T	1893	4578	Columbkille	3'6"	2'1"	16'7½"	9'0"	14x20	604	9¾	650	20	150	30-12¾	8-14	11,900	1937
10	Neilson, Reid	4-4-4T	1902	6103	Sir James	4'0"	2'3"/2'3"	26'1½"	7'3"	14x20	713	11½	1,000	50	150	38-10¾	10-13	10,413	1933
11	Neilson, Reid	4-4-4T	1902	6104	Hercules	4'0"	2'3"/2'3"	26'1½"	7'3"	14x20	713	11½	1,000	50	150	38-10¾	10-13	10,413	1933
12	Nasmyth, Wilson	4-6-4T	1904	697	Eske	3'9"	2'3"/2'3"	25'2"	9'0"	15x21	757*	12	1,000	35	160	44-10	8-16	14,280	1954
13	Nasmyth, Wilson	4-6-4T	1904	698	Owenea	3'9"	2'3"/2'3"	25'2"	9'0"	15x21	757*	12	1,000	35	160	44-10	8-16	14,280	1952
14	Nasmyth, Wilson	4-6-4T	1904	699	Erne	3'9"	2'3"/2'3"	25'2"	9'0"	15x21	757*	12	1,000	35	160	44-10	8-16	14,280	1967
15	Nasmyth, Wilson	4-6-4T	1904	700	Mourne	3'9"	2'3"/2'3"	25'2"	9'0"	15x21	757*	12	1,000	35	160	44-10	8-16	14,280	1952
16	Nasmyth, Wilson	2-6-4T	1907	828	Donegal	4'0"	2'9"/2'3"	26'3"	10'0"	14x21	713	11½	1,000	50	175	43-10	9-0	12,730	-
17	Nasmyth, Wilson	2-6-4T	1907	829	Glenties	4'0"	2'9"/2'3"	26'3"	10'0"	14x21	713	11½	1,000	50	175	43-10	9-0	12,730	-
18	Nasmyth, Wilson	2-6-4T	1907	830	Killybegs	4'0"	2'9"/2'3"	26'3"	10'0"	14x21	713	11½	1,000	50	175	43-10	9-0	12,730	-
19	Nasmyth, Wilson	2-6-4T	1908	831	Letterkenny	4'0"	2'9"/2'3"	26'3"	10'0"	14x21	713	11½	1,000	50	175	43-10	9-0	12,730	1940
20	Nasmyth, Wilson	2-6-4T	1908	832	Raphoe	4'0"	2'9"/2'3"	26'3"	10'0"	14x21	713	11½	1,000	50	175	43-10	9-0	12,730	1955
21	Nasmyth, Wilson	2-6-4T	1912	958	Ballyshannon	4'0"	2'9"/2'3"	27'3"	10'0"	15½x21	724	11½	1,500	50	160	50-8	10-6	14,295	1961
2A	Nasmyth, Wilson	2-6-4T	1912	956	Strabane	4'0"	2'9"/2'3"	27'3"	10'0"	15½x21	724	11½	1,500	50	160	50-8	10-6	14,295	-
3A	Nasmyth, Wilson	2-6-4T	1912	957	Stranorlar	4'0"	2'9"/2'3"	27'3"	10'0"	15½x21	724	11½	1,500	50	160	50-8	10-6	14,295	1961

Notes

* When superheated.

No. 1 (First) – On loan to CB&PR 1918-1922.

No. 12 – Renumbered No. 9 (1937).

No. 13 – Renumbered No. 10 (1937). Involved in Hospital Halt accident August 1949.

No. 14 – Renumbered No. 11 (1937).

No. 15 – Renumbered No. 12 (1937). Out of use and cannibalized 1940-1952.

No. 16 – Renumbered/renamed No. 4 Meenglas (1937). Currently at Foyle Valley Railway Derry.

No. 17 – Renumbered/renamed No. 5 Drumboe (1937). Currently at Donegal Railway Heritage Centre.

No. 18 – Renumbered/renamed No. 6 Columbkille (1937). Currently at Foyle Valley Railway Derry.

No. 19 – Renumbered/renamed No. 7 Finn (1937) - though never actually changed. Involved in Donemana accident 1913.

No. 20 – Renumbered/renamed No. 8 Foyle (1937).

No. 21 – Renumbered/renamed No. 1 Alice (1928)

No. 2A – Renumbered renamed No. 2 Blanche (1928). Currently at Ulster Folk & Transport Museum, Cultra.

No. 3A – Renumbered/renamed No. 3 Lydia (1928).

Railcars/Diesel

No.	Source/Builder	Wheels	Year	Engine	Weight	Seats	Withdrawn
1	Allday & Onions	4	1906	Petrol 10 hp	1 t. 4½ cwt	10	-
2	Ex-DVLR (Charles H. Roe)	4	1926	Petrol 22 hp	2 t. 7 cwt	17	1934
2 (2nd)	Ex-C&VBT	2.4	1934	Petrol 22 hp		26/30	-
3	Ex-DVLR (Charles H. Roe)	4	1926	Petrol 22 hp	2 t. 7 cwt	17	1934
3 (2nd)	Ex-D&BST	2.4.2.	1934	Petrol 35 hp		40	-
4	O'Doherty / GNR(I)	4	1928	Petrol 36 hp	2 t. 12 cwt	22/21	1947
5	O'Doherty/Knutsford	4	1929	-	3 t. 4½ cwt	29	-
6	O'Doherty / GNR(I)	2.4	1930	Petrol 32 hp	5 t. 11 cwt	30	-
7	O'Doherty / GNR(I)	2.4	1930	Diesel 6L2	7 t. 0 cwt	32	1949
8	O'Doherty / GNR(I)	2.4	1931	Diesel 6L2	7 t. 0 cwt	32	1949
9	CDRJC ex-GN bus	2.2	1933	Petrol 36 hp		20	-
10	CDRJC ex-GN bus	2.2	1933	Petrol 36 hp		20	1939
10 (2nd)	Ex-CVR & Walker Bros.	4.4	1942	Diesel Gardner 6L2 74 hp	12 t. 0 cwt	28	-
11	Ex-CVR & Atkinson Walker	4	1933	Diesel Gardner 6L2 74 hp	12 t. 0 cwt	-	-
12	Walker Bros & GNR(I)	4.4	1934	Diesel Gardner 6L2 74 hp		41	-
13	Ex-D&BST	4	1934	-		16	1944
14	Walker Bros & GNR(I)	4.4	1935	Diesel Gardner 6L2 74 hp		41	1961
15	Walker Bros & GNR(I)	4.4	1936	Diesel Gardner 6L2 74 hp		41	-
16	Walker Bros & GNR(I)	4.4	1936	Diesel Gardner 6LW 102 hp		41	-
17	Walker Bros & GNR(I)	4.4	1938	Diesel Gardner 6LW 102 hp		43	1949
18	Walker Bros & GNR(I)	4.4	1940	Diesel Gardner 6LW 102 hp		43	-
19	Walker Bros & GNR(I)	4.4	1950	Diesel Gardner 6LW 102 hp	11 t. 5 cwt	41	-
20	Walker Bros & GNR(I)	4.4	1951	Diesel Gardner 6LW 102 hp	11 t. 5 cwt	41	-

Notes

No. 1 – Rebuilt 1920. Later 22 hp/36 hp petrol engines. Currently at Ulster Folk & Transport Museum, Cultra.

No. 2 – Converted from 4 ft 8½ in. gauge (Dundalk).

No. 2 (2nd) – Originally 20 hp paraffin engine. Rebuilt as trailer 1944 (30 seats). Sold 1961. Removed to Mountcharles.

No. 3 – Converted from 4 ft 8½ in. gauge (Dundalk).

No. 3 (2nd) – Rebuilt as trailer 1944 (32 seats). Currently at Ulster Folk & Transport Museum, Cultra.

No. 4 – Seating reduced by one when offside door moved to rear. Lent to Clogher Valley Railway 1932.

No. 5 – Built as trailer. Currently at Donegal Railway Heritage Centre.

No. 6 – Rebuilt as trailer 1945. Sold 1958. Removed to Inver.

No. 7 – First diesel-engined railcar in British Isles.

No. 9 – Converted from ex-GN road bus (Stranorlar). Front end with 36 hp engine transferred to No. 1 1949.

No. 10 – Converted from ex-GN road bus (Stranorlar). Destroyed by fire Ballyshannon 27.08.1939.

No. 10 (2nd) – Railcar No. 1 on CVR. Currently at Ulster Folk & Transport Museum.

No. 11 – Named *Phœnix*. Former steam tractor. Purchased from CVR minus engine and boiler for £125. Currently at Ulster Folk & Transport Museum, Derry.

No. 12 – First bogie railcar on CDRJC. Currently at Foyle Valley Railway, Derry.

No. 13 – Originally railcar on D&BST - rebuilt as trailer 1934.

No. 14 – Half cab. Engine replaced with Gardner 5LW bus engine 1954.

No. 15 – Sold 1961. Passenger compartment preserved (Donegal Railway Heritage Centre).

No. 16 – Sold to Dr Cox 1961. Lay in Stranorlar. Cut up c.1972.

No. 17 – Destroyed in Hospital Halt crash August 1949.

No. 18 – Damaged by fire November 1949. Rebuilt. Currently at Foyle Valley Railway, Derry.

No. 19 – Sold to Isle of Man Railway (IOMR) 1961.

No. 20 – Sold to IOMR 1961.

C&VBT – Castlederg & Victoria Bridge Tramway.
D&BST – Dublin & Blessington Steam Tramway.
DVLR – Derwent Valley Light Railway.

Carriages

No.	Type	Built	Weight t. cwt	Maker	Length	Compts first	3rd	Seats	Wheel dia.	Wheel centres	Bogie centres	Withdrawn
1	Saloon (lav.) 6 wheel	1882	9-0	Railway Carriage & Wagon Co.	31'0"	4	-	28	2'7"	10'0"	-	-
2	Composite 6 wheel	1882	9-0	Railway Carriage & Wagon Co.	31'0"	2	3	42	2'7"	10'0"	-	1952
3	Composite 6 wheel	1882	9-0	Railway Carriage & Wagon Co.	31'0"	2	3	42	2'7"	10'0"	-	1953
4	Third 6 wheel	1882	8-12	Railway Carriage & Wagon Co.	31'0"	-	5	50	2'7"	10'0"	-	1960
5	Third 6 wheel	1882	8-12	Railway Carriage & Wagon Co.	31'0"	-	5	50	2'7"	10'0"	-	1960
6	Third 6 wheel	1882	8-12	Railway Carriage & Wagon Co.	31'0"	-	5	50	2'7"	10'0"	-	1960
7	Third 6 wheel	1882	8-12	Railway Carriage & Wagon Co.	31'0"	-	5	50	2'7"	10'0"	-	1960
8	Third 6 wheel	1882	8-12	Railway Carriage & Wagon Co.	31'0"	-	5	50	2'7"	10'0"	-	1960
9	Brake third 6 wheel	1882	8-15	Railway Carriage & Wagon Co.	31'0"	-	3	30	2'7"	10'0"	-	1941
10	Brake third 6 wheel	1882	8-5	Railway Carriage & Wagon Co.	31'0"	-	3	30	2'7"	10'0"	-	1960
11	Brake third 6 wheel	1882	8-15	Railway Carriage & Wagon Co.	31'0"	-	3	30	2'7"	10'0"	-	1960
12	Composite	1893	10-0	Oldbury Carriage & Wagon Co.	31'0"	2	3	42	2'7"	4'3"	19'3"	1960
13	Composite	1893	10-0	Oldbury Carriage & Wagon Co.	31'0"	1	2	50	2'7"	4'3"	19'3"	1960
14	Composite	1893	10-0	Oldbury Carriage & Wagon Co.	31'0"	2	3	42	2'7"	4'3"	19'3"	1960
15	Composite	1893	10-0	Oldbury Carriage & Wagon Co.	31'0"	2	3	42	2'7"	4'3"	19'3"	1960
16	Composite	1893	10-0	Oldbury Carriage & Wagon Co.	31'0"	2	3	42	2'7"	4'3"	19'3"	1960
17	Composite	1893	10-0	Oldbury Carriage & Wagon Co.	31'0"	2	3	42	2'7"	4'3"	19'3"	1960
18	Third	1893	9-0	Oldbury Carriage & Wagon Co.	31'0"	-	5	50	2'7"	4'3"	19'3"	1960
19	Third	1893	9-0	Oldbury Carriage & Wagon Co.	31'0"	-	5	50	2'7"	4'3"	19'3"	1960
20	Third	1893	9-0	Oldbury Carriage & Wagon Co.	31'0"	-	5	50	2'7"	4'3"	19'3"	1960
21	Third	1893	9-0	Oldbury Carriage & Wagon Co.	31'0"	-	5	50	2'7"	4'3"	19'3"	1960
22	Third	1893	9-0	Oldbury Carriage & Wagon Co.	31'0"	-	5	50	2'7"	4'3"	19'3"	1960
23	Brake third	1893	9-13	Oldbury Carriage & Wagon Co.	31'0"	-	2	20	2'7"	4'3"	19'3"	1960
24	Brake third	1893	9-13	Oldbury Carriage & Wagon Co.	31'0"	-	2	20	2'7"	4'3"	19'3"	1960
25	Brake third	1893	9-13	Oldbury Carriage & Wagon Co.	31'0"	-	2	20	2'7"	4'3"	19'3"	1960
26	Brake third	1893	9-13	Oldbury Carriage & Wagon Co.	31'0"	-	2	20	2'7"	4'3"	19'3"	1960
27	Brake third	1893	9-13	Oldbury Carriage & Wagon Co.	31'0"	-	2	20	2'7"	4'3"	19'3"	1960
28	Brake third	1893	9-13	Oldbury Carriage & Wagon Co.	31'0"	-	2	20	2'7"	4'3"	19'3"	1960
29	Corridor third	1901	8-15	Oldbury Carriage & Wagon Co.	36'0"	-	2	56	2'7"	5'0"	23'6"	1960
30	Corridor third	1901	8-15	Oldbury Carriage & Wagon Co.	36'0"	-	2	56	2'7"	5'0"	23'6"	1960
31	Third	1901	11-15	Oldbury Carriage & Wagon Co.	36'0"	-	6	60	2'7"	6'0"	22'6"	1952
32	Third	1901	11-15	Oldbury Carriage & Wagon Co.	36'0"	-	6	60	2'7"	6'0"	22'6"	1960
33	Third	1901	11-15	Oldbury Carriage & Wagon Co.	36'0"	-	6	60	2'7"	6'0"	22'6"	1957
34	Third	1901	11-15	Oldbury Carriage & Wagon Co.	36'0"	-	6	60	2'7"	6'0"	22'6"	1952
35	Lavatory composite	1905	12-0	R.Y. Pickering	36'0"	2	2	26	2'7"	5'0"	23'6"	1952
36	Lavatory composite	1905	12-0	R.Y. Pickering	36'0"	2	2	26	2'7"	5'0"	23'6"	1952
37	Lavatory composite	1905	12-0	R.Y. Pickering	36'0"	2	2	26	2'7"	5'0"	23'6"	1949
38	Lavatory composite	1905	12-0	R.Y. Pickering	36'0"	2	2	26	2'7"	5'0"	23'6"	1957
39	Corridor third	1905	9-0	R.Y. Pickering	36'0"	-	2	60	2'7"	5'0"	23'6"	1956
40	Corridor third	1905	9-0	R.Y. Pickering	36'0"	-	2	60	2'7"	5'0"	23'6"	1960
41	Brake third	1905	12-0	R.Y. Pickering	36'0"	-	2	20	2'7"	5'0"	23'6"	1952
42	Brake third	1905	12-0	R.Y. Pickering	36'0"	-	2	20	2'7"	5'0"	23'6"	1952

No.		Type	Built		Builder			Comp.	Seats				Scrapped
43	(S&LR)	Brake third	1905	11-15	R.Y. Pickering	36'0"	–	2	20	27"	5'0"	23'6"	1952
44	(S&LR)	Third	1907	11-15	Oldbury Carriage & Wagon Co.	36'0"		6	60	27"	6'0"	22'6"	1952
45	(S&LR)	Third	1907	11-15	Oldbury Carriage & Wagon Co.	36'0"		6	60	27"	6'0"	22'6"	1952
46	(S&LR)	Third	1907	11-15	Oldbury Carriage & Wagon Co.	36'0"		6	60	27"	6'0"	22'6"	1957
47	(S&LR)	Third	1907	11-15	Oldbury Carriage & Wagon Co.	36'0"		6	60	27"	6'0"	22'6"	1960
48	(S&LR)	Third	1907	11-15	Oldbury Carriage & Wagon Co.	36'0"		6	60	27"	6'0"	22'6"	1952
49	(S&LR)	Third	1907	11-15	Oldbury Carriage & Wagon Co.	36'0"		6	60	27"	6'0"	22'6"	1952
50	(S&LR)	Third	1907	11-15	Oldbury Carriage & Wagon Co.	36'0"		6	60	27"	6'0"	22'6"	1952
51	(S&LR)	Composite	1907	12-0	Oldbury Carriage & Wagon Co.	36'0"	2	4	52	27"	6'0"	22'6"	1952
52	(S&LR)	Brake third	1907	12-12	Oldbury Carriage & Wagon Co.	36'0"		3	26	27"	6'0"	22'6"	1952
53	(S&LR)	Brake third	1907	12-12	Oldbury Carriage & Wagon Co.	36'0"		3	30	27"	6'0"	22'6"	1960
54	(S&LR)	Brake third	1907	12-12	Oldbury Carriage & Wagon Co.	36'0"		3	30	27"	6'0"	22'6"	1952
55	(S&LR)	Composite	1907	12-0	Oldbury Carriage & Wagon Co.	36'0"		4	52	27"	6'0"	22'6"	1952
56	(S&LR)	Composite	1907	12-0	Oldbury Carriage & Wagon Co.	36'0"		4	52	27"	6'0"	22'6"	1960
57		Third	1928	16-0	LMS (NCC)	50'0"		3	54	27"	5'6"	38'0"	1960
58		Third	1928	13-15	LMS (NCC)	41'3½"		2	56	27"	4'9"	31'3½"	1960
59		Third	1928	16-0	LMS (NCC)	50'0"		4	53	27"	5'6"	38'0"	1960

Notes

No. 1 – Preserved, Ulster Folk & Transport Museum (Cultra).
No. 2 – Original tricomposite (32112).
No. 3 – Original tricomposite (32112).
No. 4 – Conversion to wagon 321 in 1929.
No. 5 – Conversion to wagon 324 in 1930.
No. 6 – Conversion to wagon 325 in 1930.
No. 7 – Conversion to wagon 323 in 1930.
No. 8 – Conversion to wagon 314 in 1927.
No. 10 – Underframe conversion to flat wagon 313 in 1927.
No. 11 – Conversion to wagon 315 in 1927.
No. 12 – Later all-third. Purchased by Dr Cox 1961.
No. 13 – Rebuilt 1953 as 3 Bk 3. Auctioned 1961.
No. 14 – Later all-third. Preserved FVR.
No. 15 – Later all-third. Purchased by Dr Cox 1961.
No. 16 – Later all-third. Purchased by Dr Cox 1961.
No. 17 – Later all-third. Purchased by Dr Cox 1961.
No. 18 – Conversion to wagon 317 in 1928.
No. 19 – Conversion to wagon 316 in 1927.
No. 20 – Conversion to wagon 319 in 1928.
No. 21 – Conversion to wagon 320 in 1929.
No. 22 – Conversion to wagon 318 in 1928.
No. 23 – Purchased by Dr Cox 1961.
No. 24 – Conversion to wagon 331 in 1937.
No. 25 – Conversion to wagon 330 in 1937.
No. 26 – Conversion to wagon 333 in 1939.

No. 27 – Conversion to wagon 332 in 1937.
No. 28 – Auctioned 1961. Preserved (Donegal Railway Heritage Centre).
No. 29 – Conversion to wagon 322 in 1929.
No. 30 – Given roller bearings and used as trailer. Chassis preserved FVR.
No. 32 – Auctioned 1961.
No. 34 – Out of use since 1944.
No. 37 – Converted to hut, Strabane 1949.
No. 38 – Damaged by fire Ballindrait 1956.
No. 40 – Purchased by Dr Cox 1961.
No. 47 – Converted to passenger van (30 seats) 1944. Purchased by Dr Cox 1961.
No. 51 – Original third, converted to tricomposite following fire damage 1913. Became first/third when 2nd class scrapped 1924.
No. 53 – Purchased by Dr Cox 1961.
No. 54 – Original tricomposite. Became first/3rd when 2nd class scrapped 1924.
No. 56 – Original tricomposite. Became first/3rd when 2nd class scrapped 1924. Purchased by Dr Cox 1961.
No. 57 – NCC No. 352; auctioned 1961.
No. 58 – NCC No. 318; built on 1894 B&L coach underframe. Auctioned 1961. Preserved (Donegal Railway Heritage Centre).
No. 59 – NCC No. 351; auctioned 1961.
S&LR – Strabane & Letterkenny Railway.

Wagons Nos.	Type	Built	Maker	Length	Width	Wheelbase	Bogie centre	Capacity (t. cwt)	Tare weight (t. cwt)
1-40	WDR convertible wagons	1881	Oldbury Carriage & Wagon Co.	15'6"	7'0"	8'6"		6-0	3-12
41-43	WDR open wagons	1881	Oldbury Carriage & Wagon Co.	15'6"	7'0"	8'6"			
44, 45	WDR open wagons	1893	Oldbury Carriage & Wagon Co.	15'6"	7'0"	8'6"		6-0	4-7
46-95	Sliding door vans	1893	Oldbury Carriage & Wagon Co.	15'6"	7'0"	8'6"		6-0	4-5
96-100	Cattle vans	1893	Oldbury Carriage & Wagon Co.	15'6"	7'0"	8'6"			
101-120	4-plank open	1893	Oldbury Carriage & Wagon Co.	15'6"	7'0"	8'6"		6-0	4-0
121-154	Open wagons	1900	Oldbury Carriage & Wagon Co.	15'6"	7'0"	8'6"			
155-157	Tranship wagons	1900	Oldbury Carriage & Wagon Co.	15'6"	7'0"	8'6"			
159	Bogie open	1900	Oldbury Carriage & Wagon Co.	25'0"	7'0"	42"	15'6"	14-0	7-18¾
158, 160-168	3-plank open wagons	1905	Metropolitan Carriage & Wagon Co.	15'6"	7'0"	8'6"		6-0	4-0
169-198	Sliding door vans	1905	Metropolitan Carriage & Wagon Co.	15'6"	7'0"	8'6"		7-0	4-7
199-208	Cattle vans	1905	R.Y. Pickering	15'6"	7'0"	8'6"		7-0	4-10
209, 210	Goods brake vans	1881	Oldbury Carriage & Wagon Co.	14'0"	7'2"	8'0"			
211-228	3-plank open ballast wagons	1904	Oldbury Carriage & Wagon Co.	14'0"	7'0"	8'6"		6-0	3-4
228 (2nd)	3-plank open wagons	1912	Purchased from Pauling (second-hand)	13'7"	6'11"	7'0"		6-0	
229-238	4-plank open	1907	R.Y. Pickering	16'6"	7'0"	9'0"		7-0	4-3½
239-248	Combination vans	1907	R.Y. Pickering	16'6"	7'0"	9'0"		7-0	4-10½
249-252	Tranship wagons	1908	GNR(I), Dundalk	15'6"	7'0"	8'6"		3-0	1-14
253, 254	Tranship wagons	1908	GNR(I), Dundalk	15'6"	7'0"	8'6"		3-0	1-14
255-284	Covered vans	1908	Hurst, Nelson	16'6"	7'0"	9'0"		7-0	4-11¼
285-294	Combination vans	1909	Hurst, Nelson	16'6"	7'0"	9'0"		7-0	4-14¾
295-304	4-plank open	1909	Hurst, Nelson	16'6"	7'0"	9'0"		7-0	4- 7¾
305, 306	WDR carriage trucks	1881	Oldbury Carriage & Wagon Co.	15'6"	7'0"	8'6"		6-0	
307, 308	DR carriage trucks	1893	Oldbury Carriage & Wagon Co.	15'6"	7'0"	8'6"		6-0	
309-312	Timber bolster wagons	1905	R.Y. Pickering	15'6"	7'0"	8'6"			
313	Horse box	1905	R.Y. Pickering	15'0"	7'0"	8'6"			
314, 315	Horse box	1893	Oldbury Carriage & Wagon Co.	15'0"	7'0"	8'6"			
313	6 wheel flat	1882	Railway Carriage & Wagon Co.	31'0"	7'0"	20'0"		12-0	7-15
314 (2nd)	Covered goods	1882	Railway Carriage & Wagon Co.	31'0"	7'0"	20'0"		14-0	7-4
315 (2nd)	Covered goods	1882	Railway Carriage & Wagon Co.	31'0"	7'0"	20'0"		14-0	7-4
316	Covered goods	1893	Oldbury Carriage & Wagon Co.	31'0"	7'0"		19'3"	12-0	9-2½
317	Covered goods	1893	Oldbury Carriage & Wagon Co.	31'0"	7'0"		19'3"	12-0	9-2½
318	Covered goods	1893	Oldbury Carriage & Wagon Co.	31'0"	7'0"		19'3"	12-0	9-2½
319	Covered goods	1893	Oldbury Carriage & Wagon Co.	31'0"	7'0"		19'3"	12-0	9-2½
320	Covered goods	1893	Oldbury Carriage & Wagon Co.	31'0"	7'0"		19'3"	12-0	9-2½
321	Covered goods	1882	Railway Carriage & Wagon Co.	31'0"	7'0"	20'0"		12-0	9-2½
322	Covered goods	1901	Railway Carriage & Wagon Co.	36'0"	7'0"		23'6"	12-0	10-2½
323	Covered goods	1882	Railway Carriage & Wagon Co	31'0"	7'0"	20'0"		12-0	9-2½
324	Covered goods	1882	Railway Carriage & Wagon Co	31'0"	7'0"	20'0"		12-0	9-2½
325	Covered goods	1882	Railway Carriage & Wagon Co	31'0"	7'0"	20'0"		12-0	9-2½
326	Roofed goods	1905	R.Y. Pickering	15'0"	7'0"	8'6"		7-0	4-8
327	Horse box	1893	Oldbury Carriage & Wagon Co.	15'0"	7'0"	8'6"		7-0	

No.	Type	Builder	Built						
328	Bogie open	Oldbury Carriage & Wagon Co.	1896	27'5"	6'0"	4'0"	14'6"	15-0	
329	Bogie open	R.Y. Pickering	1912	27'6"	6'6"	4'0"	16'0"	15-0	
330	Roofed goods	Oldbury Carriage & Wagon Co.	1893	31'0"	7'4"		19'3"	12-0	10-2½
331	Roofed goods	Oldbury Carriage & Wagon Co.	1893	31'0"	7'4"		19'3"	12-0	10-2½
332	Roofed goods	Oldbury Carriage & Wagon Co.	1893	31'0"	7'4"		19'3"	12-0	10-2½
333	Roofed goods	Oldbury Carriage & Wagon Co.	1893	31'0"	7'4"		19'3"	12-0	10-2½
334	Bogie 4-plank Open	Metropolitan Carriage & Wagon Co.	1904	28'6"	6'8"	4'0"		12-0	
335	Oil container flat	ex-CVR	1897	15'6"	7'0"	8			
336	Low-loader bogie flat	ex-BC&RBR	1898	40'0"	6'3"				
337-340	Shell Oil tankers	Midland RC&W	1923	15'0"	5'0"	9'0"			
341-345	Esso Oil tankers	Midland RC&W	1923	15'0"	5'0"	9'0"			
Horsebox 1	WDR Horsebox	Oldbury Carriage & Wagon Co.	1881	15'0"	7'0"	8'6"			
1, 2, 10-23	Red wagon series	Metropolitan Carriage & Wagon Co.	1887	13'8"	6'8"	8'0"			
3-9	Red wagon series	Oldbury Carriage & Wagon Co.	1884	13'6"	6'6"	7'0"			

Notes

1-40 – General merchandise/cattle. Nos. 30, 31 preserved (Donegal Railway Heritage Centre).

41-43 – 2'6" high, centre door. 42 rebuilt as tranship open 1926; 41. 43 3 plank dropsides 1949/50.

44, 45 – 2'6" high, centre door. Rebuilt as tranship wagons 1924; 45 rebuilt as 4 plank open 1950.

46-95 – one piece corrugated roof. No. 83 rebuilt with hinged doors.

96-100 – Originally without roofs. Rebuilt c.1924 with 1-piece roof and drop shutters. No. 97 rebuilt as merchandise van without shutters.

101-120 – Centre drop door. Nos. 110, 113, 115, 117-20 rebuilt as 3-plank dropsides.

121-154 – Nos. 121, 141 and 150 reblt as 3-plank dropsides 1949; No. 136 preserved (Cultra).

159 – Only purpose built bogie goods wagon. Sides increased 2'/2'6" (1923) - capacity 14 tons.

158, 160-168 – Nos. 158, 161 and 168 rebuilt as 3-plank dropsides.

169-198 – One piece corrugated roof. Merchandise only.

199-208 – Originally without roofs. Rebuilt c.1924 with 1-piece roof and drop shutters. No. 201 rebuilt as merchandise van without shutters.

209, 210 – Originally Nos. 1 & 2 of original WDR stock. No. 209 rebuilt as goods van.

211-228 – Nos. 212, 221, 222, 226 and 227 reblt as 4-plank opens; No. 228 scrapped pre-1935 (No. transferred to ex-C&VBT vehicle).

228 (2nd) – Purchased from C&VBT (ex-No. 28) 1935.

229-238 – Centre drop door. S&LR opens. 230-233 rebuilt as 3 plank dropsides.

239-248 – S&LR. Originally centre canvas roofs - rebuilt 1945 with closed roof bodies and drop shutters.

253, 254 – Had covered bodies, bodies and chassis carried number but often did not remain paired.

255-284 – One piece corrugated roofs; hinged doors.

285-294 – Originally centre canvas roofs - rebuilt pre-1923 with closed roof bodies; drop shutters later added (except 288, 294).

295-304 – Centre drop door. 301-304 out of service 1944; 297 & 298 rebuilt as 3-plank dropsides.

305 – 305 rebuilt as 7 ton open with steel underframes 1924; reblt to dropsides 1956.

307, 308 – 307 rebuilt as 7 ton open with steel underframes 1925; 308 reblt to dropsides 1956.

309-312 – 311 rebuilt as 7 ton open with steel underframes 1925; 309 scrapped following collision 1958.

313 – Originally No. 3 in separate horsebox series. Renumbered 1926. Rebuilt as roofed goods No. 326 (1927).

314, 315 – Originally Nos. 1 & 2 in separate horsebox series. Renumbered 1926. 314 rebuilt as roofed goods No. 327; 315 renumbered horsebox 1 (1927).

313 – Ex-6 wheel brake third coach No. 10. Converted 1927.

314 (2nd) – Ex-6 wheel third coach No. 8. Converted 1927. Rebuilt as flat fitted with two ex-CVR wagon bodies 1946.

315 (2nd) – Ex-6 wheel brake third coach No. 11. Converted 1927. Rebuilt with tubular sides for turf.

316 – Ex-bogie third coach No. 19. Converted 1928.

317 – Ex-bogie third coach No. 18. Converted 1928.

318 – Ex-bogie third coach No. 22. Converted 1928.

319 – Ex-bogie third coach No 20. Converted 1929. Rebuilt as flat for carrying oil tanks.

320 – Ex-bogie third coach No. 21. Converted 1929.

321 – Ex-6 wheel third coach No. 4. Converted 1929. Rebuilt with tubular sides for turf.

322 – Ex-corridor third No. 29. Converted 1929. Rebuilt as flat fitted with two ex-CVR wagon bodies 1946. Later rebuilt as flat for carrying oil tanks.

323 – Ex-6 wheel third coach No. 7. Converted 1930. Rebuilt with tubular sides for turf.

324 – Ex-6 wheel third coach No. 5. Converted 1930. Rebuilt as flat fitted with two ex-CVR wagon bodies 1946.

325 – Ex-6 wheel third coach No. 6. Converted 1930.

326 – Ex-horse box 313.

327 – Ex-horse box 314. Destroyed Bonagee derailment 1951.

328 – Purchased from C&VBT (ex-No. 24) 1935; came as bogie flat; 2' dia. wheels.

329 – Purchased from C&VBT (ex-No. 29) 1935; came as bogie flat.

330 – Ex-bogie brake third coach No. 25. Converted 1937.

331 – Ex-bogie brake third coach No. 24. Converted 1937.

332 – Ex-bogie brake third coach No. 27. Converted 1937.

333 – Ex-bogie brake third coach No. 26. Converted 1939.

334 – Ex-CVR (No. 96 or 97).

1, 2, 10-23 – Ex-CVR vans.

3-9 – Ex-C&VBT wagons.

Stranorlar, 23rd June, 1927. Railcar No. 7 or 8 crosses the massive bridge of the Glenties branch to bring the 10.50 am service into Stranorlar.   *H.C. Casserley, courtesy R.M. Casserley*

4-6-4T locomotive No. 14 *Erne* prepares to leave Stranorlar on 7th August, 1930, with a typical mixed train forming the 9.58 am departure to Strabane.   *H.C. Casserley, courtesy R.M. Casserley*

However, such rapid growth severely dented finances and resulted in the company being taken over by the GNR(I) and the Midland Railway of Britain in 1906. The Donegal Railway Company ceased to be and operation was overseen by a Board, comprising members of the Boards of the owning companies, under the title of the County Donegal Railways Joint Committee, by which name it was known until ultimate closure. Under the new arrangement all lines were operated by the CDRJC, although the Strabane to Derry section became the sole property of the MR.

The final addition to the system, and the last public narrow gauge passenger railway to be built in Ireland, was the Strabane & Letterkenny Railway (S&LR), planned to connect the CDRJC at Strabane with the Londonderry & Lough Swilly Railway at Letterkenny, which opened on 1st January, 1909. The S&LR remained independent throughout the operating life of the railway, but was always worked by the CDRJC, the new line bringing the total route mileage operated by the CDRJC to 124½ miles - the largest narrow gauge system in the British Isles.

Though operating in remote areas and serving an ever declining population, the CDRJC was resilient and competed against the rising threat of road transport through the pioneering use of railcars. A 'stop anywhere' policy introduced by General Manager Henry Forbes undoubtedly extended the life of the CDR, allowing it to compete with bus operators. This approach was in sharp contrast to the approach of the CDR's northern neighbour, the L&LSR, which saw its future in road transport as early as the 1930s.

The earlier railcars were a combination of second-hand acquisitions and conversions, produced by the successful partnership of the GNR(I) works in Dundalk and O'Doherty's, a local coachbuilder in Strabane. A noted landmark for the CDR

A characteristic view of the innovative County Donegal Railway. Letterkenny shed with diesel railcar and steam locomotive on 24th June, 1937.

H.C. Casserley, courtesy R.M. Casserley

was the introduction of the first diesel-powered railcars in these islands in 1931. The lifespan of the early cars was relatively short but as their engines wore out, many were given a new lease of life by having the engines removed and being converted to trailer units, an initiative introduced by Forbes to increase the railcars' passenger-carrying abilities. The later railcars were elegant articulated units from Walker Brothers' of Wigan, the last of which can still be seen on the Isle of Man Railway.

Railcar workings offered both economy and flexibility of operation - typical workings on the branch lines consisted of a railcar, possibly a trailer, plus one or two freight wagons. As a result, the steam engines were largely redundant in the latter days, being confined to freight workings or the occasional excursion traffic. Despite this, the soaring expenditure of the post-war years coincided with the need to invest in track renewal and new equipment at a time when the parent companies had their own financial difficulties. This combination was to sound the death knell of the company.

First to go was the Glenties branch, where regular passenger and goods services ceased in December 1947. The Derry section had been part of the rail system of the Ulster Transport Authority since 1948, and was closed by the UTA on the last day of 1954. Proposed closure of the Ballyshannon branch was only deferred by the poor state of County Donegal's roads. Formal application for complete closure was made in May 1959 and all services ceased on 31st December, 1959. The railway services were replaced by a fleet of buses and lorries, which continued to carry the name of the railway until taken over by CIÉ in 1971.

Chronology

15.05.1860	Finn Valley Railway incorporated.
07.09.1863	FVR opened Stranorlar - Strabane (broad gauge).
21.07.1879	West Donegal Railway incorporated.
25.04.1882	WDR opened from Stranorlar to Drumminin (Lough Eske) 3 ft 0 in. gauge.
16.09.1889	Opened to Donegal.
27.06.1892	FVR and WDR merge as Donegal Railway Company.
18.08.1893	Donegal to Killybegs extension opened.
16.07.1894	FVR section converted to 3 ft 0 in. gauge.
03.06.1895	Stranorlar to Glenties branch opened.
01.08.1900	Strabane to Derry extension opened.
21.09.1905	Donegal to Ballyshannon branch opened.
01.05.1906	County Donegal Railways Joint Committee formed following takeover by GNR(I) and Midland Railway of England.
01.01.1909	Strabane to Letterkenny branch opened (Strabane & Letterkenny Railway).
00.06.1931	Introduction of first diesel railcar in British Isles.
13.12.1947	End of regular passenger & freight service on Glenties branch (complete closure 10.03.1952).
31.12.1954	Strabane to Derry services terminated (abandoned 23.09.55).
31.12.1959	Complete closure.

Route

Distance	Station/Halt/Crossing	Opened	Closed	Notes
0	Stranorlar	1863	1960	
2½	Meenglas Halt	1882	1960	Closed 1918-1936.
2¾	Quinn's Crossing	1882	1960	Railcar stopping place from 1944.
5¼	Lough Gates	1882	1960	Railcar stopping place from 1944.
7¾	Derg Bridge Halt	1912	1960	
11¾	Barnesmore Halt	1891	1960	'Barrack Bridge for Barnesmore'.
12¼	Dunnion's Crossing	1889	1960	Railcar stopping place from 1938.
13¾	Lough Eske	1889	1960	Originally Drumminin. Passing place.
13¾	No. 2 Gates (Lough Eske sta.)	1882	1960	
14¼	Townawilly Crossing	1889	1956	Railcar stopping place from 1938.
15¼	No. 3 Gates (McNamee)	1889	1960	
15½	No. 4 Gates (McClanaghy)	1889	1960	
16	Clar Bridge Halt	1891	1960	
16¼	No. 5 Gates (McHugh)	1889	1960	
17	No. 6 Gates (Gorrell)	1889	1960	
18	Donegal	1889	1960	
18	No. 7 Gates (Donegal sta.)	1893	1960	
18¼	Drimark Hill	1893	1960	Railcar stopping place from 1944.
18¾	No. 8 Gates (McDaid)	1893	1960	Now restored by current owner.
19½	No. 9 Gates (McGroarty)	1893	1960	
19¾	No. 10 Gates (Bogle)	1893	1960	
20	Killymard Halt	1893	1956	Closed 1918-1936.
20¼	No. 11 Gates (Keeney)	1893	1960	
21¾	No. 12 Gates (Meehan)	1893	1960	
22	Mountcharles	1893	1960	
23½	No. 13 Gates (Freeburn)	1893	1960	
23¾	Doorin Road	1893	1960	Halt from 1921.
23¾	No. 14 Gates (Doorin Rd sta.)	1893	1960	
24	No. 15 Gates (Keeney)	1893	1960	
25¼	Mullanboy Halt	1893	1960	
25¼	No. 16 Gates (Mullanboy, Rose)	1893	1960	
25½	No. 17 Gates (Scott)	1893	1960	
26	Inver Church	1936	1960	Railcar stopping place from 1936.
26	No. 18 Gates (Conaghan)	1893	1960	
26¼	Inver	1893	1960	Passing place.
26½	No. 19 Gates (Cannon)	1893	1960	
26¾	No. 20 Gates (Battles)	1893	1960	Railcar stopping place from 1936.
28	No. 21 Gates (Meehan)	1893	1960	
28	Port	1913	1960	Halt from 1913.
29¼	No. 22 Gates (Roses)	1893	1960	
30¼	Dunkineely	1893	1960	
30¼	No. 23 Gates (Dunkineely Station)	1893	1960	
30½	No. 24 Gates (Lappin)	1893	1960	
30¾	No. 25 Gates (McMenamin)	1893	1960	
31¼	Spamount	1893	1960	
32	No. 26 Gates (McGroarty)	1944	1960	Formerly Kenny.
32½	No. 26A Gates (Bruckless sta.)	1893	1960	

Distance	Station/Halt/Crossing	Opened	Closed	Notes
32½	Bruckless	1893	1960	
32¾	No. 27 Gates (McMenamin)	1893	1960	
34¾	Ardara Road	1893	1960	
34¾	No 28 Gates (Ardara Rd sta.)	1893	1960	
35	No. 29 Gates (McGinley)	1893	1960	
35¼	No. 30 Gates (Hegarty's)	1893	1960	Railcar stopping place from 1936.
37	Killybegs	1893	1960	
37¼	Killybegs Pier	1893	1960	
18	Donegal	1889	1960	
18½	Hospital Halt	1935	1950	
19½	Drumbar Halt	1906	1960	
20½	No. 41 Gates (McHugh's)	1905	1960	Railcar stopping place from 1938.
21	No. 42 Gates (Monaghan)	1905	1960	
21¼	Laghey	1905	1960	
22¼	No. 43 Gates (Conaghan)	1905	1960	
23	Bridgetown	1905	1960	
23	No. 44 Gates (Bridgetown sta.) (Gallagher)	1905	1960	
23½	Drumhorry Bridge	1905	1960	Railcar stopping place from 1942.
25	Ballintra	1905	1960	
26	Dromore Halt	1930	1960	Railcar stopping place from 1944.
27	Dorrian's Bridge	1905	1960	
28¼	Rossnowlagh	1905	1960	
28½	Friary Halt	1953	1960	
28¾	No. 45 Gates (McAree)	1905	1960	
29	Coolmore	1905	1960	
30	Corker Crossing	1905	1960	Formerly McCann's. Railcar stop from 1940.
30¾	Creevy Halt	1911	1960	
30¾	Creevy Halt Gates	1905	1960	
31	No. 46 Gates (McIntyre)	1905	1960	
32¼	Gillen's (Kildoney) Crossing	1905	1960	Railcar stopping place from 1942.
32¾	No. 47 Gates (Culleton)	1905	1960	
33½	Ballyshannon	1905	1960	
0	Stranorlar	1863	1960	
½	Ballybofey	1895	1947	
½	No. 31 Gates (Ballybofey sta.)	1895	1952	
¾	No. 32 Gates (McConnell)	1895	1952	Also known as Gallinagh's.
1½	Ballindoon Bridge	1944	1947	Railcar stopping place 1944-47.
2¼	No. 33 Gates (McBride)	1895	1952	Also known as Double.
4	Glenmore	1895	1947	
4	No. 34 Gates (Glenmore sta.)	1895	1952	
6¾	Cloghan	1895	1947	
9	Elatagh Halt	1930	1947	
10	Cronadun Bridge	1944	1947	Railcar stopping place 1944-47.
11½	Glassagh Halt	1937	1947	
13¾	Ballinamore	1895	1947	
13¾	No. 35 Gates (Ballinamore sta.) (Doherty)	1895	1952	
14¾	No. 36 Gates (S. Doherty's)	1895	1952	Railcar stopping place 1944-47.
16	Fintown	1895	1947	Reopened CTGL (see p. 132) 1995.

Distance	Station/Halt/Crossing	Opened	Closed	Notes
20	No. 37 Gates (Brennan's)	1895	1952	Also known as Herron.
21	Shallogans Halt	1903	1947	
22¾	No. 38 Gates (McMonagle's)	1895	1952	Railcar stopping place 1944-47.
23¾	No. 39 Gates (McNelis)	1895	1952	
24	No. 40 Gates (Glenties Station)	1895	1952	
24	Glenties	1895	1947	
0	Stranorlar	1863	1960	
½	Town Bridge Halt	1863	1960	Closed c.1950.
1¾	Cavan Halt	1931	1960	
4	Killygordon	1863	1960	
5¾	Liscooly	1863	1960	
5¾	No 1 Gates (Schoales)	1863	1960	
7¾	Castlefinn	1863	1960	Rep. of Ireland Customs.
9¼	Clady	1863	1960	
11¼	Urney Bridge (over River Finn)	1863	1960	Line crossed into Republic of Ireland (post 1922).
13¾	Strabane	1894	1960	INWR station used 1863-1894.
13¾	Strabane	1894	1960	
16½	Ballymagorry	1900	1955	
18¼	Ballyheather Halt	1900	1955	
20	Donemana	1900	1955	
22	Cullion	1900	1955	
23¼	Desertone Halt	1900	1955	
25½	New Buildings	1900	1955	
28¼	Derry (Victoria Road)	1900	1955	
13¾	Strabane	1894	1960	
14¼	Lifford	1909	1960	Rep. of Ireland Customs.
16½	Ballindrait	1909	1960	
16¾	No. 48 Gates (O'Brien)	1909	1960	
17	No. 49 Gates (Devenny)	1909	1960	
17½	No. 50 Gates (Donnelly)	1909	1960	
18½	Coolaghy Halt	1909	1960	
20¼	Raphoe	1909	1960	Crossing place.
	No. 51 Gates (Kearns)	1909	1960	
21	No. 52 Gates (Chambers)	1909	1960	
	No. 53 Gates (Linney's)	1909	1960	Railcar stopping place from 1936.
22¾	Convoy	1909	1960	
	No. 54 Gates (Mulrine)	1909	1960	
	No. 55 Gates (Gillen)	1909	1960	
	No. 56 Gates (Ayton's)	1909	1960	Formerly Kelly, later Cannon, later Vance.
24¾	Cornagillagh Halt	1911	1960	
27½	Glenmaquin	1909	1960	
28¼	No. 57 Gates (Doherty)	1909	1960	
29	No. 58 Gates (Parke)	1909	1960	
29¾	No. 59 Gates (Maguire)	1909	1960	
30½	No. 60 Gates (Martin)	1909	1960	
31	No. 61 Gates (Killen's)	1909	1960	Railcar stopping place from 1944. 'Killen's Gate Signal' on tickets.
31½	No. 62 Gates (Baird's)	1909	1960	Railcar stopping place from 1944.
33	Letterkenny	1909	1960	

The Castlederg & Victoria Bridge Tramway

Steam locomotives

No.	Manufacturer	Type	Year	Works No.	Name	Driving wheel dia.	Leading/trailing wheel dia.	Total wheel-base	Coupled wheel-base	Cyls (in.)	Heating surface (sq. ft)	Grate area (sq. ft)	Water capacity (galls)	Coal capacity (cwt)	Boiler pressure (psi)	Weight (t. cwt.)	Max. axle load (t. cwt.)	Tractive effort at 85% (lb.)	Wdn
1	Kitson	0-4-0T	1884	T106	Mourne	2'9"	-	6'6"	6'6"	12x15	269	7.3	318	10	160	14-2	7-4	8,860	1904
2	Kitson	0-4-0T	1884	T107	Derg	2'9"	-	6'6"	6'6"	12x15	269	7.3	318	10	160	14-2	7-4	8,860	1912
3	Kitson	0-4-0T	1891	T257	-	2'9"	-	6'6"	6'6"	12x15	269	7.3	455	10	140	18-0	9-0	7,753	1928
4	Hudswell, Clarke	2-6-0T	1904	698	-	3'1"	1'8½"	11'2"	7'0"	13½x18	596.4	9.25	600	15	160	26-0	7-0	12,058	1942
5	Hudswell, Clarke	0-4-4T	1912	978	-	3'1"	2'0½"	14'2"	5'6"	12½x18	508.7	9	510	30	160	24-10		10,388	1934
6	Beyer, Peacock	2-4-0T	1878	1828	-	3'9"	2'0"	14'3"	6'3"	12½x18	392.3	6.85	360	20	140	19-3	7-0	7,440	1933

Notes

No. 4 – Named *Victoria* in builder's photograph but no name carried in service. Sold to CVR in 1934; rebuilt (2-6-2T). Survived to close of CVR 1941.

No. 5 – Named *Castlederg* in builder's photograph but no name carried in service.

No. 6 – As rebuilt 1889. Former NCC No. 105. Purchased by C&VBT 1928. Never carried number and referred to in record books as No 3.

Railcar/diesel locomotive

Source/Builder	Type	Year	Engine	Weight	Seats	Withdrawn	Notes
C&VBT	2.4	1925	Paraffin 20 hp Fordson	10 t. 0 cwt	28	1928	Railcar sold to CDRJC 1932 (£25).
Kerr, Stuart & Co	0-6-0	1929	McLaren-Benz 60 bhp, 4 cylinder	10 t. 0 cwt	-	1930	Diesel engine - trial only - returned to manufacturer.

Chapter Nine

The Castlederg & Victoria Bridge Tramway

The Castlederg & Victoria Bridge Tramway (C&VBT), at just over 7 miles in length, was one of the shortest of the independent Irish narrow gauge railways, linking the village of Castlederg to Victoria Bridge, on the Great Northern Railway of Ireland's Omagh to Derry line. From the outset, the undertaking was optimistic, given its rural nature and resultant small catchment population and there was a reliance on cattle fairs and markets to boost traffic.

The earliest proposals for the tramway were made in 1860, following the passing of the Tramways Act of that year, but were never advanced. A tramway connection, built to the 3 ft gauge, became more of a practicality, following the passing of the 1871 Tramways Act which, for the first time, allowed mechanical power on roadside tramways but it was to be another 10 years before a committee was formed to advance the proposal, and only after a Baronial guarantee was secured.

Despite a slow accumulation of capital and unexpected opposition from the GNR(I) the necessary Parliamentary approval for a roadside tramway, 7 miles and 5 chains in length, together with a short extension to the market place in Castlederg and an additional short spur where the tramway turned into the goods yard at Victoria Bridge, was received on the 16th July, 1883. The contract for construction of the station buildings at Castlederg was granted to Messrs Hepburn of Strabane, while that for the construction of the line was awarded to Messrs T.I. Dixon of Belfast. Construction of the line proceeded without too much difficulty, there being a good road in place between Victoria Bridge and

Castlederg & Victoria Bridge Tramway locomotive No. 5.

H.C. Casserley, courtesy R.M. Casserley

Carriages

No.	Type	Built	Maker	Length	Compts	Seats	Wheel dia.	Wheel centres	Bogie centres	Withdrawn
1	First/second composite	1884	Oldbury Carriage & Wagon Co.	21'0"	first/2nd	20	2'3"	7'6"	-	1934
2	First/second composite	1884	Oldbury Carriage & Wagon Co.	21'0"	first/2nd	20	2'3"	7'6"	-	1934
3	Second	1884	Oldbury Carriage & Wagon Co.	21'0"	All 2nd	22	2'3"	7'6"	-	1934
4	First	1884	Oldbury Carriage & Wagon Co.	21'0"	All first	20	2'3"	7'6"	-	1934
5	Bogie third	1887	Oldbury Carriage & Wagon Co.	33'6"	All 3rd	40	2'3"	4'0"	19'0"	1934
1	Brake van 4 wheel	1884	Oldbury Carriage & Wagon Co.	16'0"	-	-	2'3"	7'0"	-	1934
2	Brake van 4 wheel	1884	Oldbury Carriage & Wagon Co.	16'0"	-	-	2'3"	7'0"	-	1934

Notes

Nos. 1 and 2 – later first/third (1887).
No. 3 – Later first/third (1887).
Later all-third (1887).
Brake vans Nos. 1 & 2 rebuilt 1908. No. 2 further rebuilt 1929.

Wagons

Nos.	Type	Built	Maker	Length	Width	Wheel diameter	Wheelbase	Bogie centre	Capacity (t. cwt)
1-14	Goods/cattle	1884	Oldbury Carriage & Wagon Co.	13'6"	6'6"	2'3"	7'0"	-	-
15-20	Open	1884	Oldbury Carriage & Wagon Co.	13'6"	6'6"	2'3"	7'0"	-	-
21-23	Open catttle wagons	1890	Oldbury Carriage & Wagon Co.	13'6"	6'6"	2'3"	7'0"	-	-
24	Bogie open	1896	Oldbury Carriage & Wagon Co.	27'6"	6'6"	2'0"	4'0"	14'6"	15-0
25-27	Covered cattle wagons	1899	Oldbury Carriage & Wagon Co.	13'6"	6'6"	2'3"	7'0"	-	-
28	Open	1912	R.Y. Pickering	13'7"	6'11"	2'3"	7'0"	-	6-0
29	Bogie open	1912	R.Y. Pickering	27'6"	6'6"	2'0½"	4'0"	16'0"	15-0

Notes

Nos. 1-14 – Probably originally Goods only - dual purpose following rebuild 1903-12.
Nos. 21 and 22 – Rebuilt as dual purpose covered vans 1921 and 1917.
Nos. 25-27 – Rebuilt as dual purpose vans.

Castlederg. The Board of Trade inspection was conducted on the 5th July, 1884, passed fit for inspection and public services commenced on the 11th of that month, with three trains in each direction and an additional late service in each direction on Friday evening. There was no Sunday service during the tramway's history and special services operated on the last Friday of the month for the Castlederg fair.

The finances of the C&VBT were perilous from the outset and through the early years of its life the Tramway struggled, barely making a profit, as any excess revenue was soaked up by expenditure on the upkeep of rolling stock and permanent way. Within 20 years, the original two engines supplied to the line were worn out and were withdrawn. A new and more powerful engine arrived in 1904 which, being considerably heavier than the original engines, only increased the need to complete the replacement of sleepers being undertaken at the time. No sooner was this complete than the original rails were in need of replacement. On top of this, any changes within the local farming community that altered the movement of livestock further threatened the company's income.

The years of World War I provided a boost to traffic and a windfall payment was received in 1921 under the Settlement of Claims Act but, like many other railways, the C&VBT was to suffer from the economic changes resulting from the war, in particular rising fuel and wage costs. The British coal strike of 1926 brought a further massive increase in the cost of coal. In addition, the threat of road competition began to appear with a number of operators from Omagh and Derry competing with both themselves and the Tramway. In response to these threats, George Pollard, the locomotive superintendent, together with local tradesmen, produced a paraffin-fuelled railcar which, though underpowered and somewhat ungainly, provided a competitive mode of passenger traffic and allowed the company to survive until the financial position settled somewhat. Steam operation returned in 1928, but No. 3 was condemned and an ex-NCC 2-4-0T was acquired in 1929 to support the two remaining Hudswell, Clarke engines.

The engine shed at Castlederg on 7th August, 1930 with locomotive No. 4 (*left*) and No. 5 (*right*).   *H.C. Casserley, courtesy R.M. Casserley*

Any improvement was temporary, though, and the inexorable rise of road competition continued. Following partition, the government of Northern Ireland favoured the development of road transport at the expense of railways. In January 1933, services ceased completely following withdrawal of labour as part of the rail strike that afflicted much of Northern Ireland's railways for a period of 10 weeks. Traffic ordinarily carried by the Tramway quickly found other means of conveyance and although the strike ended in April 1933, there was little prospect of the company winning back the custom and the line remained closed. Eventually, on 30th September, 1933, the company was wound up at a special meeting of Directors and shareholders.

Following closure, the company's assets were disposed of at auction, with other narrow gauge concerns benefiting. Locomotive No. 4 was originally acquired by a Belfast contractor but was given to the Clogher Valley Railway in exchange for two of its worn-out engines. She was rebuilt as a 2-6-2T in the CVR workshops at Aughnacloy. In her rebuilt state she gave good service until the end of operations on the CVR. Other stock lived on in Donegal, the County Donegal Railways Joint Committee purchasing the derelict railcar, which was first rebuilt with a petrol engine and later rebuilt again as a railcar trailer. She survived until closure of the CDR in 1959. In addition a number of lightweight C&VBT open wagons were bought by the CDRJC and used to carry luggage behind their railcars.

Chronology

16.07.1883	Castlederg & Victoria Bridge Tramway Company incorporated.
10.07.1884	Tramway opened.
30.09.1933	Company wound up following 1933 Railway strike

Route

Distance	Station/Halt	Opened	Closed	Notes
0	Castlederg	1884	1933	
1¾	Spamount	1884	1933	
3¾	Crew	1884	1933	Referred to as 'Charlie Allen's' by locals.
5¼	Fyfin	1884	1933	
5½	Stonewalls	?	?	Unstaffed halt
6	Glen	?	?	Unstaffed halt. Opened 1912/13.
7	Victoria Bridge	1884	1933	

Chapter Ten

The Bessbrook & Newry Tramway

The Bessbrook & Newry Tramway (B&NT) was built for the water-driven Bessbrook flax mills, one of the oldest in Ireland, powered by the stream of the same name. In 1846 these mills were purchased and enlarged by the Richardson family, with the construction of a model village for their employees, though many lived in the neighbouring town of Newry. The line was promoted with the object of both transporting these workers to and from the mills and the carriage of coal, raw materials and finished goods to and from the quays at Newry.

Work was initially undertaken without any official powers, the ceremonial cutting of the first sod for the tramway taking place on the 8th September, 1883, but statutory authority for the line was subsequently obtained under the Tramways & Public Companies (Ireland) Act 1883 and the Bessbrook & Newry Tramway Company was incorporated on 26th May, 1884. Though it was initially intended to work the tramway by steam, this was changed to electric traction, on the advice of Dr Edward Hopkinson, a pioneer in electric traction, who was awarded the contract for electrical equipment.

A 29½ ft waterfall on the nearby Camlough stream was used to drive hydro-electric generators located at Millvale, approximately one mile from the Bessbrook terminus. Power from here was delivered to the railway engines by a thin conductor rail laid mid-way between the two rails, apart from one short section of approximately 150 ft at Millvale where the Newry to Bessbrook public road was crossed - here power was instead collected from an overhead cable by bow collectors on the cars.

B&NT power car No. 4 with van No. 2 and brake van No. 6 at Barbrook Mill.
W.A. Camwell/Stephenson Locomotive Society

The Bessbrook & Newry Tramway

Electric Cars & Trailers

No.	Source/Builder	Year	Wheels	Engine	Class	Weight t-c	Length	Seats	Withdrawn
1	Ashbury Carriage Co.	1885	4.4	Edison-Hopkinson dynamo motor 20 hp	Composite	8-5	33'0"	24(2nd)/10(first)	1921
2	Ashbury Carriage Co.	1885	4.4	Edison-Hopkinson dynamo motor 20 hp	Second	8-5	21'8"	24	1948
3	Starbuck Co.	1885	4.4	Trailer	Second	5-10	33'0"	44	1948
1 (2nd)	Hurst, Nelson	1921	4.4	2 x 36 hp	Second		37'1¾"	40	1948
4	Hurst, Nelson	1921	4.4	Electric Construction Co. 25 hp	Composite		29'0"	32	1948
5	Hurst, Nelson	1920	4	Trailer (open)	Second		13'9"	20	1948
6	B&NT	1922	4	Trailer	Second		13'0½"	12	1948
7	See No. 5								
2 (2nd)	Unknown	1928	4.4	Trailer	Second		19'2"	26	1948
5 (2nd)	Unknown	1928	4.4	Trailer	Second		15'7"	24	1948

Notes

No. 1 – Driving platform extension of 3 ft 7 in.

No. 2 – Driving platform extension of 3 ft 7 in. Body later replaced with body of ex-Dublin & Lucan Electric Railway (D&LER) No. 24. In latter days had 20 hp Mather & Platt motor.

No. 1 (2nd) – End platforms added a further 6 ft 4 in. to body length.

No. 4 – Luggage compartment at driving end. 2 x 22 hp engines fitted in 1928.

No. 5 – Renumbered 7 c.1935.

No. 2 (2nd) – Ex-D&LER No. 24. Overall length 23 ft 5 in.

No. 5 (2nd) – Ex-D&LER No. 27. Overall length 20 ft 10 in.

Wagons

No.	Type	Built	Maker	Capacity	Tare weight
1-22	4 wheel open/closed	1884-1887	Ashbury Carriage Co.	2 t. 0 cwt	1 t. 3¾ cwt
23-27	4 wheel open/closed			2 t. 0 cwt	1 t. 3¾ cwt

Work began on 3rd November, 1884 and the line was complete and ready for inspection by the Board of Trade on 10th September, 1885. A number of criticisms required attention, mainly with regard to provision of gates at Millvale and occupational crossings, before final approval and public traffic began on 1st October.

To show that operating costs were not greater than that of steam traction, the contractor worked the line for the first six months, which fully vindicated the choice of power, and the owning company took over formally in April 1886.

The length of the line was just over three miles. It was single throughout and rose by 185 ft almost the entire way from Newry to Bessbrook at an average gradient of 1 in 86, the steepest being 1 in 50.

The original passenger rolling stock comprised two electric motor cars and one trailer, supplied by Ashbury in 1885. All were carried on two 4-wheel bogies. Two further powered coaches and a four-wheel trailer were purchased in 1921 and two bogie trailers were acquired in 1928 from the Dublin & Lucan Tramway.

Freight stock consisted of 27 open and closed 4-wheeled goods wagons, of interest as the wheels were flangeless, to allow the wagons to run on either rail or road, greatly facilitating transhipment. This was achieved by laying lighter outside rails, seven-eighths of an inch lower than the 3 ft gauge rails, which effectively acted as flanges. The wagon wheels were loose on their axles to facilitate road operation, where they were hauled initially by horses, later by petrol driven tractors. On the tramway, the wagons always ran between a motor car and trailer.

Such innovation did not, though, stave off the rise of road transport following World War II. Services were first reduced and the line closed completely on 10th January, 1948. As one of the pioneers of electric traction it had provided a reliable service to the locality throughout its 62 years' existence.

Chronology

26.05.1884	Bessbrook & Newry Tramway Company incorporated.
01.10.1885	Tramway opened.
10.01.1948	Tramway closed.

Route

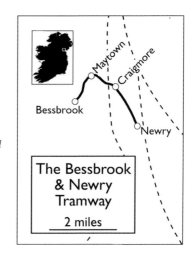

The Bessbrook & Newry Tramway

2 miles

Distance	Station/Halt	Opened	Closed
0	Newry (Edward Street)	1885	1948
1½	Craigmore	1885	1948
2	Millvale Crossing	1885	1948
2½	Maytown	?	?
3	Bessbrook	1885	1948

The Dublin & Lucan Tramway

Locomotives

No.	Manufacturer	Type	Year	Works No.	Driving wheel dia.	Total wheel-base	Coupled wheel-base	Cyls (in.)	Heating surface (sq. ft)	Grate area (sq. ft)	Boiler pressure (psi)	Water capacity (galls)	Coal capacity (cwt)	Weight (t. cwt.)	Tractive effort at 85% (lb.)	Withdrawn
	Manlove, Alliott & Fryer	2-4-2	1881		2'3"	17'6"	4'6"	7x9	116	2.27	150	160		9-0	3,680	1926
1	Kitson	0-4-0	1882	T57	2'4¼"	5'0"	5'0"	8x12	106	5.17	150	160	2½	7-5		1899
2	Kitson	0-4-0	1883	T74	2'4¼"	5'0"	5'0"	8x12	106	5.17	150	160	2½	7-5		1899
3	Kitson	0-4-0	1883	T81	2'4¼"	5'0"	5'0"	8x12	106	5.17	150	160	2½	7-5		1899
4	Kitson	0-4-0	1884	T104	2'4¼"	5'0"	5'0"	8x12	129	6.0	150	171	6½			1912
5	Kitson	0-4-0	1884	T108	2'4¼"	5'0"	5'0"	8x12	129	6.0	150	171	6½			1912
6	Kitson	0-4-0	1887	T224	2'4¼"	5'0"	5'0"	10x12	135	6.2	150	200	6½	9-0		1912
7	Thos Green & Son	0-4-0CT	1892	169	2'6"	5'0"	5'0"	9&14x14								1896

Notes

Nos. 4-6 – Converted to 3 ft 6 in. gauge 1899; survived until 1912, boiler pressure reduced to 140 psi.

No. 7 – Compound. Built for Lucan, Leixlip & Celbridge Tramway. Sold to contractor on closure in 1896.

Electric cars and trailers

No.	Source/builder	Year	Wheels	Engine	Wheel dia.	Overall wheelbase	Bogie wheelbase	Class	Length	Seats	Withdrawn
12	Dick, Kerr & Co.	1899	4.4	2 x Dick, Kerr 25 hp	2'7¾" & 1'9¾"	15'6"	4'0"	first/3rd	23'0"*	30(in)/32 (out)	1925
13	Dick, Kerr & Co.	1899	4.4	2 x Dick, Kerr 25 hp	2'7¾" & 1'9¾"	15'6"	4'0"	first/3rd	23'0"*	30(in)/32 (out)	1925
14	Dick, Kerr & Co.	1899	4.4	2 x Dick, Kerr 25 hp	2'7¾" & 1'9¾"	15'6"	4'0"	first/3rd	24'6"†	34(in)/32 (out)	1925
15	Dick, Kerr & Co.	1899	4.4	2 x Dick, Kerr 25 hp	2'7¾" & 1'9¾"	15'6"	4'0"	first/3rd	23'0"*	30(in)/32 (out)	1925
16	Dick, Kerr & Co.	1899	4.4	2 x Dick, Kerr 25 hp	2'7¾" & 1'9¾"	15'6"	4'0"	first /3rd	23'0"*	30(in)/32 (out)	1925
(a)	Rebuild, Conyngham Road	1905	4	2 x Dick, Kerr 25 hp	2'7¾"	6'0"	-	-	18'6"#	-	1925
17	British Thompson-Houston Co.	1905	4	2 x BTH GE/58 37½ hp			-	-	27'0"	-	1918
18	Milnes, Voss & Co.	1906	4.4	2 x BTH GE/58 37½ hp	2'7¾"	14'6"	4'0"	first/3rd	20'6"§	30(in)/36 (out)	1925
19	Milnes, Voss & Co.	1907	4.4	2 x BTH GE/58 37½ hp	2'7¾"	6'0"	-	-	24'1"	39	1925
26	Conyngham Road	1918	4	2 x BTH GE/58 37½ hp		7'6"	-	-	23'0"¶	10	1925

Notes

No. 12 – Rebuilt 1917-18. Body extended over platforms. Seating increased to 72. * Length over body. End platforms extra 4 ft 9 in. either end giving overall length of 32 ft 6 in.

No. 13 – Renumbered 17 in 1918.

No. 16 – Rebuilt 1917-18. Body extended over platforms. Seating increased to 74.

No. 14 – End platforms extra 4 ft 9 in. either end giving overall length of 34 ft 0 in. † Length over body.

(a) – Unnumbered vehicle. Conversion from steam bogie trailer. Used for mails. # Length over body. End platforms extra 4 ft 3 in. either end giving overall length of 27 ft 0 in.

No. 17 – Electric locomotive for goods working.

No. 18 – § Length over body. End platforms extra 5 ft 6 in. either end giving overall length of 32 ft 6 in.

No. 19 – Ex-All-Red Railway vehicle.

No. 26 – Rebuild of No 17. ¶ Length over body. End platforms extra 2'0" either end giving overall length of 25 ft 0 in.

Chapter Eleven

The Dublin & Lucan Steam Tramway

Unlike the majority of Irish 3 ft gauge lines which were built in rural and often sparsely populated areas, the Dublin & Lucan tramway ran through suburban Dublin, though its time built to that gauge was short. Lucan was a village in the Liffey Valley, eight miles from the centre of Dublin, and in the latter half of the 19th century had a token rail service from distant stations on both the Great Southern & Western and Midland Great Western railways. A clothing factory and a flour mill, both using the waters of the River Liffey as a power source were situated there. But it was the visitors to the Spa Hotel, to avail of the healing powers of the local sulphur springs, that prompted the hotel proprietors, together with local businessmen to press for improved transport to the village.

Probably largely due to the local topography a roadside tramway was the chosen option and the Dublin and Lucan Steam Tramway (D&LST) was incorporated in 1880 and authorized to construct a tramway from Lucan to connect with Dublin United Tramways (DUT) at their Conyngham Road terminus, by the Phoenix Park, some six miles distant. The D&LST was to be built as a 3 ft gauge line and as DUT was to the Irish standard gauge of 5 ft 3 in., the choice is surprising but was likely chosen to save on the cost of construction.

The line ran by the side of the public road, the only exception to this being where it moved to the centre while crossing the bridge over the Liffey at Chapelizod. It was opened for traffic from Conyngham Road, to Chapelizod,

Electric car No. 26 c.1919. *John Langford Collection*

about a mile, in June 1881, and completed through to Lucan on 2nd July, 1883. From Conyngham Road, passengers would continue to the centre of Dublin via the horse-drawn trams of DUT. The D&LST did give some consideration to proposals for achieving their own access to the city centre - these included the laying of a third rail to allow access over the DUT rails and an independent route to the centre, but neither was advanced. There were also proposals for extensions, through a separate company, the Lucan, Leixlip & Celbridge Steam Tramway, who obtained powers to extend the line from Lucan to Leixlip, with a branch to Celbridge and plans for further extension to the village of Clane, in County Kildare. Of these, only the Lucan to Leixlip extension was built, opening in 1889 and operated by the D&LST.

But the Leixlip extension was not to last long, closing in 1896, by which time D&LST were struggling financially. In addition, the original line was in a bad state of repair and in need of replacement. The Leixlip extension did not earn sufficient revenue to justify replacement though an independent contractor worked the line with his own rolling stock for a short time before giving up.

For the rest of the D&LST, powers were obtained, in 1896, to electrify the line between Dublin and Lucan and at the same time the decision was made to widen the gauge to 3 ft 6 in. It would have been more logical to extend the gauge to 5 ft 3 in., as the DUT was also undergoing conversion to electric traction, which would have allowed the D&LST to run through to the centre of Dublin over DUT rails. The poor finances of the D&LST and the need to complete the works as cheaply as possible, were probably the reasons the wider gauge was not adopted. At the same time the name of the company was changed to Dublin & Lucan Electric Railway. To power the new line a new power station was built at Fonthill, 1½ miles from Lucan. It was equipped with two 100 hp steam engines. These drove dynamos that generated the supply rated at 500 volts. In addition to the tramway's own requirements, current was also supplied to some houses along the route for lighting. Electric working between Dublin and Lucan commenced on 8th March, 1900, and allowed the journey from Dublin (Conyngham Road) to Lucan, to be accelerated to 40-45 minutes. A short extension to the Spa Hotel was reopened in 1909.

Traffic was never heavy and with the outbreak of World War I, the wage and material cost increase that resulted brought the company to its knees. A strike by staff closed the line. It reopened when the Government took control of Irish railways and remained under Government control until 1921. When independent control was restored the financial position was hopeless. Increased operating costs, the emergence of competition from buses and the need for investment in the infrastructure brought closure on 1st January, 1925.

The Dublin United Tramways Company, at the behest of Dublin Corporation, agreed to take over the line. They regauged to 5 ft 3 in., reopening as such in May 1928, this allowing through running into the centre of Dublin. Eventually, competition from road transport took its toll and the DUT closed on 12th April, 1940.

The Lucan tramway was the only line in Ireland to operate on three different gauges during its existence. It was also the only case of the gauge being widened from 3 ft to 5 ft 3 in. although the reverse operation took place in three cases.

Chronology

19.04.1880	Application to County Dublin Grand Jury for Approval.
01.06.1881	Tramway opened to Chapelizod.
11.1881	Opened as far as Palmerstown.
20.02.1883	Official opening to Lucan
June 1890	Lucan & Leixlip Steam Tramway opened, operated by D&LST.
1896	Converted to 3 ft 6 in. gauge and electrified (Not L&LST).
31.10.1897	Lucan & Leixlip Steam Tramway service terminated.
8.03.1900	Dublin and Lucan Electric Railway opened.
1911	Short extension to Spa Hotel reopened.
01.01.1925	Closed to traffic.
1927	Purchased by DUTC and regauged to 5 ft 3 in.
14.05.1928	Reopened to Chapelizod.
31.05.1928	Reopened to Lucan.
12.04.1940	Complete closure.

Route

Distance	Station/Halt	Opened	Closed	Notes
0	Conyngham Road	1881	1940	
½	Islandbridge	1881	1940	
1¾	Chapelizod	1881	1940	Passing loop.
2	Saint Laurence	1881	1940	Passing loop.
4½	Palmerstown	1881	1940	Passing loop.
5¼	Quarryvale	1881	1940	
5½	Cursis Stream	1881	1940	Passing loop.
?	Hermitage	1881	1940	Passing loop.
6½	Ballydowd	1881	1940	Passing loop.
7	Lucan	1881	1940	
7½	Dodsborough	1881	1927	Closed 1896. Reopened 1911 to serve Spa Hotel.
8	Lucan Spa Hotel	1881	1896	
9	Leixlip	1881	1896	

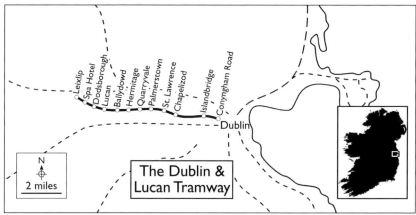

The Clogher Valley Railway

Locomotives

No.	Manufacturer	Type	Year	Works No.	Name	Driving wheel dia.	Leading/trailing wheel dia.	Total wheel-base	Coupled wheel-base	Cyls (in.)	Heating surface (sq. ft)	Grate area (sq. ft)	Boiler pressure (psi)	Water capacity (galls)	Coal capacity (cwt)	Weight (t. cwt.)	Max. axle load (t. cwt.)	Tractive effort at 85% (lb.)	Wdn
1	Sharp, Stewart	0-4-2T	1886	3369	Caledon	3'0"	2'3"	10'4"	4'9"	13½x18	514	10	140	600	20	23-16	8-2	10,850	1934
2	Sharp, Stewart	0-4-2T	1886	3370	Errigal	3'0"	2'3"	10'4"	4'9"	13½x18	514	10	140	600	20	23-16	8-2	10,850	1942
3	Sharp, Stewart	0-4-2T	1887	3371	Blackwater	3'0"	2'3"	10'4"	4'9"	13½x18	514	10	140	600	20	23-16	8-2	10,850	1942
4	Sharp, Stewart	0-4-2T	1887	3372	Fury	3'0"	2'3"	10'4"	4'9"	13½x18	514	10	140	600	20	23-16	8-2	10,850	1929
5	Sharp, Stewart	0-4-2T	1887	3373	Colebrooke	3'0"	2'3"	10'4"	4'9"	13½x18	514	10	140	600	20	23-16	8-2	10,850	1936
6	Sharp, Stewart	0-4-2T	1887	3374	Erne	3'0"	2'3"	10'4"	4'9"	13½x18	514	10	140	600	20	23-16	8-2	10,850	1942
7	Hudswell, Clarke	0-4-4T	1910	914	Blessingbourne	3'4"	2'0"	14'6"	5'3"	14x20	605	12¼	160	700	25	29-14	9-2	13,350	1934
8	Atkinson-Walker	0-4-0T	1928	114		2'6"	-	6'6"	6'6"	7x10	60	3⅜	280	500	10	12-0	-	5,700	1932
4 (2nd)	Hudswell, Clarke	2-6-2T	1904	698		3'1"	18½"/2'6"	16'6"	7'0"	13½x18	596	9¼	160	600	30	28-10	7-0	12,058	1942

Notes

Nos. 1 & 7 – Exchanged as scrap for ex-C&VBT 2-6-0T No. 4.

No. 7 – Little used due to poor performance. Lay out of use 1926-34.

No. 8 – Steam tractor, trial only; sold to CDR - converted to diesel. A larger boiler with total heating surface of 90 sq. ft and grate area of 5 ft was supplied but probably never fitted.

No. 4 (2nd) – Ex-C&VBT 2-6-0T. Acquired by CVR in 1934; rebuilt (2-6-2T). Survived to close of CVR 1941.

Railcar, diesel locomotive

No.	Source/builder	Wheels	Year	Engine	Weight (t. cwt)	Seats	Cost	Wdn	Notes
1	Walker Bros	4.4	1932	Diesel 6L2	12-0	29	£1,950	-	Sold to CDRJC for £315; renumbered No. 10. Preserved Cultra.
2	Walker Bros (rail tractor, wagon body)	4	1933	Diesel 6L2	-	-		1941	Sold to CDRJC less engine. Cab used to repair No. 10 1946.

Chapter Twelve

The Clogher Valley Railway

The Clogher Valley Railway (CVR) is of historic interest as the first light railway to have been built following the passing of the Tramways and Public Companies (Ireland) Act 1883. This act removed restrictions on use of mechanical power and speed and provided Government aid to the Baronies, to offset, to some extent, the effects of the Baronial Guarantee. With the passing of the Act, long term plans for a railway for the area were finally realized with approval granted on the 7th August, 1884 for the Clogher Valley Tramway Company Ltd to construct a roadside tramway linking the GNR(I) stations of Maguiresbridge and Tynan, through the villages of Fivemiletown, Clogher and Ballygawley.

Work proceeded without undue delay, the line being ready for the Board of Trade inspection on 11th April, 1887, and opened to the public on 3rd May, 1887. A name change to the Clogher Valley Railway Company Ltd followed in 1894, as recognition as a railway was necessary to enable through bookings to locations on other rail networks.

From the outset, traffic receipts did not meet expectations and the company was only kept going by the guaranteeing areas. Despite this, a number of ambitious extension schemes were considered, none of which came to fruition. The shortfall in income was to continue for the life of the railway and the CVR was a continual tax burden on the ratepayers. Rises in coal and staff costs, particularly following World War I, together with strikes in the coal industry,

A busy moment at Fivemiletown station on 25th June, 1937. No. 3 has just brought in its train from Tynan while, to the left, railcar No. 1 and van No. 5 form the 12 noon departure.
H.C. Casserley, courtesy R.M. Casserley

Carriages

No.	Type	Built	Maker	Length	Compts	Seats	Wheel dia.	Wheel centres	Bogie centres	Withdrawn
1	4 wheel luggage, parcel & brake van	1886	Metropolitan Carriage & Wagon Co.	14'0"	-	-	2'0"	6'6"	-	
2	4 wheel luggage, parcel & brake van	1886	Metropolitan Carriage & Wagon Co.	14'0"	-	-	2'0"	6'6"	-	
3	4 wheel luggage, parcel & brake van	1886	Metropolitan Carriage & Wagon Co.	14'0"	-	-	2'0"	6'6"	-	
4	4 wheel luggage, parcel & brake van	1886	Metropolitan Carriage & Wagon Co.	14'0"	-	-	2'0"	6'6"	-	
5	4 wheel luggage, parcel & brake van	1886	Metropolitan Carriage & Wagon Co.	14'0"	-	-	2'0"	6'6"	-	
6	4 wheel luggage, parcel & brake van	1886	Metropolitan Carriage & Wagon Co.	14'0"	-	-	2'0"	6'6"	-	1900
7	Bogie first	1886	Metropolitan Carriage & Wagon Co.	24'0"	-	18	2'0"	4'0"	11'6"	1942
8	Bogie first	1886	Metropolitan Carriage & Wagon Co.	24'0"	-	18	2'0"	4'0"	11'6"	1942
9	Bogie first	1886	Metropolitan Carriage & Wagon Co.	24'0"	-	18	2'0"	4'0"	11'6"	1942
10	Bogie first/third composite	1886	Metropolitan Carriage & Wagon Co.	29'6"	1 3 3	8/25	2'0"	4'0"	17'0"	1942
11	Bogie first/third composite	1886	Metropolitan Carriage & Wagon Co.	29'6"	1 3 3	8/25	2'0"	4'0"	17'0"	1942
12	Bogie third	1886	Metropolitan Carriage & Wagon Co.	29'6"	-	40	2'0"	4'0"	17'0"	1942
13	Bogie third	1886	Metropolitan Carriage & Wagon Co.	29'6"	-	40	2'0"	4'0"	17'0"	1942
14	Bogie third	1886	Metropolitan Carriage & Wagon Co.	29'6"	-	40	2'0"	4'0"	17'0"	1942
15	Bogie third	1886	Metropolitan Carriage & Wagon Co.	29'6"	-	40	2'0"	4'0"	17'0"	1942
16	Bogie third	1886	Metropolitan Carriage & Wagon Co.	29'6"	-	40	2'0"	4'0"	17'0"	1942
17	Bogie third	1886	Metropolitan Carriage & Wagon Co.	29'6"	-	40	2'0"	4'0"	17'0"	1942
18	Bogie third	1886	Metropolitan Carriage & Wagon Co.	29'6"	-	40	2'0"	4'0"	17'0"	1942
19	Bogie third	1886	Metropolitan Carriage & Wagon Co.	29'6"	-	40	2'0"	4'0"	17'0"	1942
20	4 wheel horse box	1887	Metropolitan Carriage & Wagon Co.	12'6"	-	-	2'0"	5'9"	-	1942
21	4 wheel horse box	1887	Metropolitan Carriage & Wagon Co.	12'6"	-	-	2'0"	5'9"	-	1942

Notes

All 13 coaches had end verandahs.
Nos. 1-6 – 14'0" over buffers, body 12'0".
Nos. 7-9 – 24 ft over end platforms. First class abolished 1st September, 1928.
Nos. 10-19 – 29 ft 6 in. over end platforms, 24 ft over bodies.

Wagons

Type	Built	Maker	Length	Width	Wheelbase	Capacity	Notes
Cattle wagons (30)		Metropolitan Carriage & Wagon Co.	14'0"	6'8"		5 tons	Nos. 1-5, 7, 8, 10-13,15-20, 22, 25, 27, 29-32, 34, 35, 76, 79, 82, 84.
Covered wagons (18)		Metropolitan Carriage & Wagon Co.	13'8"	6'8"		5 tons	Nos. 6, 9, 14, 21, 23, 24, 26, 28, 33, 38-40, 75, 77, 78, 80, 81, 83.
Butter wagons (2)		Metropolitan Carriage & Wagon Co.	13'8"	6'8"		5 tons	Nos. 36, 37 (converted from goods vans).
Open wagons (40)		Metropolitan Carriage & Wagon Co.	13'6"	6'6"		5 tons	Nos. 41, 42, 45, 47-55, 57-61, 63-71, 73, 74, 85-95. No. 62 converted to spray wagon (weedkiller).
Timber trucks (4)		Metropolitan Carriage & Wagon Co.	13'0"	6'8"		6 tons	Nos. 43, 44, 106, 107.
Ballast wagons (8)		Metropolitan Carriage & Wagon Co.	13'6"	6'0"		6 tons	Nos. 98-105.
Bogie open wagons (2)	1904	Metropolitan Carriage & Wagon Co.	28'6"	6'8"		15 tons	Nos. 96, 97.
Covered wagons (12)	1884	Oldbury Carriage & Wagon Co.	15'4"	6'6"	7'0"		Purchased from C&VBT. Never converted or numbered and lay in Aughnacloy out of use.
Covered wagons (2)	1890	Oldbury Carriage & Wagon Co.	15'4"	6'6"	7'0"		Purchased from C&VBT. Never converted or numbered and lay in Aughnacloy out of use.
Covered wagons (3)	1894	Oldbury Carriage & Wagon Co.	15'4"	6'6"	7'0"		Purchased from C&VBT. Never converted or numbered and lay in Aughnacloy out of use.

affected the CVR badly. Unlike many other Irish railways, the political unrest in Ireland following the war, and subsequent partition, had little effect on the CVR, though the creation of the border, only a mile from the Ballygawley-Tynan section of the line removed the Monaghan hinterland from the Clogher Valley Traders and changed established attendance at fairs and other events, which in turn effected CVR traffic.

The company's perpetual poor finances were under continued scrutiny with the county councils seeking to close the railway and remove the financial burden. A committee of management was formed to manage the company, comprising members of the county councils of Tyrone and Fermanagh and two appointed by the government - Robert Darragh, an old Belfast & Northern Counties railwayman and Henry Forbes, Manager and Secretary of the County Donegal Railways Joint Committee

One of the first actions of the committee was to approach the GNR(I) with a view to amalgamation or some other arrangement but the GNR(I) would not entertain the proposal. Darragh and Forbes, as practical railwaymen, recommended abolition of first class travel and fares and an acceleration of passenger services, by separation of passenger and goods workings. A steam tractor came on trial from Atkinson-Walker in January 1929 but was to prove a dismal failure. Forbes, with his growing experience of railcar operations in Donegal, arranged a highly successful trial of CDR railcar No. 4 on the CVR in May 1932, following which an articulated railcar was purchased from Walker Bros of Wigan, entering service in December of that year. An additional power bogie unit with a removable wagon body, which also served as a reserve power unit when the railcar's unit was in for repair or overhaul, was also purchased, arriving in September 1933.

Having just introduced the new railcar, the company was then faced with the consequences of the strike which paralysed virtually all the railways of Ireland from 31st January to 7th April. The CVR were not affected directly by the strike but the GNR(I) was, and this had a knock-on effect on CVR traffic. The committee initially considered closing the line but instead laid off considerable numbers of staff, maintaining sufficient only to keep the railcar operating. Without a regular service, the public made alternative arrangements and as a result, with the ending of the strike, traffic remained poor.

The company continued to lose money and the burden of the Baronial Guarantee continued to tax the public. Ever increasing costs meant the end was inevitable though the introduction of railcar operations and the improved service resulting gave something of a stay of execution. The councils continued to agitate to have the Baronial Guarantee removed and eventually the government capitulated passing the Clogher Valley Railway and Roads (N.I.) Act 1941, whereby the railway was to cease operations on the last day of December 1941. The last train to run was a special railcar operation packed with local people, late on the evening of the 31st. It reached Fivemiletown at midnight and returned to Ballygawley at 1.23 am, the CVR thus officially kept running into 1942!

Following closure, some of the CVR stock lived on, as the CDRJC acquired the diesel railcar and the rail tractor unit (minus the engine) together with a number of wagons and vans all of which played a major part in the successful railcar operations in County Donegal.

No. 6 pauses at Stoneparkcross on 25th June, 1937 with the 9.50 am from Maguiresbridge with van No. 4 and coach No. 12.   *H.C. Casserley, courtesy R.M. Casserley*

The CVR railcar at Augher on 3rd May, 1938.   *W.A. Camwell/Stephenson Locomotive Society*

Chronology

26.05.1884	Clogher Valley Tramway Company incorporated under Tramways Act of 1883.
03.05.1887	Opened to traffic.
16.07.1894	Name changed to Clogher Valley Railway.
28.06.1928	Committee of Management appointed to oversee operation.
31.12.1941	Closed to all traffic (though last train ran until after midnight - into 1942!).

Route

Distance	Station/Halt	Opened	Closed	Notes
0	Tynan	1887	1942	
¼	Lemnagore Gate Lodge	1887	1942	Tramway joined road. Obligatory stop.
1	Caledon	1887	1942	No station. Obligatory stop in main street opposite courthouse.
1½	Kilsampson Halt	1887	1942	
3	Ramaket Halt	1887	1942	
3	Crossing	1887	1942	
4¼	Emyvale Road	1887	1942	Originally named Curlagh ('Curlough' in timetable) to c.1914.
5¼	Cumber Halt	1887	1942	
6¼	Glenkeen Halt	1887	1942	
7	Crilly Halt	1887	1942	
8¼	Glencrew Halt	1887	1942	
8½	Crossing	1887	1942	Tramway left road.
9½	Crossing - 'Absolute Stop'	1887	1942	Aughnacloy-Dungannon Road.
9½	Aughnacloy	1887	1942	
11¾	Tullyvar	1887	1942	
12¼	Crossing	1887	1942	Tramway left road.
12½	Tullywinney Gate Lodge	1887	1942	Known locally as Dempsey's Crossing. Compulsory stop for down trains.
13¼	Crossing	1887	1942	
13½	Ballygawley	1887	1942	Tramway left road after station.
14½	Crossing	1887	1942	Tramway rejoined road.
14½	Lisdoart Halt	1887	1942	
15	Tramway left road	1887	1942	
15½	Annaghilla	1887	1942	Level Crossing (secondary road).
16¾	Tramway rejoined road	1887	1942	
16¾	Roughan	1887	1942	Crossing place.
18½	Crossing	1887	1942	Crossed Main Street - 'Compulsory stop'.
18½	Augher	1887	1942	Siding to Augher Creamery.
19¼	Farranetra	1887	1942	Originally Summer Hill Halt. Tramway left road.
20	Clogher	1887	1942	
20¼	Crossing	1887	1942	
21	Carryclogher	1887	1942	
22	Findermore Halt	1887	1942	Tramway rejoined road.

Distance	Station/Halt	Opened	Closed	Notes
23¼	Ballagh	1887	1942	
25¼	Kiltermon Halt	1887	1942	
26½	Ballyvaden Halt	1887	1942	
27½	Fivemiletown	1887	1942	Tramway left road.
28½	Cranbrooke Halt	1887	1942	
28¾	Tattynuckle	1887	1897	
29½	Corralongford Halt	1887	1942	Tramway rejoined road.
30¼	Killarbran Halt	1887	1942	Tramway left road. Gates replaced by cattle grid 1913.
31	Claraghy Halt	1887	1942	
31½	Colebrooke	1887	1942	Tramway rejoined road.
31¾	Stonepark Halt	1887	1942	Tramway left road.
32¾	Skeoge Halt	1887	1942	
32¾	Crossing	1887	1942	'Absolute stop'. Tramway left road.
33½	Brookeborough	1887	1942	Tramway rejoined road.
34¼	Crossing	1887	1942	Tramway left road.
34¾	Aghavea Halt	1887	1942	
36	Tramway rejoined road	1887	1942	
36½	Maguiresbridge Fair Green	1887	1942	Originally 'Maguiresbridge Town' - renamed 1907.
37	Maguiresbridge	1887	1942	Originally 'Maguiresbridge Station' - renamed 1907.

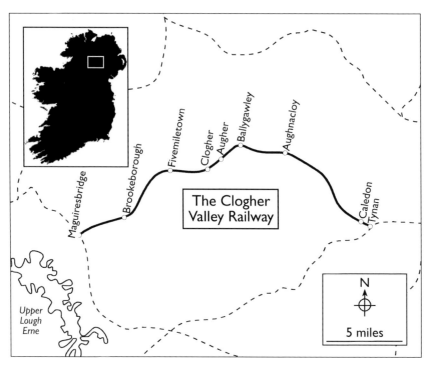

Chapter Thirteen

The Cavan & Leitrim Railway

The Cavan & Leitrim Railway (C&LR) was built to improve transport connections between the villages and towns of, initially, Cavan, Leitrim & Roscommon, a thinly-populated area of predominantly poor land divided in smallholdings, dotted among the many lakes and rivers that characterized the region. Railways extended in the region when the Midland Great Western Railway (MGWR) opened the Dublin to Sligo line in 1862, followed by the GNR(I) branch to Belturbet in 1885.

A number of early proposals for an extended rail network into Co. Leitrim collapsed but the passing of the Tramways & Public Companies (Ireland) Act 1883 prompted the proposal of a light railway connecting Dromod, on the MGWR with Belturbet, on the GNR(I) with, in addition, a roadside, steam, tramway to Drumshanbo and Boyle - this to both satisfy local transport requirements and those of the Arigna coal districts - and built to the 3 ft gauge. This led to the incorporation of the Cavan, Leitrim & Roscommon Light Railway & Tramway Company Ltd on 3rd December, 1883, under the terms of the 1883 Act, which provided for financial guarantees from the ratepayers of the districts served by the railway, in return for which the Grand Jury could elect Directors to the Board of the company. In the end, the Roscommon Grand Jury withdrew its guarantee, so the line to Boyle never progressed, as a result of which the company name was changed to the 'Cavan & Leitrim Railway Company Ltd' in 1895.

Bawnboy Road, 25th September, 1957. Hugh Davies, Railway Enthusiast Club organizer, talks to the driver of ex-CB&PR 2-4-2T No. 10L.   *John Langford*

The Cavan & Leitrim Railway

Locomotives

No.	Manufacturer	Type	Year	Works No.	Name	Driving wheel dia.	Leading/trailing wheel dia.	Total wheel-base	Coupled wheel-base	Cyls (in.)	Heating surface (sq. ft)	Grate area (sq. ft)	Water capacity (galls)	Coal capacity (cwt)	Boiler pressure (psi)	Weight (t. cwt.)	Max. axle load (t. cwt.)	Tractive effort at 85% (lb.)	Wdn
1	R. Stephenson	4-4-0T	1887	2612	Isabel	3'6"	2'1"	16'9"	6'0"	14x20	548	8½	600	20	150	27-0	9-5	11,900	1959
2	R. Stephenson	4-4-0T	1887	2613	Kathleen	3'6"	2'1"	16'9"	6'0"	14x20	548	8½	600	20	150	27-0	9-5	11,900	1959
3	R. Stephenson	4-4-0T	1887	2614	Lady Edith	3'6"	2'1"	16'9"	6'0"	14x20	548	8½	600	20	150	27-0	9-5	11,900	1959
4	R. Stephenson	4-4-0T	1888	2615	Violet	3'6"	2'1"	16'9"	6'0"	14x20	548	8½	600	20	150	27-0	9-5	11,900	1959
5	R. Stephenson	4-4-0T	1888	2616	Gertrude	3'6"	2'1"	16'9"	6'0"	14x20	548	8½	600	20	150	27-0	9-5	11,900	1925
6	R. Stephenson	4-4-0T	1888	2617	May	3'6"	2'1"	16'9"	6'0"	14x20	548	8½	600	20	150	27-0	9-5	11,900	1927
7	R. Stephenson	4-4-0T	1888	2618	Olive	3'6"	2'1"	16'9"	6'0"	14x20	548	8½	600	20	150	27-0	9-5	11,900	1945
8	R. Stephenson	4-4-0T	1888	2619	Queen Victoria	3'6"	2'1"	16'9"	6'0"	14x20	548	8½	600	20	150	27-0	9-5	11,900	1959
9	R. Stephenson	0-6-4T	1904	3136	King Edward	3'3"	2'1"	18'3"	7'5"	15x20	749½	14	700	30	150	36-12	8-12	14,710	1934
10L	Neilson, Reid	2-4-2T	1899	5561	-	4'6"	3'0"	21'0"	8'0"	14½x22	801	12	1,000	50	160	37-3	11-11	11,650	1959
11L	Neilson, Reid	2-4-2T	1899	5562	-	4'6"	3'0"	21'0"	8'0"	14½x22	801	12	1,000	50	160	37-3	11-11	11,650	1939
12L	Neilson, Reid	2-4-2T	1899	5563	-	4'6"	3'0"	21'0"	8'0"	14½x22	801	12	1,000	50	160	37-3	11-11	11,650	1959
13L	Neilson, Reid	2-4-2T	1899	5564	-	4'6"	3'0"	21'0"	8'0"	14½x22	801	12	1,000	50	160	37-3	11-11	11,650	1954
3T	Hunslet Engine Co.	2-6-0T	1889	479	-	3'0½"	2'0"	15'7"	8'9"	13x18	560	9¾	750	15	150*	30-11	8-10	9,900	1959
4T	Kerr, Stuart	2-6-0T	1903	836	-	3'0"	2'0"	15'0"	9'1"	12½x20	478	7½	750	20	160	31-0		11,806	1959
5T	Hunslet Engine Co.	2-6-2T	1890	555	-	3'0½"	2'0"	21'2"	9'0"	13½x18	601	10¾	780	17	150*	32-0		10,695	-
6T	Hunslet Engine Co.	2-6-0T	1898	677	-	3'0½"	2'0"	15'7"	8'9"	13x18	560	9¾	730	15	150	30-11	8-10	10,626	1959

Notes

* BP originally 140 psi. Increased when reboilered on T&DR.
No. 2 – Acquired 'Tramway-style' cab of No. 7 in 1940.
No. 7 – Out of use for several years and cannabilized. Scrapped 1945.
No. 10L – Ex CB&PR No 4P.
No. 11L – Ex CB&PR No 5P.
No. 12L – Ex CB&PR No 6P.
No. 13L – Ex CB&PR No 7P.
No. 3T – Transferred from T&DR 1939. 'T' later dropped.
No. 4T – Originally No. 8 on T&DR. Renumbered 1907. Transferred from T&D 1941.
No. 5T – Transferred from T&DR 1950. Preserved.
No. 6T – Transfer to WCR 1953; to C&L 1957. Worked Dromod section demolition train.

Work commenced on the line in the autumn of 1885, with labour gangs employed from both the Belturbet and Dromod ends and at the chosen headquarters site at Ballinamore. Progress was good, despite objections from the MGWR with threats to introduce a road cart service in opposition and from local activists causing damage to the infrastructure to inhibit progress, and was completed in July 1887, with the official inspection by the Board of Works on 5th October. The line was passed with little amendment required and officially opened for goods traffic on 17th October and for passenger traffic a week later.

From the start, facilities were inadequate, predictions of traffic having been grossly underestimated and extensions to platforms and additional rolling stock were soon necessary. Worse, was the underestimation of running costs, which could be as high as 97 per cent of receipts. As result, the C&LR was never a profitable concern and for the duration of its independent working life was dependent on the ratepayers to pay shareholders' dividends, a source of disillusionment in the company for the people of Co. Leitrim, who shouldered the majority of the burden. Despite the financial struggle, a number of expansion schemes were considered, including the ambitious Ulster & Connaught Light Railway scheme to link Newry via the CVR and C&LR to Clifden in Connemara, which never progressed despite attaining the necessary Parliamentary approval.

The C&LR formed other partnerships, notably with the Arigna Mining Company, aimed both at providing extra traffic for the railway and supplying it with cheap coal. In return for which the C&LR provided accommodation and services, including that of station masters acting as agents for the supply of coal. The C&LR Board had always been dominated by the landed gentry, later by shareholder Directors and the more democratically appointed County Council Directors could not enjoy a majority, which only increased local resentment.

For some long time, the question of extending from Arigna to the mines had been discussed but progress had faltered over who should pay for such an extension - either the mining company or the C&LR. The latter prospect was not supported by the Leitrim tax payers, on whom much of the financial burden of supporting the C&LR fell, as the extension line was entirely in Co. Roscommon. In 1906 the Government offered a grant of £24,000 towards the cost of construction but disagreement among the Directors led to the offer being rejected. The opportunity was finally afforded with the advent of World War I, when wartime coal shortages persuaded the British Government to invest in Irish railways to facilitate extraction of available coal resources, with the Arigna mines identified as one resource for support. The C&LR came under the control of the Irish Railway Executive Committee on 1st January, 1917 and the Executive provided the finance for the construction of a 4¼ mile extension to facilitate the speedy transport of coal from the Derreenavoggy and Aughabehy pits, which ultimately opened in June 1920. The line remained under the care of the Board of Works, being worked by the C&LR. The Aughabehy workings soon diminished and eventually ceased in 1930, when the extension was reduced back to Derreenavoggy, which kept working, and was a valuable source of traffic for the C&LR up to closure.

Carriages No.	Type	Built	Weight (t. cwt)	Maker	Length	Seats	Wheel dia.	Wheel centres	Bogie centres	Withdrawn
1	Composite first/third	1887	7-12	Metropolitan Carriage & Wagon Co.	40'0"*	14(first)/34(third)	2'0"	4'0"	26'0"	1961
2	Composite first/third	1887	7-12	Metropolitan Carriage & Wagon Co.	40'0"*	14(first)/34(third)	2'0"	4'0"	26'0"	1950
3	Composite first/third	1887	7-12	Metropolitan Carriage & Wagon Co.	40'0"*	14(first)/34(third)	2'0"	4'0"	26'0"	1950
4	Composite first/third	1887	7-12	Metropolitan Carriage & Wagon Co.	40'0"*	14(first)/34(third)	2'0"	4'0"	26'0"	1951
5	Composite first/third	1887	7-12	Metropolitan Carriage & Wagon Co.	40'0"*	14(first)/34(third)	2'0"	4'0"	26'0"	-
6	Composite first/third	1887	7-12	Metropolitan Carriage & Wagon Co.	40'0"*	14(first)/34(third)	2'0"	4'0"	26'0"	1959
7	Composite first/third	1887	7-12	Metropolitan Carriage & Wagon Co.	40'0"*	14(first)/34(third)	2'0"	4'0"	26'0"	-
8	Composite first/third	1887	7-12	Metropolitan Carriage & Wagon Co.	40'0"*	14(first)/34(third)	2'0"	4'0"	26'0"	1943
9	Third	1887	7-12	Metropolitan Carriage & Wagon Co.	40'0"*		2'0"	4'0"	26'0"	1943
10	Third	1887	7-12	Metropolitan Carriage & Wagon Co.	40'0"*	50	2'0"	4'0"	26'0"	1950
11	Third	1887	7-12	Metropolitan Carriage & Wagon Co.	40'0"*	50	2'0"	4'0"	26'0"	1959
12	Third	1887	7-12	Metropolitan Carriage & Wagon Co.	40'0"*	50	2'0"	4'0"	26'0"	1943
13	4 wheel passenger brake van	1887		Metropolitan Carriage & Wagon Co.	15'6"†	-	2'0"	7'0"	-	1941
14	4 wheel passenger brake van	1887		Metropolitan Carriage & Wagon Co.	15'6"†	-	2'0"	7'0"	-	1959
15	4 wheel passenger brake van	1887		Metropolitan Carriage & Wagon Co.	15'6"†	-	2'0"	7'0"	-	1941
16	4 wheel passenger brake van	1887		Metropolitan Carriage & Wagon Co.	15'6"†	-	2'0"	7'0"	-	1959
17	4 wheel passenger brake van	1887		Metropolitan Carriage & Wagon Co.	15'6"†	-	2'0"	7'0"	-	1959
18	4 wheel passenger brake van	1887		Metropolitan Carriage & Wagon Co.	15'6"†	-	2'0"	7'0"	-	1959
19	Horse box	1887		Metropolitan Carriage & Wagon Co.	15'6"		2'0"	7'0"	-	1957
20	Horse box	1887		Metropolitan Carriage & Wagon Co.	15'6"		2'0"	7'0"	-	1957
21L	Composite first/third	1907		Midland Carriage & Wagon Co.	30'1½"	18(first)/14(third)	2'0"	4'0"	21'0"	1957
22L	Bogie brake	1890								-

Notes

* 34 ft coach body, 3 ft verandah either end.

† 12 ft 6 in. body, 3 ft end verandah.

No. 1 – Rebuilt all-third. Transferred WCR June 1959 (retained 1L). Sold to Bord na Móna in Bellacorrick.

No. 2 – Converted to all-third 1900-07. Scrapped 1950.

No. 3 – Converted to all-third 1900-07. Scrapped 1950.

No. 4 – 'Cardboard' sides added in Inchicore (? when). Little used after.

No. 5 – Converted to brake/composite. 1945/46. To Belfast Transport Museum on closure.

No. 6 – Converted to brake/composite 1950. Out of use at end. Sold to Gaelic Athletic Association 1959.

No. 7 – Sent to Inchicore with No. 4. Rebuilt as 36 seat third brake with 'Bus body' 1953. Sold to Bord na Móna on closure - later to C&L Dromod.

No. 8 – Converted to all-third 1899. Scrapped 1943.

No. 11 – Lay derelict for a number of years before closure.

No. 13 – 'Birdcage' roof removed before World War I.

No. 14 – 'Birdcage' roof removed before World War I.

No. 15 – 'Birdcage' roof removed before World War I.

No. 16 – 'Birdcage' roof removed before World War I.

No. 17 – 'Birdcage' roof removed before World War I.

No. 18 – 'Birdcage' roof removed before World War I.

No. 19 – Body scrapped; frame and wheels used to make new coal wagon.

No. 20 – Body scrapped; frame and wheels used to make new coal wagon.

No. 21L – T&D No 18T. Transferred to WCR (42C) 1940; to C&L 1954; returned to WCR 1959; preserved in USA.

No. 22L – Some dispute regarding the original identity of this vehicle. Coakham, D., (Narrow Gauge Rolling Stock: An Irish Railway Pictorial) and Rowlands, D., McGrath, W., Francis, T., (The Dingle Train) state 2T became 51C in 1954 with 5T transferring to C&L 1954 as 22L. Taylor, P., (The West Clare Railway) 2T to WCR 1953 then to C&L as 22L 1954. Return to WCR. Preserved in USA. No record 5T. Flanagan, Patrick J., (The Cavan & Leitrim Railway) states 22L was a Bristol Carriage & Wagon Co. vehicle of 1890. Originally brake third, rebuilt Whitehouse, P.B., (The Tralee & Dingle Railway). 2T Transferred to WCR 1954 (number not stated). No record of further transfer. 5T converted to brake van 1947. Scrapped 1954.

Wagons (after renumbering 1918)

Nos.	Type	Built	Maker	Length	Width	Wheelbase	Capacity (t. cwt)	Tare weight
1-40	4 plank open	1886	Metropolitan Carriage & Wagon Co.	13'6"	7'3"	6'8"	5-0	
41-50	C&L open	1889-1917	C&L, Ballinamore					
51-60	Open	1912	R.Y. Pickering					3-1
61-80	Covered wagons*	1886	Metropolitan Carriage & Wagon Co.	15'6"	7'0"	7'6"	6-0	
81-100	Cattle wagons	1886	Metropolitan Carriage & Wagon Co.	15'6"	7'0"	7'6"		
101-102	Timber	1886	Metropolitan Carriage & Wagon Co.					
103-109	Covered wagons	1889	Metropolitan Carriage & Wagon Co.					
110	Covered wagons	1886	Metropolitan Carriage & Wagon Co.					
111-112	Covered wagons	1903	C&L, Ballinamore					
113-132	Covered wagons	1904	R.Y. Pickering	15'6"	7'0"	7'0"		
133-142	Covered wagons	1912	R.Y. Pickering					
143-161	Covered wagons*	1886	Metropolitan Carriage & Wagon Co.	15'6"	7'0"	7'6"		
162-163	Timber	1918						
164-169	2 plank ballast wagon	1888	Bristol Carriage & Wagon Co.					
170L-189L	Open	1900	?	15'9"	7'0"	7'9"	5-0	3-10
190L-191L	Goods brake vans	1900	?	17'0"	7'0"	8'4"		
192L-203L	Open	1900	?	15'9"	7'0"	7'9"	5-0	3-10
204L-209L	Open	1934	Inchicore Works				5-0	
210L-211L	Open	?	?				5-0	
212L	Covered cattle	1941	Inchicore Works					
213L	Covered cattle	1941	Inchicore Works					
214L-215L	Covered wagons (corrugated iron roofs)	1942	?					
216L-217L	Covered wagons (ordinary full roofs)	1942	?					
218L-225L	Open	1942	?					
226L-228L	Ballast wagons	1953						
231L-240	Open	1957						

Notes
* Half 'convertible' - open centre portion for cattle use.
170L-189L and 192L-203L – Ex-CB&PR - for coal traffic on Arigna branch.
190L-191L – Ex-CB&PR.
204L-209L – New bodies, some parts of ex-C&MLR wagons used - for coal traffic on Arigna branch.
210L-211L – Ex-C&MLR - altered from 6T to 5T capacity.
212L – Rebuild of open wagon No. 6.
213L – Rebuild of original C&LR open wagon.
214L-225L – Ex-CVR.
226L-228L – Ex-T&DLR.
231L-240 – From WCR. Ex-C&MLR(8) and CVR(2). Little used.

Ballinamore, 19th April, 1955, with a train of empties preparing to leave for Arigna. On shed, right, are locomotives Nos. 8L, 3L, 5T, 2L.   *H.C. Casserley, courtesy R.M. Casserley*

Deep in coal country. Locomotive No. 5L, facing towards Ballinamore, shunts a coach at Arigna on 19th April, 1955.   *H.C. Casserley, courtesy R.M. Casserley*

As was the case on other Irish Railways, costs had soared during Executive control, Government compensation doing little to guarantee financial security and, as a result, the Government recommended amalgamation of all railway companies in the Free State, with the formation of the Great Southern Railway, which came into being on 1st January, 1925. Under the GSR, the suffix 'L' was added to the C&LR rolling stock numbers. The Ballinamore workshops were downgraded, heavy repairs transferring to Inchicore and in the early 1930s all carriage sheds were removed, the subsequent overnight exposure to the local weather conditions leading to the early demise of many of them. The C&LR did benefit from the transfer of locomotives from the Cork, Blackrock & Passage Railway and the Tralee & Dingle Railway when passenger services ceased on these lines.

The advent of motor transport also reached County Leitrim but despite this the C&LR continued to benefit from coal traffic, which even increased with reorganization of Dereenavoggy mines in 1934, to cater for which wagons were transferred from the CB&PR. The advent of World War II once again boosted the need for coal.

The GSR and the Dublin United Transport Company merged to form CIÉ with effect from 1st January, 1945. For the C&LR little changed. Over the years rolling stock deteriorated, transfer to Inchicore for major repair or scrapping proving necessary, with some respite offered by transfer of stock from other lines. But the real threat to the line's survival came with a reduction in coal traffic in the early 1950s which saw losses begin to mount. The final nail in the C&LR's coffin came with the announcement by the Government of plans for the construction of Arigna power station which would use the entire output of Arigna mines, depriving the C&LR of any regular source of income. By 1959, annual losses were reportedly reaching £40,000 and with no money to heal the ailing infrastructure, the decision to close was made, with the last train running on the 31st March, 1959.

Chronology

03.12.1883	Cavan, Leitrim & Roscommon Light Railway & Tramway Company incorporated under Tramways Act of 1883.
17.10.1887	Opened for goods traffic from Belturbet to Dromod.
24.10.1887	Opened for passenger traffic from Belturbet to Dromod.
02.05.1888	Ballinamore to Arigna branch opened.
16.10.1895	Title changed to Cavan & Leitrim Railway.
02.06.1920	Extension from Arigna to Aughabehy (Arigna Mining Co.) opened.
01.01.1925	C&LR became a part of Great Southern Railways.
1930	Aughabehy to Derreenavoggy section closed.
01.01.1945	CIÉ formed from amalgamation of GSR and Dublin United Transport Co.
31.03.1959	Closed to all traffic.

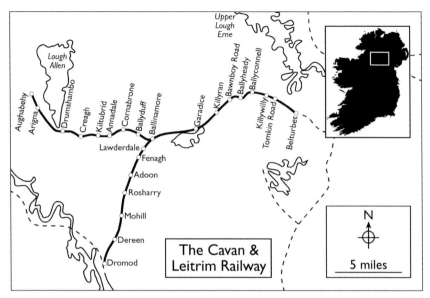

Route

Distance	Station/Halt/Crossing	Opened	Closed	Notes
0	Dromod	1887	1959	
½	Clooncolry Crossing No. 27	1887	1959	
1¾	Corrycramp Crossing No. 26	1887	1959	
2½	Dereen	1887	1959	Originally to have been named Lough Rhyn.
2½	Dereen Station Gates No. 25	1887	1959	
4¾	Clooncahir Crossing	1887	1959	Accommodation crossing.
5¾	Mohill	1887	1959	
5¾	Mohill Station Gates	1887	1959	
6	Hill Street Crossing No. 24	1887	1959	
7⅛	Gortfada Crossing No. 23	1887	1901	Market Day Stopping place to 1901 - also 'Rosharry No. 1'.
7½	Rosharry Crossing No. 22	1901	1920	Rosharry Gates, stopping place 1901-1920.
10¼	Adoon Station Gates No. 21	1887	1959	
10¼	Adoon	1887	1959	
10½	Annaghderry Crossing No. 20	1887	1959	aka Adoon Crossing.
11⅓	Sallyfield Crossing No. 19	1887	1959	
12½	Drumharkan Crossing No. 18	1887	1959	
12¾	Fenagh Station Gates No. 17	1887	1959	aka Ardagh Gates.
12¾	Fenagh	1887	1959	
14¼	Lawderdale Station Gates No. 16	1887	1959	
14¼	Lawderdale	1887	1959	Proper name Drumrane. Aghoo Bridge also proposed.
15½	Cornacreegh	1887	1959	Accommodation crossing.
16	Tully Crossing No. 15	1887	1959	

Distance	Station/Halt/Crossing	Opened	Closed	Notes
16¼	Cannaboe Crossing			
	(Ballinamore Station)	1887	1959	
16¼	Ballinamore	1887	1959	
17⅔	Corgar Crossing No. 14	1887	1959	
19½	Garadice Crossing No. 13	1887	1959	
20¼	Glebe Crossing No. 12	1887	1959	Accommodation crossing.
21¼	Killyran Station Gates No. 11	1887	1959	
21½	Killyran	1887	1959	
22¼	Killymoriarity Crossing No. 10	1887	1959	Accommodation crossing.
23	Bawnboy Rd	1887	1959	Crossing place.
23	Bawnboy Rd Station Gates	1887	1959	
24½	Currin Crossing No. 9	1887	1959	aka Killycluggin Crossing.
24¾	Ballyheady	1887	1959	Officially Bellaheady.
24¾	Ballyheady Station Gates No. 8	1887	1959	
27½	Ballyconnell Station Gates	1887	1959	
27½	Ballyconnell	1887	1959	
28	Cavanagh Crossing No. 7	1887	1959	
29½	Killywilly Crossing No. 5	1887	1959	aka Ardue Crossing.
30½	Tomkin Road	1887	1959	
30½	Tomkin Rd Station Gates No. 5	1887	1959	aka Drumrush Gates.
30¾	Carrowfarnaghan			
	Crossing No. 4	1887	1959	
32	Raffian Crossing No. 3	1887	1959	aka Drumary Crossing.
32½	Drumacon Crossing No. 2	1887	1959	Accommodation crossing
33¾	Straheglin Crossing No. 1	1887	1959	
33¾	Belturbet	1887	1959	
0	Ballinamore	1887	1959	
	Cannaboe Crossing	1887	1959	
¼	Tully Crossing No. 15	1887	1959	
½	Lower Town Gates	1887	1959	
¾	Stradermot Quarry siding			
3	Ballyduff	1887	1959	Tramway joined road.
3¾	Dromkeen Wood Siding	1918	1919	
5¾	Cornabrone	1887	1959	Roadside stopping place.
6½	Aughacashlaun ballast siding	1896	1952	
7½	Annadale	1887	1959	Roadside stopping place.
8	Driney	1887	1959	Excursions only.
8½	Kiltubrid Crossing	1887	1959	
8¾	Kiltubrid	1887	1959	
9	Crossing	1887	1959	Ungated.
10¼	Creagh	1887	1959	Roadside stopping place.
12¼	Drumshambo	1887	1959	
12½	Carrignabrack Crossing	1887	1959	Ungated.
13¼	Mahanagh Gates	1887	1959	
14¾	Arigna	1887	1959	
14¾	Arigna (Aghafin) crossing	1920	1959	Ungated.
16	Arigna-Keadue Rd Crossing	1920	1959	
16½	Dereenavoggy Crossing	1920	1959	Ungated.
16½	Rover Road Crossing	1920	1930	
18¾	Aughabehy	1920	1930	

The West Clare Railway

Locomotives

No.	Manufacturer	Type	Year	Works No.	Name	Driving wheel dia.	Leading/ trailing wheel dia.	Total wheel-base	Coupled wheel-base	Cyls (in.)	Heating surface (sq. ft)	Grate area (sq. ft)	Water capacity (galls)	Coal capacity (cwt)	Boiler pressure (psi)	Weight (t. cwt.)	Max. axle load (t. cwt.)	Tractive effort at 85% (lb.)	Wdn
1	W.G. Bagnall	0-6-0T	1886	730	-	3'6"	-	11'0"	11'0"	13x20	510	9	600	20	140	24-0	8-0	9,576	1912
2	W.G. Bagnall	0-6-0T	1886	738	-	3'6"	-	11'0"	11'0"	13x20	510	9	600	20	140	24-0	8-0	9,576	1900
3	W.G. Bagnall	0-6-0T	1887	792	Clifden	3'6"	-	11'0"	11'0"	14x20	540	9	600	20	140	24-0	8-0	11,106	1915
4	W.G. Bagnall	0-6-0T	1887	793	Besborough	3'6"	-	11'0"	11'0"	14x20	540	9	600	20	140	24-0	8-0	11,106	1901
5	Dübs & Co.	0-6-2T	1892	2890	Slieve Callan	4'0"	4'0"	15'0"	9'6"	15x20	740.5	11.18	938	40	150	35-12	9-3	11,900	-
6	Dübs & Co.	0-6-2T	1892	2891	Saint Senan	4'0"	4'0"	15'0"	9'6"	15x20	740.5	11.18	938	40	150	35-12	9-3	11,900	1956
7	Dübs & Co.	0-6-2T	1892	2892	Lady Inchiquin	4'0"	4'0"	15'0"	9'6"	15x20	740.5	11.18	938	40	150	35-12	9-3	11,900	1922
8	Dübs & Co.	2-6-2T	1894	3169	Lisdoonvarna	3'6"	2'6"	18'0"	9'3"	15x20	743	11.18	900	30	150	36-9	9-7	13,607	1925
9	Thos Green & Sons	2-6-2T	1898	229	Fergus	3'6"	2'6"	18'0"	9'3"	15x20	743.5	11.18	900	40	150	36-10	9-7	13,607	1954
2	Thos Green & Sons	2-6-2T	1900	234	Ennis	3'6"	2'6"	18'0"	9'3"	15x20	743.5	11.18	900	40	150	36-10	9-7	13,607	1955
4	Thos Green & Sons	2-6-2T	1901	236	Liscannor	3'6"	2'6"	18'0"	9'3"	15x20	743.5	11.18	900	40	150	36-10	9-7	13,607	1928
10	Kerr, Stuart	4-6-0T	1903	818	Lahinch	3'0"	2'0"	19'0"	8'0"	15x20	700	12	800	35	150	39-10		14,000	1952
11	W.G. Bagnall	4-6-0T	1908	1881	Kilkee	3'6"	2'3"	19'1½"	8'4"	15x20	696	11.5	860	40	160	36-0		14,571	1953
1	Hunslet Engine Co.	4-6-0T	1912	1098	Kilrush	3'9"	2'3"	19'1½"	8'10½"	15x20	604	11.5	860	35	160	39-10	10-4	13,600	1953
3	Hunslet Engine Co.	4-6-0T	1922	1432	Ennistymon	3'9"	2'3"	19'1½"	8'10½"	15x20	604	11.5	860	35	160	39-10	10-4	13,600	1953
7	Hunslet Engine Co.	4-6-0T	1922	1433	Malbay	3'9"	2'3"	19'1½"	8'10½"	15x20	604	11.5	860	35	160	39-10	10-4	13,600	1956
6T	Hunslet Engine Co.	2-6-0T	1898	677	-	3'0½"	2'0"	15'7"	8'9"	13x18	560	9.75	730	15	150	30-11	8-10	10,626	1960
8T	Hunslet Engine Co.	2-6-0T	1910	1051	-	3'0½"	2'0"	15'7"	8'9"	13x18	560	9.75	730	15	150	31-0	8-10	10,626	1956

Notes

No. 3 – Rebuilt 1905/06; given frames and side tanks of No. 4 - became No. 3 *Besborough*.
No. 4 – Withdrawn 1901; cannibalized to keep No. 3 running.
No. 5 – Owned by SC Rly. Wheels 3 ft 6 in. after 1904 - TE 13,607 lb. No. 5C under GSR. Restored to running order on West Clare Railway Moyasta 2009.
No. 6 – Owned by SC Rly. Wheels 3 ft 6 in. after 1893 - TE 13,607 lb.
No. 7 – Owned by SC Rly. Wheels 3 ft 6 in. after 1906 - TE 13,607 lb. Rebuilt by Thos Green 1902. Out of use from 1916.
No. 8 – Scrapped by GSR on takeover - out of use for some years.
No. 9 – No. 9C under GSR.
No. 2 (2nd) – No. 2C under GSR.
No. 4 (2nd): No. 4C under GSR.
No. 10 - No. 10C under GSR. Reboilered. BP 160 psi, TE 17,000.
No. 11 – No. 11C under GSR.
No. 1 (2nd) – No. 1C under GSR. Withdrawn 1953.
No. 3 (2nd) – No. 3C under GSR. Last engines built for the Irish narrow gauge.
No. 7 (2nd) – Owned by SC Rly. No. 7C under GSR. Last engines built for the Irish narrow gauge.
No. 6T – Transferred from T&D 1953. Withdrawn 1955 and sent to Inchicore for scrapping. Reconditioned and sent to C&L 1957.
No. 8T – Transferred from T&D Nov. 1953. Never known to have run. Boiler transferred to 6T 1954.

Chapter Fourteen

The West Clare Railway

The West Clare Railway was the outcome of a number of schemes proposed to link the coastal towns of Clare with the county town of Ennis, already linked to the Irish standard gauge system. The company was incorporated following the passing of the Tramways and Public Companies (Ireland) Act 1883 with powers for the construction of 27 miles of railway of 3 ft gauge from Ennis to Miltown Malbay, the capital guaranteed by the ratepayers of county Baronies. Construction began in January 1885 and, after initial progress, the company ran into financial difficulty, due to slow uptake of the guaranteed shares and a loan was necessary from the Board of Works to allow completion of the line. The line was passed for operation following a Board inspection on 29th June, 1887, and service commenced on 2nd July.

In the meantime, approval had been granted for a southerly extension to Kilrush and Kilkee to the South Clare Railway Company Ltd. Although a separate company to the WCR, much of the Board membership and many key managerial positions were shared with the WCR, who provided rolling stock and operated the line. Construction commenced in October 1890 and, following a number of Board of Trade inspections, full service commenced on 23rd December, 1892.

From the outset, the traffic was largely seasonal, the resort towns being very popular during the summer season. Resources were stretched at these busy

No. 11C with an excursion train from Ennis at Kilkee on Sunday 15th July, 1934. The front coach is No. 23C. *H.C. Casserley, courtesy R.M. Casserley*

Railcars/diesel locomotives

No.	Source/builder	Wheels	Year	Engine	Weight (t. cwt)	Seats	Wdn	Notes
395	Drewry/Baguley	4	1927	Petrol 45 bhp	5-10	30	1943	Withdrawn 1936. Transferred to Inchicore 1939. Scrapped 1943.
396	Drewry/Baguley	4	1927	Petrol 45 bhp	5-10	30	1943	Withdrawn 1936. Transferred to Inchicore 1939. Scrapped 1943.
6	T&DLR Workshops/Baguley Chassis	4	1922	Ford Model 'T'		4	1961	Transferred WCR 1926. Rebuilt with Ford 8 engine. Ennis, 1938.
3386	Walker Bros/Inchicore	4.4	1952	Diesel 6LW 107 bhp	11-0	41	1961	Driving sections scrapped, passenger saloons sold to BNM.
3387	Walker Bros/Inchicore	4.4	1952	Diesel 6LW 107 bhp	11-0	41	1961	Driving sections scrapped, passenger saloons sold to BNM.
3388	Walker Bros/Inchicore	4.4	1952	Diesel 6LW 107 bhp	11-0	41	1961	Driving sections scrapped, passenger saloons sold to BNM.
3389	Walker Bros/Inchicore	4.4	1952	Diesel 6LW 107 bhp	11-0	41	1961	Driving sections scrapped, passenger saloons sold to BNM.
46C	Bristol Wagon & Carriage Co./Ennis		1952	-		40	1961	Ex-T&D No. 1T. Transferred to WCR 1940; converted to railcar trailer (bus body on carriage underframe) 1951.
47C	Bristol Wagon & Carriage Co./Ennis		1952	-		40	1961	Ex T&D No. 6T. Transferred to WCR 1940; converted to railcar trailer (bus body on carriage underframe) 1951.
48C	Bristol Wagon & Carriage Co./Ennis		1952	-		40	1961	Ex-T&D No. 8T. Transferred to WCR 1940; converted to railcar trailer (bus body on carriage underframe) 1951.
F501	Walker Bros/Inchicore	BoBo	1955	Diesel 6LW 107 bhp (2x)	23-0	-	1961	Stored in Inchicore while CIE attempted to sell. Scrapped 1968/69.
F502	Walker Bros/Inchicore	BoBo	1955	Diesel 6LW 107 bhp (2x)	23-0	-	1961	Stored in Inchicore while CIE attempted to sell. Scrapped 1968/69.
F503	Walker Bros/Inchicore	BoBo	1955	Diesel 6LW 107 bhp (2x)	23-0	-	1961	Stored in Inchicore while CIE attempted to sell. Scrapped 1968/69.

times and, as a tight construction budget had provided insufficient rolling stock and left little provision for workshops, stock was soon run down, resulting in delays and inefficiencies.

Despite this, traffic steadily increased, peaking just before World War I. During the war years, the service was initially increased from four to five trains in each direction daily, though in 1916, this was reduced to three, due to wartime coal shortages. Excursion trains were particularly affected. Government control of Irish Railways took effect on 1st January 1917, and this period saw a steep rise in costs for coal and materials, together with an increase in staff pay.

World War I was followed by, first, the War of Independence and thereafter by the Civil War, which followed on the creation of the Irish Free State in 1921. With the level of Republican activity in the county, the railway suffered a number of incidents which resulted in military guards accompanying all trains, until matters settled in 1923.

Under the Irish Railways Act, of July 1924, all railways wholly within the Irish Free State, were absorbed into the Great Southern Railways and on 1st January, 1925, the WCR duly became part of the GSR. Under the new owners, the suffix 'C' was added to numbers of the engines and rolling stock, and engine repair and maintenance transferred to Inchicore. As an economy measure, two petrol-engined railcars were purchased in 1927 and operated with variable success until 1936. As other narrow gauge lines closed, the GSR transferred stock to work on the WCR. With the advent of World War II, services were again badly affected by coal shortages and a minimum service of one goods and one passenger train in each direction was only maintained by the burning of local turf in the locomotives.

On 1st January, 1945, the GSR was merged with the Dublin United Transport Co. to form Córas Iompair Éireann. Under CIÉ the transfer of stock from other, closed, lines continued and in the early 1950s a decision was taken to introduce diesel power. Four articulated diesel railcars were purchased from Walker Bros and the same firm supplied three diesel locomotives in 1955 to work the goods traffic. While these measures enabled the WCR to survive longer than it otherwise might have done, in reality, they simply delayed the inevitable end. Like the other narrow gauge concerns, improvements to the road infrastructure led to increasing competition from road transport and in September 1960, faced with mounting losses, CIÉ made the decision to close the line. Some local opposition to closure was mounted but failed. The last passenger service operated from Kilrush into Ennis on the afternoon of 31st January, 1961 while the last train to run was a down goods train which ran from Ennis to Kilkee, arriving late in the night of the 31st.

Locomotive No. 5 *Slieve Callan* was saved from the scrap man and stood on a length of track on Ennis platform for many years. A revival was to come in the mid-1990s when a restoration group was formed, based at the old Moyasta station. As part of the restoration project, *Slieve Callan* was moved to Moyasta, later being shipped to England for restoration to working order. For details of the West Clare Railway restoration project see Chapter Twenty.

Carriages

No.	Type	Built	Maker	Length	Compts 1st	Compts 3rd	Seats dia.	Wheel	Wheel centres	Bogie centres	Withdrawn
1*	6 wheel brake	1887	Bristol Carriage & Wagon Co.	30'0"	-	-	-	2'0"	9'9"	-	1905
2	4 wheel brake	1887	Bristol Carriage & Wagon Co.	14'3"	-	-	-	2'0"	-	-	1909
3*	Third 6 wheel	1887	Bristol Carriage & Wagon Co.	30'0"	-	6	48	2'0"	9'9"	-	1941
4*	Composite first/third 6 wheel	1887	Bristol Carriage & Wagon Co.	30'0"	3	2	34	2'0"	9'9"	-	1957
5*	Third 6 wheel	1887	Bristol Carriage & Wagon Co.	30'0"	-	6	48	2'0"	9'9"	-	1957
6*	Composite first/third 6 wheel	1887	Bristol Carriage &- Wagon Co.	30'0"	3	2	34	2'0"	9'9"	-	1939
7*	Third 6 wheel	1887	Bristol Carriage & Wagon Co.	30'0"	-	6	48	2'0"	9'9"	-	1957
8*	Composite first/third 6 wheel	1887	Bristol Carriage & Wagon Co.	30'0"	3	2	34	2'0"	9'9"	-	1957
9*	Third 6 wheel	1887	Bristol Carriage & Wagon Co.	30'0"	-	6	48	2'0"	9'9"	-	1957
10*	Third 6 wheel	1887	Bristol Carriage & Wagon Co.	30'0"	-	6	48	2'0"	9'9"	-	1941
11*	Third 6 wheel	1887	Bristol Carriage & Wagon Co.	30'0"	-	6	48	2'0"	9'9"	-	1957
12	4 wheel brake	1887	Bristol Carriage & Wagon Co.	14'3"	-	-	-	2'0"	-	-	1905
13*	6 wheel brake	1887	Bristol Carriage & Wagon Co.	30'0"	-	-	-	2'0"	9'9"	-	1908
14*	Composite first/third 6 wheel	1893	Bristol Carriage & Wagon Co.	30'0"	3	2	34	2'0"	9'9"	-	1941
15*	Third 6 wheel	1893	Bristol Carriage & Wagon Co.	30'0"	-	6	48	2'0"	9'9"	-	1941
16*	Third 6 wheel	1893	Bristol Carriage & Wagon Co.	30'0"	-	6	48	2'0"	9'9"	-	1957
17*	6 wheel brake	1893	Bristol Carriage & Wagon Co.	30'0"	-	-	-	2'0"	9'9"	-	1961
18*	6 wheel brake	1893	Bristol Carriage & Wagon Co.	30'0"	-	-	-	2'0"	9'9"	-	1961
19*	Composite first/third 6 wheel	1894	Bristol Carriage & Wagon Co.	30'0"	3	2	34	2'0"	9'9"	-	1957
20*	Composite first/third 6 wheel	1894	Bristol Carriage & Wagon Co.	30'0"	3	2	34	2'0"	9'9"	-	1941
21*	Third 6 wheel	1892	Bristol Carriage & Wagon Co.	30'0"	-	6	48	2'0"	9'9"	-	1957
22*	Third 6 wheel	1892	Bristol Carriage & Wagon Co.	30'0"	-	6	48	2'0"	9'9"	-	1957
23*	Third 6 wheel	1892	Bristol Carriage & Wagon Co.	30'0"	-	6	48	2'0"	9'9"	-	1957
24*	Third 6 wheel	1892	Bristol Carriage & Wagon Co.	30'0"	-	6	48	2'0"	9'9"	-	1952
25*	Composite first/third 6 wheel	1892	Bristol Carriage & Wagon Co.	30'0"	3	2	34	2'0"	9'9"	-	1944
26*	Composite first/third 6 wheel	1892	Bristol Carriage & Wagon Co.	30'0"	3	2	34	2'0"	9'9"	-	1957
27*	Third 6 wheel	1894	Bristol Carriage & Wagon Co.	30'0"	-	6	48	2'0"	9'9"	-	1957
28	4 wheel horse box	1897	Bristol Carriage & Wagon Co.	14'3"	-	-	4	2'0"	-	-	1959
29	First 6 wheel	1901	Metropolitan Carriage & Wagon Co.	30'10"	5	-	30	2'1"	9'9"	-	1957
30	First 6 wheel	1901	Metropolitan Carriage & Wagon Co.	30'10"	5	-	30	2'1"	9'9"	-	1952 (?)
31	Brake/third 6 wheel	1904	WCR Ennis	30'0"	-	2	24	2'0"	9'9"	-	1961
32	Third saloon 6 wheel	1905	WCR Ennis	32'0"	-	1	52	2'0"	9'9"	-	1957
33	Third saloon 6 wheel	1905	WCR Ennis	32'0"	-	1	52	2'0"	9'9"	-	1957
34	First saloon 6 wheel	1906	WCR Ennis	32'0"	-	1	30	2'0"	9'9"	-	1944
35	Third saloon 6 wheel	1906	WCR Ennis	32'0"	-	1	52	2'0"	9'9"	-	1957
36	6 wheel ballast brake	1909	WCR Ennis	30'0"	-	-	-	2'0"	9'9"	-	1961
37	Brake/third 6 wheel	1910	WCR Ennis	30'0"	-	2	24	2'0"	9'9"	-	1940
38	Brake/third 6 wheel	1910	WCR Ennis	30'0"	-	2	24	2'0"	9'9"	-	1958
39C	Third	1890	Bristol Wagon & Carriage Co.	27'0"	-	1	34	2'0"	3'6"	15'6"	1961
40C	Composite first/third	1907	Midland Carriage & Wagon Co.	30'0"	1	1	32	2'0"	4'0"	21'0"	1953
41C	Bogie brake	1904	T&DLR Tralee	32'0"	-	-	-	2'0"	-	-	1958
42C	Composite first/third	1907	Midland Carriage & Wagon Co.	30'0"	1	1	32	2'0"	4'0"	21'0"	-

No.	Type	Builder	Built							Withdrawn
43C	Composite first/third	Bristol Carriage & Wagon Co.	1890	27'0"	2	34	2'0"	3'6"	15'6"	1958
44C	Third	Bristol Carriage & Wagon Co.	1891	27'0"	1	34	2'0"	3'6"	15'6"	-
45C	Third	Bristol Carriage & Wagon Co.	1890	27'0"	1	34	2'0"	3'6"	15'6"	1958
46C	Third	Bristol Carriage & Wagon Co.	1890	27'0"	1	34	2'0"	3'6"	15'6"	1961
47C	Third	Bristol Carriage & Wagon Co.	1890	27'0"	1	34	2'0"	3'6"	15'6"	1961
48C	Third	Bristol Carriage & Wagon Co.	1890	27'0"	1	34	2'0"	3'6"	15'6"	1961
49C	Third	T&DLR Tralee	1896	27'0"	1	34	2'0"	-	-	1961
50C	Brake third	Bristol Wagon & Carriage Co.	1903	27'0"	1	26	2'0"	-	-	1957
12(2nd)	4 wheel breakdown van	WCR Ennis	1905	30'0"	-	-	2'0"	-	-	1959
2(2nd)	4 wheel Directors' saloon	WCR Ennis	1908	14'3"	1	-	2'0"	-	-	1958
13(2nd)	6 wheel brake	WCR Ennis	1908	30'0"	-	-	-	-	-	1961
51C	Bogie brake	Bristol Wagon & Carriage Co.	1890	27'0"	-	-	2'0"	3'6"	15'6"	1961
52C	Bogie brake	Bristol Wagon & Carriage Co.	1891	27'0"	-	-	2'0"	3'6"	15'6"	-
1L	Third	Metropolitan Carriage & Wagon Co.	1887	41'8"	1	50	2'0"	4'0"	26'0"	1961
200C	4 wheel luggage	CIE Limerick	1951	13'6"	-	-	-	7'8"	-	1961
201C	4 wheel luggage	CIE Limerick	1951	13'6"	-	-	-	7'8"	-	1961
202C	4 wheel luggage	CIE Limerick	1951	13'6"	-	-	-	7'8"	-	1961

Notes

* Cleminson patent design.

No. 1 – withdrawn following collision 1905. Scrapped 1913.

No. 2 – Converted to inspection saloon 1908; parts used to build wagon No. 143 1909.

No. 3 – Converted to all first 1895; reverted to third 1901.

No. 12 – Rebuilt as cattle wagon No. 93 1905; some parts may have been used in replacement No. 12.

Nos. 21-26 – For opening of South Clare Railways. No. 24C destroyed by fire 1952.

No. 29 & No. 30 – 5 compartments. No. 30 destroyed by fire 1952 (?).

No. 31 – 2 compartments tourist.

No. 32-35 – tourist saloons.

No. 39C – Ex-T&D No. 3T 1940.

No. 40C – Ex-T&D No. 17T 1940.

No. 41C – Ex-T&D No. 16T 1940; former composite first/third; converted to brake on WCR.

No. 42C – Ex-T&D No. 18T 1940; to C&L 1954 (21L); returned to WCR 1959, retaining No 21L; preserved in USA.

No. 43C – Original full third; converted to composite 1904. Ex-T&D No. 4T 1940.

No. 44C – Ex-T&D No. 10T 1940; body extant Dromod C&LR.

No. 45C – Ex-T&D No. 7T 1940.

No. 46C – Ex-T&D No. 1T 1940; converted to railcar trailer 1951 (40 seats).

No. 47C – Ex-T&D No. 6T 1940; converted to railcar trailer 1951 (40 seats).

No. 48C – Ex-T&D No. 8T 1940; converted to railcar trailer 1951 (40 seats).

No. 49C – Ex-T&D No. 11T 1940.

No. 50C – Ex-T&D No. 14T 1940.

No. 2 (2nd) – Used parts Nos. 1 and 2; officially a 'conversion'.

No. 51C – Ex-T&D No. 2T 1953; preserved in USA.

No. 52C – Ex-T&D No. 9T 1953. Transferred to C&L 1954 as 22L.

No. 1L – Original first/third composite from C&L. Rebuilt Ballinamore 1958. Transferred to WCR 1959. Sold to BNM in 1961.

No. 200C – Built on underframe of ex-Clogher Valley Railway wagon (No. 187C under GSR) for railcar traffic. Original Metropolitan C&W Co.

No. 201C – Built on underframe of ex-Clogher Valley Railway wagon (No. 188C under GSR) for railcar traffic. Original Metropolitan C&W Co.

No. 202C – Built on underframe of ex-Clogher Valley Railway wagon (No. 190C under GSR) for railcar traffic. Original Metropolitan C&W Co. Preserved USA.

No. 22L – see page 86.

Wagons

Type	Built	Maker	Length	Width	Wheelbase	Capacity (t. cwt)	Notes
Covered goods (25)	1887	Bristol Wagon & Carriage Works Co.	14'2"	7'3"	7'4"	5-0	Nos. 1-3, 14, 15, 20, 21, 27, 28, 30-34, 36, 38-40, 45, 46, 48, 50-53. Ten were 'open-centres' - also used for cattle.
Cattle wagons (10)	1887	Bristol Wagon & Carriage Works Co.	14'2"	7'3"	7'4"	5-0	Nos. 4, 6-8, 13, 18, 22-24, 37.
Open goods (15)	1887	Bristol Wagon & Carriage Works Co.	14'2"	7'3"	7'4"	5-0	Nos. 5, 9-12,16, 17, 19, 35, 41-44, 47, 49.
Flat (3)	1887	Bristol Wagon & Carriage Works Co.	14'2"	7'3"	7'4"	5-0	Nos. 25, 26, 29.
Timber wagon	1887	Bristol Wagon & Carriage Works Co.	14'2"	7'3"	7'4"	5-0	No. 54.
Ballast wagon	1887	Bristol Wagon & Carriage Works Co.	14'2"	7'3"	7'4"	5-0	Nos. 55-66.
Covered goods (10)	1899	Bristol Wagon & Carriage Works Co.	14'3"	7'3"	7'4"	5-0	Nos. 67-76.
Open cattle (5)	1902	Bristol Wagon & Carriage Works Co.	14'3"	7'3"	7'4"	5-0	Nos. 77-82.
Covered cattle (17)	1904	WCR Ennis	14'3"	7'3"	7'4"	5-0	Nos. 83-92, 94-99, 122.
Covered cattle (1)	1905	WCR Ennis	14'3"	7'3"	7'4"	5-0	No. 93. Rebuild of coach No.12.
Water tank	1905	WCR Ennis	14'3"	7'3"	7'4"	5-0	No. 100. Rebuilt as timber 1922.
Covered goods (6)	1892	WCR Ennis	14'2"	7'3"	7'4"	5-0	Nos. 101-106.
Covered cattle (16)	1892	Bristol Wagon & Carriage Works Co.	14'2"	7'3"	7'4"	5-0	Nos. 107-122.
Large open (6 wheel) (2)	1907	Bristol Wagon & Carriage Works Co.	30'0"	7'3"	7'4"	7-0	Nos. 123, 124.
Ballast wagon	1904	WCR Ennis	14'3"	7'3"	7'4"	5-0	No. 125.
Open coal (7)	1904	WCR Ennis	14'3"	7'3"	7'4"	5-0	Nos. 126-132.
Open ballast (3)	1907	WCR Ennis	14'3"	7'3"	7'4"	5-0	Nos. 133-135.
Luggage van (6)	1908	WCR Ennis	14'2"	7'3"	7'4"	5-0	Nos. 136-141.
Open goods (1)	1908	WCR Ennis	14'2"	7'3"	7'4"	5-0	No. 142.
Cattle wagons (1)	1909	WCR Ennis	14'3"	7'3"	7'4"	5-0	No. 143. Built from parts of coach 2.
Covered cattle (6)	1911	WCR Ennis	14'3"	7'3"	7'4"	5-0	Nos. 144-149.
Open coal (6)	1912	WCR Ennis	14'3"	7'3"	7'4"	5-0	Nos. 150-155.
Covered goods (5)	1912	WCR Ennis	14'2"	7'3"	7'4"	5-0	Nos. 156-160.
Covered cattle (10)	1913	WCR Ennis	14'2"	7'3"	7'4"	4-0	Nos. 161-170.
Open goods (6)	1887	WCR Ennis				6-0	Nos. 171-176. Ex-C&MLR (Nos. 7K, 10K, 2K, 4K, 3K, 1K).
Open goods (4)	1887	WCR Ennis				6-0	Nos. 177, 181-183. ex-C&MLR (Nos. 49K, 48K, 33K, 50K).
Open goods (3)	1887	WCR Ennis				6-0	Nos. 178-180. Ex-C&MLR (Nos. 82K, 83K, 80K).
Open goods (1)	1897	-	13'6"			5-0	No. 184. Ex-Clogher Valley Railway.
Open goods (7)		Metropolitan Carriage & Wagon Co.	13'6"	7'0"		5-0	Nos. 185-191. Ex-CVR.
Covered goods (4)		Metropolitan Carriage & Wagon Co.	13'8"	7'3"		5-0	Nos. 192-195. Ex-CVR.
Covered goods (1)	1943	Metropolitan Carriage & Wagon Co.				5-0	No. 196. Ex-C&LR No. 121L.
Spray wagons (3)	1946	Inchicore	15'6"	7'0"	7'6"	5-0	Nos. 197-199.
Covered goods (7)	1886	Inchicore	13'6"	7'3"	6'8"	5-0	Nos. 203-209. Ex-C&LR Nos. 144L, 145L, 149L, 153L, 154L, 216L, 217L.
4-plank open (9)	1886	Metropolitan Carriage & Wagon Co.				6-0	Nos. 210-218. Ex-C&LR Nos. 1L, 3L, 4L, 18L, 26L, 27L, 29L, 35L, 36L.
Open goods (7)	1934	Metropolitan Carriage & Wagon Co.				6-0	Nos. 219-224. Ex-C&LR Nos. 171L, 181L, 204L-207L.
Open goods (2)	1887	Inchicore	13'6"	7'3"		6-0	Nos. 225-226. Ex-C&LR 219L, 223L. ex-CVR.
Open goods (7)	1957	Metropolitan Carriage & Wagon Co.	15'6"	7'3"		6-0	No. 227. Ex-C&Lr 229l. ex-CVR underframe.
Open goods (18)	1929	Inchicore	15'0"	7'0"		5-0	Nos. 14850-14867.
Covered goods (17)	1929	Inchicore	15'0"	7'0"		5-0	Nos. 19750-19766.
Cattle (15)	1929	Inchicore	15'0"	7'3"		5-0	Nos. 22850-22864.

Chronology

15.12.1883	West Clare Railway incorporated.
09.06.1884	South Clare Railway incorporated.
02.07.1887	Line opened Ennis-Milltown Malbay.
03.08.1892	Milltown Malbay-Kilrush/Kilkee opened to freight traffic.
23.12.1892	Milltown Malbay-Kilrush/Kilkee opened to passenger traffic.
01.01.1925	WCR became a part of Great Southern Railways.
01.01.1945	CIÉ formed from amalgamation of GSR and Dublin United Transport Co.
31.01.1961	Line closed to all traffic.

Route

Distance	Station/Halt/Crossing	Opened	Closed	Notes
0	Ennis	1887	1961	
1¼	Curravorrin Crossing	1887	1961	
1¾	Lifford	1952	1961	Railcar stopping place May 1952.
1¾	Lifford Crossing	1887	1961	aka Asylum Gates.
3½	Erinagh Crossing	1887	1961	
4¾	Ballygriffey Crossing	1887	1961	Ballast Siding opened in 1904.
6¾	Ruan Halt	1888	1961	Closed 1898, reopened 1904. Closed 1921. Railcar stopping place 1952.
6¾	Ruan Crossing	1887	1961	
7	Laurel Vale Crossing	1887	1961	
7⅓	Dromcavan Crossing	1887	1961	aka Murphy's Crossing.
7½	Cragmoher No. 1 Crossing	1887	1961	aka Ballycullinan No. 1.
8¼	Cragmoher No. 2 Crossing	1887	1961	aka Ballycullinan No. 2.
8¾	Corofin	1887	1961	
8¾	Corofin Station Gates	1887	1961	
9¾	Roxton Halt and Gates	1887	1961	
10¾	Newton Crossing	1887	1961	
11¾	Willbrook	1888	1961	Closed 1898, reopened 1904. Closed 1921. Reopened by GSR 1929.
11¾	Willbrook Crossing	1887	1961	
14	Clouna Halt	1954	1961	Opened May 1954 as railcar stopping place.
15¾	Monreal Halt and Gates	1952	1961	Opened December 1952 as railcar stopping place.
17½	Knockdromagh No. 1 Crossing	1887	1961	
17½	Knockdromagh No. 2 Crossing	1887	1961	
18½	Ennistymon	1887	1961	
19½	Workhouse	1887	1961	Closed 1925. Reopened for diesel working June 1953.
20	Lahinsey No. 1 Crossing	1887	1961	
20¼	Lahinsey No. 2 Crossing	1887	1961	
20¾	Lahinch	1887	1961	Passing place from 1911. Turntable added August 1953.
20¾	Lahinch Station Gates	1887	1961	
21¼	Gregg Crossing	1887	1961	

At Ennis, 30th June, 1938, locomotive No. 6C shunts stock for the 12 noon departure to Kilkee.
H.C. Casserley, courtesy R.M. Casserley

The WCR's unique Ford inspection car.   *John Langford Collection*

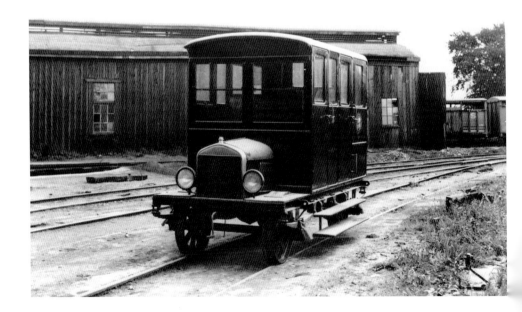

Distance	Station/Halt/Crossing	Opened	Closed	Notes
22¼	Hanrahan's Bridge	1958	1961	Originally Moy Bridge. Opened as railcar stopping place October 1958.
22¾	Moymore No. 1 Crossing	1887	1961	
23	Moymore No. 2 Crossing	1887	1961	
24½	Rineen	1952	1961	Opened May 1952 as railcar stopping place. Request stop previously.
27	Miltown Malbay	1887	1961	
27	Miltown Malbay Station Gates	1892	1961	
27¼	Flag Road No. 1 Crossing	1892	1961	
27½	Flag Road No. 2 Crossing	1892	1961	
28½	Braffa Crossing	1892	1961	
28¾	Annagh No. 1 Crossing	1892	1961	
29½	Annagh No. 2 Crossing	1892	1961	Opened May 1952 as railcar stopping place.
29¾	Emalough Crossing	1892	1961	
30¾	Quilty East Crossing	1892	1961	
31	Quilty Station Gates	1892	1961	
31½	Quilty	1892	1961	
32¼	Kilmurry Station Gates No. 1	1892	1961	
32½	Kilmurry	1892	1961	
32½	Kilmurry Station Gates No. 2	1892	1961	
33½	Clonadrum Crossing	1892	1961	
33¾	Lisseynealon Crossing	1892	1961	
34½	Craggaknock Station Gates	1892	1961	
34½	Craggaknock	1892	1961	
35⅓	Clohans No. 1 Crossing	1892	1961	
35½	Clohans No. 2 Crossing	1892	1961	
36¼	Caherfeenich No. 1 Crossing	1892	1961	
36⅓	Caherfeenich No. 2 Crossing	1892	1961	
36½	Caherfeenich No 3 Crossing	1892	1961	
37⅓	Caherfeenich No 4 Crossing	1892	1961	
37½	Doonbeg Station Gates	1892	1961	
37¾	Doonbeg	1892	1961	
39¾	Shragh Siding Halt and Gates	1892	1961	Opened May 1952 as railcar stopping place.
41¼	Moanmore Crossing	1892	1961	
43	Moyasta Junction	1892	1961	Reopened 1997 as base for West Clare Railway.
43	Moyasta No. 4 Gates	1892	1961	
43¾	Moyasta West No. 5 Gates	1892	1961	
44	Bawnmore Crossing	1892	1961	
44¾	Gurrane Crossing	1892	1961	
45¼	Blackweir	1892	1961	Downgraded to Halt and request stop early 1900s.
45¼	Blackweir Station Gates	1892	1961	
46¾	Lisdeen Crossing	1892	1961	
47	Dough Crossing	1892	1961	
48	Kilkee	1892	1961	

Distance	Station/Halt/Crossing	Opened	Closed	Notes
43	Moyasta Junction	1892	1961	
43	Moyasta No. 1 Gates	1892	1961	
43	Moyasta No. 2 Gates	1892	1961	
43	(Moyasta No 3 Gates)	1892	1961	Situated on the 'Loop' - for through workings Kilkee-Kilrush.
43¾	Carnacalla No. 1 Crossing	1892	1961	Carrowncalla on Ordnance Survey maps.
44¾	Carnacalla No. 2 Crossing	1892	1961	
46	Leadmore No. 1 Crossing	1892	1961	
46¾	Leadmore No. 2 Crossing	1892	1961	
47	Dock Crossing	1892	1961	
47	Kilrush	1892	1961	
47	Kilrush Station Gates	1892	1961	
47¾	Cappagh Crossing	1892	1961	
48	Cappagh Pier	1892	1916	

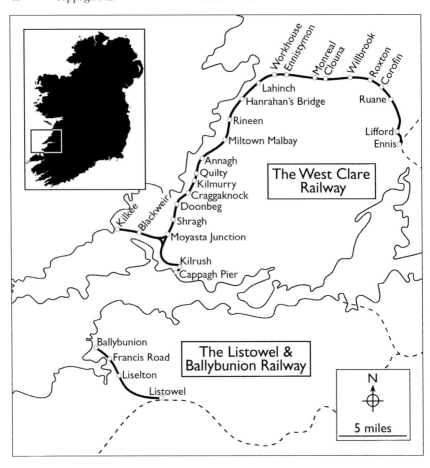

Chapter Fifteen

The Listowel & Ballybunion Railway

Ballybunion, a small seaside town in north Kerry is renowned for its resort, its golf course, as the birthplace of Lord Kitchener and for the one-time transport link to the main line at Listowel which was a unique experiment in light railway technology. The origins of this railway curiosity are to be found in the desert sands of north Africa. It was here that Charles Francois Marie Therese Lartigue (1834-1907), in looking to design a cheap, portable railway which could be used in difficult terrain, was inspired by the sight of camels carrying heavy loads balanced in panniers either side of their humps and came up with the idea of the monorail system that bears his name. It consisted of a single elevated running rail carried on the apex of A-shaped iron trestles approx 3 ft 6 in. high, anchored at the bottom onto iron or wooden sleepers, with a metal cross brace for rigidity. The object of the design was intended to avoid the need and expense of levelling the ground.

The rolling stock ran on the top rail on vertical double flanged wheels which bore all the weight. Light guide rails ran along the outside of the trestles, 2 ft below the running rails. Horizontal double-flanged wheels were fitted on either side of the vehicles to run on these guide rails to control lateral movement and give stability. The triangular nature of the track intruded into the vehicles and, though carriages had similar widths to 3 ft gauge stock, this intrusion limited their carrying capacity.

A postcard view of L&BR locomotive No. 3 at Listowel.   *John Langford Collection*

The Listowell & Ballybunion Railway

Locomotives

No.	Manufacturer	Type	Works No.	Year	Driving wheel dia.	Wheelbase	Cyls (in.)	Heating surface (sq. ft)	Grate area (sq. ft)	Water capacity (galls)	Coal capacity (cwt)	Boiler pressure (psi)	Weight (t. cwt.)	Max. axle load (t. cwt.)	Tractive effort at 85% (lb.)	Withdrawn
1	Hunslet Engine Co.	0-3-0	431	1887	2'0"	5'8"	7x12	143	5	200	8	150	10-0*	2-0	3,112	1924
2	Hunslet Engine Co.	0-3-0	432	1887	2'0"	5'8"	7x12	143	5	200	8	150	10-0*	2-0	3,112	1924
3	Hunslet Engine Co.	0-3-0	433	1887	2'0"	5'8"	7x12	143	5	200	8	150	10-0*	2-0	3,112	1924
	Tubize, Belgium†	0-2-0	-	1886	1'3"		4½x7	70				100	2-10			1900

Notes

* Manufacturer's quoted weight in working order - engine plus tender.

† Known as the 'Coffee Pot'. Not numbered. Believed to have been built for Westminster Exhibition 1886. Probably used in construction. Withdrawn early - lay at Listowel until about 1900.

Carriages

No.	Type	Maker	Built	Compts	Seats	Length	Wheel dia.	Wheel centres	Bogie centres	Withdrawn
A3	First & third composite	Falcon Engine & Car Co.	1887	3		16'10"	1'10"	2'6"	9'3"	1924
A5	Third	Falcon Engine & Car Co.	1887	2	24	16'10"	1'10"	2'6"	9'3"	1924
A6	First	Falcon Engine & Car Co.	1887	2	20	16'10"	1'10"	2'6"	9'3"	1924
A7	First	Falcon Engine & Car Co.	1887	3	20	16'10"	1'10"	2'6"	9'3"	1924
A8	First & third composite	Falcon Engine & Car Co.	1887	2		16'10"	1'10"	2'6"	9'3"	1924
B1	Brake third (with stairs)	Falcon Engine & Car Co.	1887	1		16'10"	1'10"	2'6"	9'3"	1924
B2	First & third brake composite	Falcon Engine & Car Co.	1887	2		16'10"	1'10"	2'6"	9'3"	1924

Exact makeup of passenger stock unknown. Above details for individual vehicles from Newham. Wheel dimensions etc. an estimate from drawings.

Wagons

Quantity	Type	Maker	Built	Capacity
28 (total)	Covered goods	Achille LeGrand, Belgium	1887	4 ton
	Sand wagons	Achille LeGrand, Belgium	1887	5 ton
	Cattle wagons			

Lartigue's first system was assembled in the deserts of Algeria - a 90 km line for the transport of esparto grass in wagons hauled by mules. The claimed advantages were that track could be easily lifted and relaid, that it was quick to construct, easy to operate and cheap, while the monorail structure would allow for sharper curves and steeper gradients. The Lartigue Railway Construction Co. was formed to market his invention and, in an attempt to gain a foothold in Britain, a demonstration was staged in Westminster, London in 1886.

Meanwhile, the people of Ballybunion had been trying for a number of years for a connection to the main line in Listowel, which had been opened in 1880 by the Limerick and Tralee section of the Waterford & Limerick Railway. Proposals included lines to the Irish standard gauge of 5 ft 3 in. as well as the 3 ft gauge, which was gaining in popularity. Both proposals required Baronial Guarantees and failed to raise sufficient support and both had been rejected by 1885. But it is believed the requirements of the north Kerry people lay on the desk of a minister of Parliament in Westminster when the Lartigue exhibition arrived there some few months later and may explain how the Lartigue company and the town of Ballybunion came together. Anxious for a permanent display of their system, the company agreed to build and equip the line for £33,000 and without the requirement for a Baronial Guarantee.

The Listowel & Ballybunion Railway gained the necessary approval on the 16th April, 1886, under the Listowel & Ballybunion Railway Act. Work began in the autumn of 1887. The official opening ceremony took place on 29th February, 1888 and the line opened for regular service on 1st March, 1888. The Managing Director of the Lartigue Railway Construction Company, Mr F.H. Behr, was appointed Managing Director of the L&BR. The line covered the 9¼ miles from Listowel to Ballybunion with a short extension running on to the pier in Ballybunion for the purpose of sand transport.

The Lartigue system differed in many ways from conventional railways and in so doing had a number of drawbacks. There were no platforms, passengers entering the train from ground level. A major disadvantage was the need to balance the train - for passenger services, by the guard and station master each walking down one side of the train and calling to the other the number in each half of the coach. If there was any imbalance then some of the passengers would have to move to the other side of the carriage and to enable this, a staircase on wheels was included in each passenger train.

Conventional points were not possible, access to different roads was achieved by use of turntables - this severely limited shunting operations as only a single vehicle could be accommodated on the turntable at any one time. It necessitated the trestle track being unbolted from the ground, disconnected from its current line, moved into position and connected with the new line and again bolted in place. How different from the pull of a lever to change conventional points!

For 'level crossings', two options were used. For occupation crossings, a section of the railway was hinged, converting it into a gate which was locked and could only be opened by the person having the right of way. A warning signal arm was raised when the gate was opened and the key could only be removed when the gate was locked. For crossing roads, a wooden drawbridge was constructed which could be raised by pulleys to allow trains to pass; the bridge could then be lowered with the two halves resting on the elevated rail to allow road traffic to pass.

Despite these drawbacks, the company was optimistic about the prospects for the L&BR and extensions of the line to Ballylongford and Tarbert, on the Shannon estuary, were proposed, though this required a Baronial Guarantee which may have hindered its progress. They were also optimistic about the Lartigue system's chances of being used for the construction of further cheap railways in Ireland. Their optimism, though, was unfounded and the L&BR not only remained the only example of its kind, but failed to prosper. Lack of support for the system resulted in the Lartigue Company being wound up in 1890. The L&BR relied on summer tourist traffic to help pay its way but receipts in winter generally did not cover operating costs and in 1897 it went into receivership and was to remain so until eventual closure. There followed a number of years of struggle with small profits or losses until 1917, when wartime government control of railways came into effect. When control ended in 1921, the railway had already sustained some damaged in the aftermath of the Republican activity following the Rising of 1916. This only worsened during the Civil War of 1922, when the carriage of Free State troops resulted in rolling stock being targeted and damage. With no funds for repair, efforts were made for the railway to be included in the Great Southern Railways merger of 1924. These proved unsuccessful, the need for substantial repairs and the unconventional nature of the system probably proving its undoing. With no other option for survival, an order of the High Court for closure was obtained and the line closed to all traffic on 14th October, 1924.

Chronology

16.04.1886	Listowel & Ballybunion Railway incorporated.
01.03.1888	L&BR opened.
1897	L&BR went into receivership.
01.01.1917	Under wartime government control.
01.08.1921	End of wartime government control.
14.10.1924	L&BR closed to all traffic.

Route

Distance	Station/Halt/Crossing	Opened	Closed
0	Listowel	1888	1924
4½	Lisselton	1888	1924
7	Francis Road	1912	1924
9¼	Ballybunion	1888	1924
9¾	Sand Pits	1888	1924

Chapter Sixteen

The Tralee & Dingle Railway

In the latter half of the 19th century, a major source of income for the people of Dingle was fishing and road transport difficulties meant that the catch was usually transported by sea. With the passing of the Tramways & Light Railways (Ireland) Act of 1883, consideration was given to the construction of a light railway between Dingle and Tralee, to benefit the shipment of fish from Dingle and goods in the opposite direction. Approval was granted in September 1888 for construction of a 31½ mile-long main line and a 6 mile branch to Castlegregory. As with other lines finance was secured with the aid of a Baronial Guarantee.

Construction began late in 1888 and took three years, disagreement over the precise route into Tralee causing delays. The line terminated near to the terminus of the north Kerry line of the Waterford, Limerick and Western Railway, to which it was connected by a short line through the streets for exchange of goods. The contractor was charged with providing rolling stock and supplied four locomotives, three 2-6-0 side tanks and one 0-4-2 side tank built by Hunslet and 47 carriages and wagons, originally supplied by the Bristol Wagon Works, much of which had been used in construction and required overhaul before entering service. The Board of Trade passed the line in March 1891 and service commenced on 1st April.

From the beginning the company was in financial difficulty, with receipts never sufficient to cover working expenses. The cheap nature of construction soon became apparent as farmers complained of poor fencing and loss of

The furthest west. Dingle station and engine shed on 14th July, 1934. No. 5 receives some attention. *H.C. Casserley, courtesy R.M. Casserley*

The Tralee & Dingle Railway

Locomotives

No.	Manufacturer	Type	Year	Works No.	Driving wheel dia.	Leading/trailing wheel dia.	Total wheel-base	Coupled wheel-base	Cyls (in.)	Heating surface (sq. ft)	Grate area (sq. ft)	Water capacity (galls)	Coal capacity (cwt)	Boiler pressure (psi)	Weight (t. cwt.)	Max. axle load (t. cwt)	Tractive effort at 85% (lb.)	Wdn
1	Hunslet Engine Co.	2-6-0T	1889	477	3′0½″	2′0″	15′7″	8′9″	13x18	560	9¾	730	15	140	30-11	8-10	9,900	1955
2	Hunslet Engine Co.	2-6-0T	1889	478	3′0½″	2′0″	15′7″	8′9″	13x18	560	9¾	750	15	140	30-11	8-10	9,900	1955
3	Hunslet Engine Co.	2-6-0T	1889	479	3′0½″	2′0″	15′7″	8′9″	13x18	560	9¾	750	15	140	30-11	8-10	9,900	1959
4	Hunslet Engine Co.	0-4-2T	1890	514	3′0½″	1′10″	11′4″	4′6″	11x18	404	6⅓	500	13	140	24-0		7,101	1907
5	Hunslet Engine Co.	2-6-2T	1892	555	3′0½″	2′0″	20′8″	8′9″	13½x18	601	10¾	780	30	140	32-0		10,695	-
6	Hunslet Engine Co.	2-6-0T	1898	677	3′0½″	2′0″	15′7″	8′9″	13x18	560	9¾	730	15	150	30-11	8-10	10,626	1959
7	Kerr, Stuart & Co.	2-6-0T	1902	800	3′0″	2′0″	15′0″	9′0″	12½x20	478	7½	750	20	160	31-0		11,806	1928
8 (4)	Kerr, Stuart & Co.	2-6-0T	1903	836	3′0″	2′0″	15′0″	9′0″	12½x20	478	7½	750	20	160	31-0		11,806	1959
8	Hunslet Engine Co.	2-6-0T	1910	1051	3′0½″	2′0″	15′7″	8′9″	13x18	560	9¾t	730	15	150	31-0	8-10	10,626	1956

Notes

No. 1 – Rebuilt 1894-5. No. 1T under GSR.
No. 2 – No. 2T under GSR.
No. 3 – No. 3T under GSR. Transferred to C&L 1939 (not renumbered).
Nos. 1-3 – Boiler Pressure increased to 150 psi when reboilered.
No. 4 (1st) – Castlegregory branch engine. Out of service since 1902.
No. 5 – Initially oil burning, converted 1904. New boiler 1906, 150 psi, tractive effort 11,459. No. 5T under GSR; transferred to C&L 1950. Preserved.
No. 6 – No. 6T under GSR. Transferred to WCR 1953; to C&L 1957. Worked Dromod section demolition train.
No. 7 – No. 7T under GSR. Cylinders bored to 13½ in. and pressure to 160 psi to increase power.
No. 8 (2nd No. 4) – Renumbered 4 in 1908; little used. No. 4T under GSR. Transferred to C&L 1941.
No. 8 (2nd) – No. 8T under GSR. Transferred to WCR 1954.

Railcar

No.	Source/builder	Wheels	Year	Engine	Seats	Withdrawn
*	T&DLR Workshops/Baguley Chassis	4	1922	Ford T	4	1961

Notes

* Inspection vehicle. No. 6 in GSR Engineer's department railcars. Transferred WCR 1926. Rebuilt with Ford 8 engine, Ennis, 1938.

livestock as a consequence of straying onto the line and was deemed a factor in the fatal accident of 1893, when a livestock train derailed approaching Curraduff viaduct resulting in the deaths of the crew and much of the livestock.

It was not long before the ratepayers began to feel the effects of the Baronial Guarantee and in 1896, the company came under the control of a committee of management under a clause of the Act of Incorporation which allowed for the Grand Jury to take control if the Baronies had to pay money for four years to maintain the line. They succeeded in obtaining £80,000 from the government, which was used to reduce the guaranteed capital from £120,000 to £40,000 and thereby reduced the annual burden on the ratepayers by £800.

The company continued to struggle financially with the onset of World War I bringing further problems. By early 1915, the cost of coal, excessive due to shortages, resulted in train cancellations. 1917 saw the beginning of government control of Irish railways, during which general wage increases resulted in greatly increased operating costs. The ending of the war was followed by the 'Troubles', a period of hostilities between the IRA and the British forces, and the subsequent Civil War, following the creation of the Irish Free State. Service was disrupted by drivers refusing to drive trains carrying British soldiers and by damage done to stock and buildings which closed the railway on a number of occasions.

After the formation of the Irish Free State, all railways wholly within the state were to amalgamate as the Great Southern Railway and the Tralee & Dingle was duly taken over on 1st January, 1925. The suffix 'T' was added to serial numbers of the engines and rolling stock.

Amalgamation was followed by a period of greater political stability. The railway continued to be an important transport link to Dingle and the intermediate villages, as roads in the area were still poor and competition from road transport had yet to rear its head. The GSR introduced economies, to reduce unnecessary costs, as a result of which the company's works were closed and locomotives in need of heavy repairs were sent to Limerick or Inchicore, while day to day maintenance was carried out in the Tralee main line shed. A great deal of passenger revenue continued to come from weekend excursions, particularly on the Castlegregory branch.

In 1927, flooding occurred at Tralee around the canal basin when the river Lee breached its walls. The breach was never repaired and, thereafter, the railway was regularly flooded during spring tides, resulting in long delays. By this time, the condition of Lispole viaduct was causing increasing concern and, although some repairs were carried out, a prohibition on double heading was introduced, which remained in force until closure.

The 1930s saw the creeping growth of road competition as the roads in the district were gradually improved. At the same time train journey times were becoming excessive due to the limitations imposed by the gradients and tight curves and the general deterioration of the line. When the road to Dingle was properly surfaced in 1939, the company would have had to replace the permanent way, to offer any competition to road transport, and as finance was not available the decision was made to suspend passenger services on the Dingle line, with effect from the 17th April, a single daily goods continuing to operate. All services on the Castlegregory branch were terminated.

Carriages

No.	Type	Built	Maker	Length	Compts 1st	Compts 3rd	Seats	Wheel dia.	Wheel centres	Bogie centres	Withdrawn
1	Third	1890	Bristol Wagon & Carriage Co.	27'0"	-	1	34	2'0"	3'6"	15'6"	1961
2	Brake third	1890	Bristol Wagon & Carriage Co.	27'0"	-	1	26	2'0"	3'6"	15'6"	-
3	Third	1890	Bristol Wagon & Carriage Co.	27'0"	-	1	34	2'0"	3'6"	15'6"	1961
4	Composite first/third	1890	Bristol Wagon & Carriage Co.	27'0"	2	1	32	2'0"	3'6"	15'6"	1958
5	Brake third	1890	Bristol Wagon & Carriage Co.	27'0"	-	1	26	2'0"	3'6"	15'6"	1954
6	Third	1890	Bristol Wagon & Carriage Co.	27'0"	-	1	34	2'0"	3'6"	15'6"	1961
7	Third	1890	Bristol Wagon & Carriage Co.	27'0"	-	1	34	2'0"	3'6"	15'6"	1958
8	Third	1890	Bristol Wagon & Carriage Co.	27'0"	-	1	34	2'0"	3'6"	15'6"	1961
9	Brake third	1891	Bristol Wagon & Carriage Co.	27'0"	-	1	26	2'0"	3'6"	15'6"	1961
10	Third	1891	Bristol Wagon & Carriage Co.	27'0"	-	1	34	2'0"	3'6"	15'6"	-
11	Third	1896	T&DLR Tralee	27'0"	-	1	34	2'0"	3'6"	15'6"	1961
12			Unknown	-	-	-	-	2'0"	-	-	c.1940
13	Brake - first/third composite	1898	Bristol Wagon & Carriage Co.	27'0"	-	1	34	2'0"	3'6"	15'4"	1954
14	Brake third	1903	Bristol Wagon & Carriage Co.	30'0"	-	1	26	2'0"	-	-	1957
15	Brake third	1903	Bristol Wagon & Carriage Co.	30'0"	-	1	26	2'0"	-	-	1922
16	Composite first/third	1904	T&DLR Tralee	32'0"	2	1	32	2'0"	-	-	1958
17	Composite first/third	1907	Midland Carriage & Wagon Co.	30'0"	1	1	32	2'0"	4'0"	21'0"	1953
18	Composite first/third	1907	Midland Carriage & Wagon Co.	30'0"	1	1	32	2'0"	4'0"	21'0"	-
19	Brake third	1907	Midland Carriage & Wagon Co.	30'0"	-	1	26	2'0"	4'0"	21'0"	1954
20	Brake third	1907	Midland Carriage & Wagon Co.	30'0"	-	1	26	2'0"	4'0"	21'0"	1954
1	Horsebox	1890	Bristol Wagon & Carriage Co.	31'0"	-	-	-	2'0"	-	-	1954

Notes

No. 1 – Transferred to WCR (46C) 1940; converted to railcar trailer 1952.

No. 2 – Converted to bogie brake for cattle train operation 1940; transferred to WCR (51C) 1953; preserved in USA.

No. 3 – Transferred to WCR (39C) 1940.

No. 4 – Original full third; converted to composite 1904. Transferred to WCR (43C) 1940.

No. 5 – Converted to brake for cattle traffic 1940.

No. 6 – Transferred to WCR (47C) 1940; converted to railcar trailer 1952.

No. 7 – Transferred to WCR (45C) 1940.

No. 8 – Transferred to WCR (48C) 1940; converted to railcar trailer 1951.

No. 9 – Converted to brake for cattle traffic 1940; transferred to WCR (52C) 1953; transferred to C&L 1954 as 22L.

No. 10 – Transferred to WCR (44C) 1940; body extant Dromod C&LR.

No. 11 – Transferred to WCR (49C) 1940.

No. 12 – Converted to breakdown van 1919.

No. 13 – Converted to brake for cattle traffic 1940. Scrapped on closure.

No. 14 – Transferred to WCR (50C) 1940.

No. 15 – Destroyed in the 'Troubles' 1922.

No. 16 – Transferred to WCR (41C) 1940; converted to brake van.

No. 17 – Transferred to WCR (40C) 1940.

No. 18 – Transferred to WCR (42C) 1940; to C&L 1954 (21L); returned to WCR 1959; preserved in USA.

No. 19 – Converted to brake for cattle traffic 1940. Scrapped on closure.

No. 20 – Converted to brake for cattle traffic 1940. Scrapped on closure.

No. 1 – (Horse box). Derelict in Tralee 1940.

Wagons

Nos.	Type	Built	Maker	Length	Width	Wheelbase	Bogie centre	Capacity (t. cwt)
1T, 2T, 4T, 10T, 14T, 15T, 18T-20T, 23T	Covered cattle & goods (10)	1890	Bristol Wagon & Carriage Works Co.	14'0"	6'8"	7'6"		5-0
3T, 5T-9T, 11T-13T, 16T	Covered goods (10)	1890	Bristol Wagon & Carriage Works Co.	14'0"	6'8"	7'6"		5-0
17T	Butter wagon	1890	Bristol Wagon & Carriage Works Co.					5-0
25T, 27T, 30T, 32T, 35T	Ballast trucks (dropside, 5)	1890	Bristol Wagon & Carriage Works Co.					5-0
39T	Bogie covered goods	1892	Bristol Wagon & Carriage Works Co.					10-0
40T	Bogie covered goods	1892	Tubular Wagon Co.	30'3"	6'8"	4'6"	21'0"	10-0
81T, 82T	Open (5 plank, 2)	1890/92	Oldbury Carriage & Wagon Co.					6-0
80T	Covered Goods (1)	1893 ?	Oldbury Carriage & Wagon Co.					5-0
21T, 34T, 36T, 44T, 45T	Open (3 plank, 5)	1894	Bristol Wagon & Carriage Works Co.					5-0
26T, 28T, 37T, 41T, 43T	Covered goods (5)	1894	Bristol Wagon & Carriage Works Co.	14'0"	6'6"	7'6"		5-0
22T, 31T, 33T, 46T	Open cattle (4)	1897	Bristol Wagon & Carriage Works Co.					5-0
24T, 29T	Covered cattle (2)	1897	Bristol Wagon & Carriage Works Co.					5-0
42T	Bogie covered goods	1904	T&DLR	30'7"	6'6"	4'0"	21'0"	10-0
53T-62T	Open cattle (10)	1904	R.Y. Pickering	14'6"	6'6"	7'6"		5-0
47T-52T	Open cattle (6)	1905	Hurst, Nelson & Co.					5-0
64-66T	Covered goods (3)	1907	Midland Carriage & Wagon Co.					5-0
63T, 69T, 70T, 74T, 75T	Open cattle* (5)	1907	Midland Carriage & Wagon Co.	14'1"		7'7"		5-0
67T, 68T, 71T-73T, 76T	Covered cattle (6)	1907	Midland Carriage & Wagon Co.	14'1"	6'3"	7'7"		5-0
38T, 77T	Bogie bolsters (2)	1911	T&DLR					10-0
78T	Covered cattle & goods (1)	1922	T&DLR					5-0
79T	Bogie covered goods	1922	T&DLR					10-0

Notes
No. 23T built 1894.
Nos. 25T, 27T and 30T transferred to C&LR as 226L-228L.
No. 43T built 1897.
No. 80T – ex-C&MLR No. 61K.
Nos 81T, 82T – ex-C&MLR Nos. 34K, 46K.
* Originally covered.

No. 8T arrives at Castlegregory Junction with a mixed train for Tralee on 29th April, 1938. An unidentified locomotive has just left with a service to Castlegregory.

W.A. Camwell/Stephenson Locomotive Society

A typical scene on the T&DR as locomotive No. 8T hauls its cattle train across an ungated road at Glenmore on 29th June, 1951.   *W.A. Camwell/Stephenson Locomotive Society*

The daily goods service continued until 1944, when as a result of fuel shortages this was reduced to an 'as required' service. In 1947, Córas Iompair Éireann, the successor to the GSR in 1945, reduced this to a monthly cattle working to service the Dingle fair, on the last Saturday of the month. For the cattle fair workings, trains of empty cattle wagons would be worked out from Tralee the day before, with the loaded wagons returning the following day. By 1950, only about three dozen serviceable cattle wagons remained in service and the number diminished almost monthly. The necessary cost of repair or replacement plus repair of the permanent way meant the cattle fair trains were too uneconomic to survive and in 1953 CIÉ gave notice of intent to close the section. Local opposition to closure was low-key and the last cattle trains ran on 26th and 27th June, 1953. The final train ran on 22nd July when an engine ran light to Dingle and brought some wagons back to Tralee.

Chronology

17.09.1888	Tralee & Dingle Light Railway incorporated.
31.03.1891	Line opened to traffic.
21.04.1896	Management transferred to Grand Jury and Committee of Management.
01.01.1925	T&DLR became a part of Great Southern Railways.
17.04.1939	T&DLR closed to passenger traffic.
17.04.1939	Castlegregory branch closed to all traffic.
01.01.1945	CIÉ formed from amalgamation of GSR and Dublin United Transport Co.
27.06.1953	Line closed to all traffic.

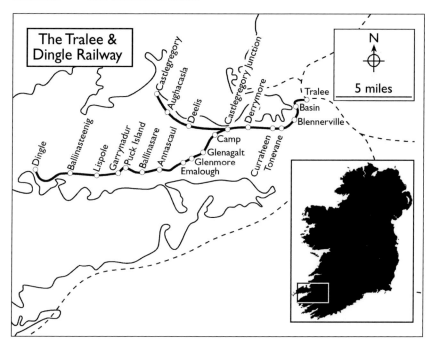

Route

Distance	Station/Halt/Crossing	Opened	Closed	
0	Tralee	1891	1953	
	Rock Street Crossing	1891	1953	
⅓	Pembroke Street Crossing	1891	1953	
¾	Strand Street Crossing	1891	1953	Obligatory stop.
1	Basin Road Crossing	1891	1953	
1	Basin Halt	1891	1920s	Tralee (Ballyard) re-opened 1993.
1	Dingle Road Crossing	1891	1953	
2½	Blennerville	1891	1953	Reopened 1993.
2½	Dingle Road Crossing	1891	1953	Ungated.
3¼	Tonevane	1891	1908	
5¾	Curraheen	1891	1953	
7½	Derrymore	1891	1953	aka Derry Quay.
9¾	Castlegregory Junction	1891	1953	Originally Camp Jn. Renamed 1895. Closed as Junction 1939.
11¼	Camp	1914	1939	
12	Scrallaghbeg Gate (Driscoll)	1891	1953	aka Skirlough Crossing.
13¾	Glenagalt Bridge Halt	1895	1939	
15¾	Glenmore Crossing	1897	1939	Blind crossing, scene of many accidents.
16	Glenmore	1891	1939	Originally Lougher.
17½	Emalough Cross	1891	1953	Also Gortbreagogue Crossing.
20¾	Annascaul	1891	1953	
20¾	Annascaul Station Gates	1891	1953	
21¼	Ballinclare Gate	1891	1953	
22¼	Gortacurraun Gate	1891	1953	
22½	Ballinacourty Gate	1891	1953	
23	Ballynasare	1891	1939	
24¾	Garrynadur	1891	1939	
26	Lispole	1891	1939	
27¾	Ballinasteenig	1891	1939	
31¼	Dingle	1891	1953	
31¼	Dingle Station Gates	1891	1939	
31¾	Dingle Pier	1891	1930	
0	Castlegregory Junction	1891	1953	
2½	Deelis	1891	1939	
4	Aughacasla	1891	1939	
6	Castlegregory	1891	1939	

Chapter Seventeen

The Schull & Skibbereen Railway

The village of Schull, in the district of West Carbery, west county Cork, is built by a sheltered natural harbour, which led to its development as an important fishing port for the area. In the latter half of the 19th century, the area, like many other rural parts of Ireland, was a target for Government support, to help the local population recover from the devastation of the 'famine' era of the late 1840s. Improvements in transport, particularly with the provision of rail links were seen as a necessary tool for development of local industries such as fishing. The hills around Schull were also, at the time, an area of active copper mining.

Rail connections reached out from Cork when the broad gauge lines of what was to become the Cork, Bandon & South Coast Railway (CB&SCR) opened for traffic, first to Bandon in 1851, to Dunmanway in 1866 and to Skibbereen in 1877. With the arrival of trains in Skibbereen, moves for a link to Schull, 15½ miles around Roaring Water bay, began. A number of proposals were advanced, but the passing of the Tramways and Public Companies (Ireland) Act on the 25th August, 1883, with its provisions for Baronial Guarantee moved matters along and within months, the West Carbery Tramways & Light Railways Co. Ltd was incorporated. Its brief was to construct two tramways - the Skibbereen & Schull Tramways & Light Railways and the Skibbereen, Glandore and Union Hall Tramways & Light Railways, though the second proposal was later dropped due to strong local opposition.

Locomotive No. 4S takes on water at Crooked Bridge on 1st July, 1938.
H.C. Casserley, courtesy R.M. Casserley

The Schull & Skibbereen Railway

Locomotives

No.	Manufacturer	Type	Year	Works No.	Name	Driving wheel dia.	Leading/trailing wheel dia.	Total wheelbase	Coupled wheelbase	Cyls (in.)	Heating surface (sq. ft)	Grate area (sq. ft)	Water capacity (galls)	Coal capacity (cwt)	Boiler pressure (psi)	Weight (t. cwt.)	Max. axle load (t. cwt.)	Tractive effort at 85% (lb.)	Wdn
1	Dick, Kerr & Co.	0-4-0T	1886	A	Marion	2'6"	-	6'0"	6'0"	9½x16			350		-	15-0	-	-	1906
2	Dick, Kerr & Co.	0-4-0T	1886	B	Ida	2'6"	-	6'0"	6'0"	9½x16			350		140	16-0	-	5,730	1926
3	Dick, Kerr & Co.	0-4-0T	1886	C	Ilen	2'6"	-	6'0"	6'0"	9½x16			350		-	15-0	-	-	1914
4	Nasmyth, Wilson & Co.	4-4-0T	1888	342	Erin	3'4"	1'10"	15'3"	5'6"	12x18	508		500	10	140	24-0	-	7,720	1954
1	Peckett & Sons	4-4-0T	1906	1085	Gabriel	3'0½"	2'0"	15'0"	5'0"	12x18	575	8	500	25	160	26-10	-	9,650	1937
3	Peckett & Sons	4-4-0T	1914	-	Kent	3'0½"	2'0"	15'0"	5'0"	12x18	514	7.58	500	18	160	25-10	-	9,650	1954
6S	Thos Green & Sons	0-4-4T	1893	200		3'6"	2'0"	14'10"	6'0"	14x20	600	10½	500	20	140	25-0	8-0	11,100	1954

Notes

No. 2 – Dimensions and figures as rebuilt in 1905; survived to GSR takeover but withdrawn.

No. 4 – Boiler replaced 1908 - pressure increased to 150 psi. No. 4S under GSR.

No. 1 (2nd) – No. 1S under GSR.

No. 3 (2nd) – Originally named *Conciliation* - changed to *Kent* (after Thomas Kent) in 1916. No. 3S under GSR.

No. 6S – Former C&MLR No. 6 *The Muskerry*; transferred by GSR 1938. Required extensive modification.

Carriages

No. Type	Maker	Built	Length	Compts	Seats	Wheel dia.	Wheel centres	Bogie centres	Wdn	Notes
1 First 4 wheel	Dick, Kerr	1888	12'6"	2		2'0"	8'0"		1953	Open balcony end platforms. Divided 1/3 smoking, 2/3 non-smoking. Heavily reconditioned 1913.
2 First 4 wheel	Dick, Kerr.	1888	12'6"		16	2'0"	8'0"	-	1953	Rebuilt 1910-12 open balcony end platforms closed in - body length 17ft.
3 Third 4 wheel	Dick, Kerr	1888	12'6"			2'0"	8'0"	-	1953	Heavy repairs 1910.
4 Third 4 wheel	Dick, Kerr	1888	12'6"			2'0"	8'0"		1953	Heavy repairs 1906.
5 Bogie composite	Gloucester Railway Carriage & Wagon Co.	1890	34'6"		40	2'0"	4'6"	24'6"	1953	Major rebuild 1905. Original balcony ends closed in.
6 Bogie third	Gloucester Railway Carriage & Wagon Co.	1897	27'6"			2'0"	4'6"	24'6"	1953	Length over body. End balcony 2'6".
7 Bogie third	Gloucester Railway Carriage & Wagon Co.	1903	27'6"			2'0"	4'6"	24'6"	1953	Length over body. End balcony 2'6".
8 Third 4 wheel	Dick, Kerr	1912	17'0"			2'0"	8'0"		1953	

Wagons

Nos.	Type	Built	Maker	Length	Width	Wheelbase	Notes
1-5	Open wagons 4-plank	1886	Dick, Kerr	10'0"	6'0"	6'0"	
6-9	Timber bolster wagons	1886	Dick, Kerr	10'0"	6'0"	6'0"	
10-35	Small livestock ventilated van	1886	Dick, Kerr	10'0"	6'0"	6'0"	
36-45	Small box van	1886	Dick, Kerr	10'0"	6'0"	6'0"	
46	Guard's goods brake van	1886	Dick, Kerr	12'0"	6'3"	6'0"	
47-49	12 ft box vans	1886	Dick, Kerr	12'0"	6'0"	8'0"	
50, 51	Open full drop side ballast wagons	c.1908	Running gear external; bodies Skibbereen	18'0"	6'0"	9'0"	
52	Large cattle wagon	c.1908	Running gear external; bodies Skibbereen	15'0"	6'0"	9'0"	No. 23 roofless.
53, 54	Guard's brake vans	1909	Running gear external; bodies Skibbereen	17'0"	6'0"	8'0"	
55-60	Large box van	1909-1912	Running gear external; bodies Skibbereen	15'0"	6'0"	9'0"	No. 43 rebuilt as cattle wagon, original No. retained.

Construction of the line commenced at three points - at Schull and Skibbereen, where materials could be transported by sea and the CB&SCR respectively and at Ballydehob, with the construction of a 12-arched viaduct, the only major civil engineering work on the line. The line largely followed the course of the road, deviations being made only to avoid excessive curves or gradients. The initial Board of Trade inspection in August 1886 was unsatisfactory and, while a second inspection in September allowed the commencement of operations, this was only with an overall speed restriction of 15 mph, with 4 mph at some points.

The first train to run was a special train on 7th September, 1886, operated for the monthly pig fair at Ballydehob, the train carrying the animals to Skibbereen. Thereafter, the improved transport for the fair allegedly resulted in the farmers receiving a higher price for the animals, but this was to prove their only solace as over the following years faults resulting from poor construction, together with low receipts, were to prove a continuing financial burden under the terms of the Baronial Guarantee. As a consequence, a committee of management was appointed by the Grand Jury to take over the running of the line, commencing in August 1892 under the name of the Schull & Skibbereen Tramway & Light Railway Company. The following year, 1893, the only extension - a short line to the pier at Schull - opened.

In 1907, the tramway was inspected as part of a Vice-regal Commission investigation of Irish railways. They recommended a grant of £15,000 towards improving the line, in view of the unsatisfactory condition in which it was handed over to the managing committee in 1892 but this, in fact, never happened. The need for improvement to permanent way and rolling stock were a continuing drain on the company's resources and contributed to ongoing annual losses.

All Irish railways came under state control early in 1917. Escalating wartime costs had a crippling effect on finances only partially offset when under the Irish Railways (Settlement of Claims) Act the Tramway received £15,716 compensation for the period of Government control. During the 'Troubles' (1919-21), extensive damage was caused to the line, including the derailment and overturning of a locomotive at Ballydehob.

The new Irish government, after recommendations by a commission, introduced a Bill to merge all the railways, other than cross-border lines, into a single entity, to be known as the Great Southern Railways, the Act becoming operative on 1st January, 1925. Under the new owners, few changes were made to services, apart from the withdrawal of Sunday trains. The suffix 'S' was added to serial numbers of the engines and rolling stock, while bilingual, black-and-white enamelled nameplates of GSR pattern were erected at the stations and halts. Heavy locomotive repairs were carried out at Inchicore and the rolling stock acquired standard GSR livery. One advantage of the unified company was that men from the CB&SCR section could be rostered to the S&S section in times of difficulty. Otherwise the S&S settled into the new era of political calm and although receipts continued to be poor, it could now call on the substantial resources of the GSR.

But such support for unprofitable lines affected the GSR's finances, which were also suffering from the emergence of road competition in the 1930s. The

In sunshine and shadow, No. 4S pauses her train near Skibbereen on 19th June, 1939.
W.A. Camwell/Stephenson Locomotive Society

No. 3 at Skibbereen.   *W.A. Camwell/Stephenson Locomotive Society*

outbreak of World War II brought more problems, particularly a shortage of locomotive coal. By 1944, the GSR had suspended services on many lines including the S&SR. The GSR itself was to disappear, merging with the Dublin United Transport Co. to form Córas Iompair Eireann, which took control on 1st January, 1945. Things did not improve, though, as with the ongoing fuel shortage, all services on the S&SR were suspended. At the same time, road bus services were expanding and the Cork to Skibereen passenger service was extended to Schull.

Services briefly resumed on 11th December, 1945 but 13 months later a further fuel crisis resulted in further reductions in service and all S&SR services were again withdrawn. The last passenger train left Schull on Saturday 25th January, 1947. There was no ceremony to mark the occasion - the assumption being that services would once again resume when the fuel crisis was over. One final train ran on 15th August, 1947 when a special return excursion from Skibbereen for the Schull regatta was organized by the local curate - this was sanctioned by CIÉ despite local concerns over the state of the line. There was no further activity and with the passing years, the elements began to take their toll on the line and the stock, much of which had been left in the open. CIÉ applied for an order to abandon the section in 1952. The county council had considered raising objection but was dissuaded by local indifference to the continued existence of the line. The official notice of the Abandonment Order for the section was given on the 16th August, 1956, by which time the lines had been lifted and much of the rolling stock disposed of.

Chronology

07.12.1883	West Carbery Tramways & Light Railways Co. (Schull & Skibbereen Branch) incorporated.
07.09.1886	Line opened to traffic.
06.04.1887	Line closed - locos unfit.
02.01.1888	Line reopened.
04.08.1892	Line taken over by Grand Jury (later County Council). Committee of Management formed.
04.08.1892	Name changed to Schull & Skibereen Tramways & Light Railway Co.
October 1893	Schull Pier Extension opened.
01.01.1925	S&SLR became a part of Great Southern Railways.
24.04.1944	Emergency closure due to wartime fuel shortage.
01.01.1945	CIÉ formed from amalgamation of GSR and Dublin United Transport Co.
25.01.1947	Last timetabled train
17.08.1956	Section officially abandoned.

Route

Distance	Station/Halt/Crossing	Opened	Closed	Notes
0	Skibereen	1886	1947	
0	Skibereen Station Gates	1886	1947	
1	New Bridge Crossing	1886	1947	
3	New Court Gates	1886	1947	Official halting place. Known locally as 'Young's House'.
4½	Church Cross	1886	1947	Also unofficial stops at 4m for Post office and school.
5	Hollyhill Crossing	1886	1947	
5½	Hollyhill	1886	1947	
6	Kilcoe No. 1 Crossing	1886	1947	
6½	Kilcoe No. 2 Crossing	1886	1947	
7	Kilcoe	1886	1947	
7¼	Crooked Bridge	1886	1947	Watering place.
7½	Ardura Crossing	1886	1947	
8¾	Skeaghanore Crossing	1886	1947	aka 'Driscoll's'.
9½	Ballydehob	1886	1947	Passing place.
	Ballydehob Viaduct	1886	1947	
9¾	Shanvanagh No. 1 Crossing	1886	1947	aka 'Sullivan's'.
10¼	Shanvanagh No. 2 Crossing	1886	1947	
10½	Shanvanagh No. 3 Crossing	1886	1947	aka 'Connor's'.
12	Woodlands	1886	1947	
14¼	Schull Station Gates	1886	1947	
14½	Schull	1886	1947	
14¼	Schull Station Gates	1886	1947	
14½	Pier Extension level crossing	1893	*	* Exact closure date unknown - out of use in late 1930s.
14¾	Schull Pier	1893	†	† Exact closure date unknown - out of use in late 1930s.

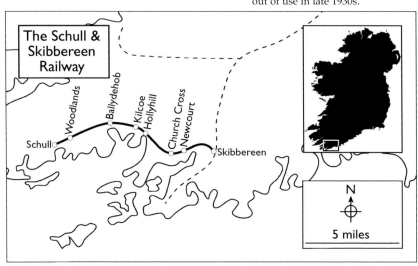

Chapter Eighteen

The Cork, Blackrock & Passage Railway

The Cork, Blackrock & Passage Railway (CB&PR) began life as a suburban standard gauge line, serving the western shore of Cork harbour. The idea of a railway connection between Cork and Passage was originally prompted by the large volume of steamer traffic operating on the river Lee from Cork via Passage to Cobh (or Queenstown), a railway link to Passage being far quicker than the corresponding steamer trip. The necessary Parliamentary approval was granted on 16th July, 1846 for the construction of a line just over 6½ miles in length, which opened for traffic on the 8th June, initially from the Cork terminus of City Park, until in 1873, when the corporation diverted the line to Albert Street, nearer the city, when drainage works in the Lee estuary were necessary.

The company also operated steamers, serving the coastal towns, but when competing concerns went out of business in 1890, and the cost of maintaining had to be justified, particularly as railway returns were good, a decision to extend the railway to Crosshaven and end the steamer services was made. In considering the Crosshaven extension, it was suggested that, if it was laid to 3 ft gauge, considerable savings could be made. It was therefore decided to adopt this gauge and to convert the existing line, powers for which were obtained under the Cork, Blackrock & Passage Railway Extension Act, passed on the 7th August, 1896, and within 12 months the necessary finance had been secured. Electric traction was briefly considered but rejected.

CB&PR locomotive No. 7P approaches Cork with the 12.05 pm working from Crosshaven.
H.C. Casserley, courtesy R.M. Casserley

The Cork, Blackrock & Passage Railway

Locomotives

No.	Manufacturer	Type	Year	Works No.	Name	Driving wheel dia.	Leading/trailing wheel	Total wheel-base	Coupled wheel-base	Cyls (in.)	Heating surface (sq. ft)	Grate area (sq. ft)	Water capacity (galls)	Coal capacity (cwt)	Boiler pressure (psi)	Weight (t. cwt)	Max. axle load (t. cwt)	Tractive effort at 85% (lb.)	Wdn
4	Neilson, Reid & Co	2-4-2T	1899	5561	-	4'6"	3'0"	21'0"	8'0"	14½x22	801	12	1,000	50	160	37-3	11-11	11,650	1959
5	Neilson, Reid & Co	2-4-2T	1899	5562	-	4'6"	3'0"	21'0"	8'0"	14½x22	801	12	1,000	50	160	37-3	11-11	11,650	1939
6	Neilson, Reid & Co	2-4-2T	1899	5563	-	4'6"	3'0"	21'0"	8'0"	14½x22	801	12	1,000	50	160	37-3	11-11	11,650	1959
7	Neilson, Reid & Co	2-4-2T	1899	5564	-	4'6"	3'0"	21'0"	8'0"	14½x22	801	12	1,000	50	160	37-3	11-11	11,650	1954
*	Sharp, Stewart	2-4-0T	1881	3023	Alice	3'6"	2'6"	11'6"	6'0"	13x20	555	9¾	500	20	120	20-0	8-0	8,200	1926

Notes
No. 4 – No. 4P under GSR. Trans to C&L 1934 (10L).
No. 5 – No. 5P under GSR. Trans to C&L 1934 (11L).
No. 6 – No. 6P under GSR. Trans to C&L 1934 (12L).
No. 7 – No. 7P under GSR. Trans to C&L 1934 (13L).
* On loan from the CDRJC 1918-1921.

Wagons

Nos.	Type	Built	Capacity (t. cwt)	Notes
1-4	Open goods	1901/2	6-0	Transferred to C&LR 192L-195L.
5-12	Covered goods	1903/4	6-0	Transferred to C&LR 170L-177L.
13-18	Cattle wagon	1903	6-0	Originally built as 6T Covered Vans. Transferred to C&LR 180L-185L.
19, 20	Brake van	1903		Transferred to C&LR 190L, 191L.
21,22	Covered goods	1903	6-0	Transferred to C&LR 178L, 179L.
23-26	Cattle wagon	1903	6-0	Originally built as 6T Covered Vans. Transferred to C&LR 186L-189L.
27-34	Open goods	1909-15	6-0	Transferred to C&LR 196L-203L.

The scheduled date for completion, March 1900, proved far too optimistic - among the delays was the unexpected discovery of a spring, during the boring of a 1,500 ft tunnel between Passage and Glenbrook. It became obvious that the Crosshaven extension would involve far greater expenditure than had been anticipated and the company was running short of capital. Disputes with the contractor ended in the courts, with the company forced to pay a large award and they were only saved from insolvency by a loan from the Public Works Commissioners.

Following this the company elected to use its own staff for the conversion of the existing line and this was carried out by the initial laying of a third rail. At the same time, the Cork-Blackrock section was converted to a double line, the only instance of this on an Irish narrow gauge system. The gauge conversion to Cork was completed on Sunday 29th October, 1900 when the line was closed for the day, the last broad gauge train having left Passage at 9.30 on Saturday night.

On 24th January, 1902 the Passage tunnel was finally finished and the section to Monkstown was completed and opened on 1st August, 1902. The remaining section to Crosshaven finally opened on 1st June, 1904, at greatly increased cost.

An ambitious timetable of frequent trains, with express services, was offered, as a result of which passenger numbers steadily increased and finances were healthy, allowing debts to be cleared. The CB&PR was inspected as part of the Vice-regal Commission of Inquiry into Irish railways during 1907-09, and some financial awards were recommended but, as with many other systems, the commission's recommendations were not implemented.

The company's fortunes were to suffer a reversal with the outbreak of the World War I, when within days, Crosshaven station and the surrounding area were commandeered by the military and the public were excluded. The company's rolling stock was pressed into serving the military needs, often at the expense of passenger services. By the end of 1915, the company was in serious financial difficulty as a consequence of the loss of revenue, due to this closure to Crosshaven, together with increased wages and fuel costs, and closure was threatened. However, revenue picked up the following year and financial pressures eased.

Cork Albert Street terminus of the CB&PR on 10th June, 1932 with the 1.15 pm service to Monkstown about to depart.   *H.C. Casserley, courtesy R.M. Casserley*

Carriages

No.	Type	Built	Weight (t. cwt)	Maker	Length	Compts	Seats	Wheel dia.	Wheel centres	Bogie centre	Withdrawn
1	Bogie first	1900-2	12-0	Brown, Marshalls & Co.	36'0"	6	36				1923
2	Bogie first saloon	1900-2	12-0	Brown, Marshalls & Co.	36'0"						1933
3	Bogie first	1900-2	12-0	Brown, Marshalls & Co.	36'0"	6	36				1923
4	Bogie first	1900-2	12-0	Brown, Marshalls & Co.	36'0"	6	36				1933
5	Bogie first	1900-2	12-0	Brown, Marshalls & Co.	36'0"	6	36				1933
6	Bogie first	1900-2	12-0	Brown, Marshalls & Co.	36'0"	6	36				1933
7	Bogie first	1900-2	12-0	Brown, Marshalls & Co.	36'0"	6	36				1933
8	Bogie first	1900-2	12-0	Brown, Marshalls & Co.	36'0"	6	36				1933
10	Brake first saloon	1900-2	12-0	Brown, Marshalls & Co.	36'0"	2 + saloon					1923
11	Brake first	1900-2	12-0	Brown, Marshalls & Co.	36'0"						1933
12	Brake first	1900-2	12-0	Brown, Marshalls & Co.	36'0"						1933
13	Brake first	1900-2	12-0	Brown, Marshalls & Co.	36'0"						1933
15	Bogie third	1900-2	12-0	Brown, Marshalls & Co.	36'0"	6	48				1933
16	Bogie third	1900-2	12-0	Brown, Marshalls & Co.	36'0"	6	48				1933
17	Bogie third	1900-2	12-0	Brown, Marshalls & Co.	36'0"	6	48				1923
18	Bogie third	1900-2	12-0	Brown, Marshalls & Co.	36'0"	6	48				1933
19	Bogie third	1900-2	12-0	Brown, Marshalls & Co.	36'0"	6	48				1933
20	Bogie third	1900-2	12-0	Brown, Marshalls & Co.	36'0"	6	48				1933
21	Bogie third	1900-2	12-0	Brown, Marshalls & Co.	36'0"	6	48				1933
22	Bogie third	1900-2	12-0	Brown, Marshalls & Co.	36'0"	6	48				1933
23	Bogie third, saloon	1900-2	12-0	Brown, Marshalls & Co.	36'0"		36				1933
24	Bogie third	1900-2	12-0	Brown, Marshalls & Co.	36'0"	6	48				1923
25	Bogie third, saloon	1900-2	12-0	Brown, Marshalls & Co.	36'0"		36				1933
26	Bogie third	1900-2	12-0	Brown, Marshalls & Co.	36'0"	6	48				1933
31	Brake thid	1900-2	12-0	Brown, Marshalls & Co.	36'0"		32				1933
32	Brake thid	1900-2	12-0	Brown, Marshalls & Co.	36'0"		32				1933
33	Brake third/saloon	1900-2	12-0	Brown, Marshalls & Co.	36'0"		?				1923
34	Brake third	1900-2	12-0	Brown, Marshalls & Co.	36'0"		30				1933
1 (2nd)	Bogie first	1924		Metropolitan Carriage & Wagon & Finance Co.	36'0"	6	36	2'9"	4'9"	24'0"	1933
4 (2nd)	Bogie first	1924		Metropolitan Carriage & Wagon & Finance Co.	36'0"	6	36	2'9"	4'9"	24'0"	1933
11 (2nd)	Bogie third	1924		Metropolitan Carriage & Wagon & Finance Co.	36'0"	6	48	2'9"	4'9"	24'0"	1933
18 (2nd)	Bogie third	1924		Metropolitan Carriage & Wagon & Finance Co.	36'0"	6	48	2'9"	4'9"	24'0"	1933
24 (2nd)	Bogie third	1924		Metropolitan Carriage & Wagon & Finance Co.	36'0"	6	48	2'9"	4'9"	24'0"	1933
33 (2nd)	Brake third	1924		Metropolitan Carriage & Wagon & Finance Co.	36'0"	3	24	2'9"	4'9"	24'0"	1933

Notes

No. 1 – Destroyed in 'Troubles' 1922.
No. 4 – Destroyed in 'Troubles' 1922.
No. 10 – Converted to third 1915; conv to composite 1921.
No. 11 – Converted to third 1915. Destroyed in 'Troubles' 1922.
No. 12 – Converted to third 1915; conv to composite 1921.

No. 13 – Converted to third 1915; conv to composite 1921.
No. 18 – Destroyed in 'Troubles' 1922.
No. 24 – Destroyed in 'Troubles' 1922.
No. 33 – Destroyed in 'Troubles' 1922.

The CB&PR came under the government control of Irish railways, which came into force on 1st January, 1917, and the following year saw passenger traffic increased to such an extent that the Railway Executive transferred three third-class coaches from the Londonderry & Lough Swilly Railway together with 2-4-0T engine No. 1, *Alice*, from the County Donegal Railways Joint Committee. This locomotive remained for three years and proved so popular with the crews that an offer to purchase her was made but she was returned to Donegal after sustaining accidental damage.

Shortage of coal supplies following the ending of the war was to result in restrictions in service, while legislation leading to the introduction of the eight-hour working day in 1919 resulted in a 25 per cent increase in staff and consequent larger wage bill. Staff unrest led to strike action. Worse was to occur following the creation of the Irish Free State, when the resulting Civil War, resulted not only in physical damage to the railway but to costly restrictions in service. The damage included the burning of a number of coaches for which replacements were ordered in 1923.

With the ending of the Civil War, work began to repair the damage to bridges, signal cabins and the infrastructure generally and to get rail services back in operation. The company showed an operating loss for 1923, some, ominously attributable to increasing competition from motor transport.

Meanwhile, a government-recommended amalgamation of all railway companies in the Free State came into being, with the formation of the Great Southern Railway on 1st January, 1925 and the CB&PR duly came under the GSR banner, the suffix 'P' being added to the rolling stock numbers. While efforts were made to maintain a frequent train service, competition from trams and road transport grew. To cut costs, the line between Cork and Blackrock was reduced to single track in 1927 but losses mounted as passengers deserted to the buses and, early in 1932, the GSR applied for closure. The Monkstown-Crosshaven section was the first to close, on 31st May, 1932, and the last train, from Albert Street station to Monkstown, ran on 10th September of that year, bringing to an end a unique suburban narrow gauge service. The company's passenger services transferred to buses, but its four steam engines and a number of open wagons saw further service for many years following transfer by the GSR to the Cavan & Leitrim section.

Chronology

16.07.1846	Cork, Blackrock & Passage Railway incorporated.
08.06.1850	Line opened from Cork to Passage (broad gauge).
06.02.1873	Albert Street station opened.
07.08.1896	Cork, Blackrock & Passage Extension Act passed (to Crosshaven, 3 ft 0in. gauge).
29.10.1900	Cork to Passage line converted to 3 ft 0 in. gauge.
01.08.1902	Passage to Monkstown section opened.
15.06.1903	Monkstown to Carrigaline section opened.
01.06.1904	Carrigaline to Crosshaven section opened.
01.01.1925	Became a part of Great Southern Railways.
31.05.1932	Monkstown to Crosshaven section closed.
10.09.1932	Complete closure.

Route

Distance	Station/Halt/Crossing	Opened	Closed	
0	Cork (Albert Street)	1873	1932	
2	Blackrock	1873	1932	End of double track section.
2½	Ballinure Halt	1909	1920s	
4	Rochestown	1850	1932	Originally 'Douglas'. Converted to passing station 1906.
6½	Passage	1850	1902	Old terminus.
6½	Passage	1902	1932	Through station - Crosshaven extension.
	Passage tunnel	1902	1932	535 yds long.
6¾	Glenbrook	1902	1932	
6¾	Glenbrook Station Gates	1902	1932	
7¾	Monkstown Station Gates	1902	1932	
7¾	Monkstown	1902	1932	Passing place.
9¾	Raffeen Station Gates	1903	1932	
9¾	Raffeen	1903	1932	
11½	Carrigaline	1903	1932	Subway connection between main and island platform.
	Owenboy Bridge	1904	1932	
15	Hoddersfield Halt	1904	1932	
	Crosshaven viaduct	1904	1932	
16	Crosshaven	1904	1932	

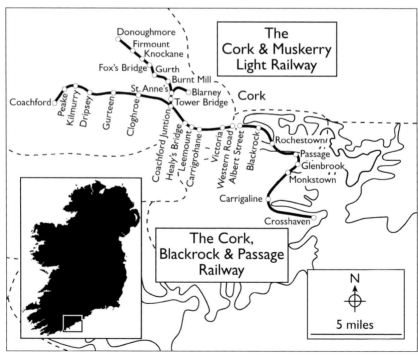

Chapter Nineteen

The Cork & Muskerry Light Railway

The Cork & Muskerry Light Railway, was another of the light railways constructed following the passing of the Tramways and Public Companies (Ireland) Act 1883, promoted by the landowners and farmers of the Muskerry district, to the north west of Cork city, as a means of improving transport between the area and the city and to capitalize on the tourist traffic to Blarney. The proposed route was from Western Road in Cork, through Carrigrohane, Leemount, Inishbeg and Dripsey, to Coachford, with a branch to Blarney, more circuitous than the main road through Blackpool but availing of the more lucrative traffic offered by the Western Road. Objections lodged by some local ratepayers, fearful of the financial burden of the Baronial Guarantee if the line proved non-profitable, delayed approval but supported by some Dublin-based nobles and the MP for mid-Cork, Parliamentary approval was granted on 26th June, 1886.

Work commenced in February 1887 and proceeded rapidly, with the aim to open to Blarney in time for the early autumn traffic. Following a successful Board of Trade inspection in July, the Blarney section opened to traffic on the 8th August. Work, meanwhile, continued on the Coachford section, which opened to traffic on 19th March, 1888.

Cork & Muskerry No. 2 makes a brave show under the tram wires as it leaves Cork on 10th June, 1932 with the 3.00 pm service to Coachford.

H.C. Casserley, courtesy R.M. Casserley

The Cork & Muskerry Light Railway

Locomotives

No.	Manufacturer	Type	Year	Works No.	Name	Driving wheel dia.	Leading/ trailing wheel dia.	Total wheel-base	Coupled wheel-base	Cyls (in.)	Heating surface (sq. ft)	Grate area (sq. ft)	Water capacity (galls)	Coal capacity (cwt)	Boiler pressure (psi)	Weight (t. cwt.)	Max. axle load (t. cwt)	Tractive effort at 85% (lb.)	Wdn
1	Falcon Engineering Co.	4-4-0T	1887	137	City of Cork	3'6"	2'0"	15'3"	6'0"	11½x18	472	8¼	500	20	140	25-0	8-0	6,720	1934
2	Falcon Engineering Co.	4-4-0T	1887	136	Coachford	3'6"	2'0"	15'3"	6'0"	11½x18	472	8¼	500	20	140	25-0	8-0	6,720	1934
3	Falcon Engineering Co.	4-4-0T	1887	138	St Annes	3'6"	2'0"	15'3"	6'0"	11½x18	472	8¼	500	20	140	25-0	8-0	6,720	1924
4	Kitson & Co.	0-4-2WT	1888	235	Blarney	3'6"	2'0"	11'3"	5'6"	11x15	383	7.3	400	20	150	18-10	6-6	5,500	1911
5	Thos Green & Sons	0-4-4T	1892	180	Donoughmore	3'6"	2'0"	14'10"	6'0"	14x20	600	10½	500	20	140	25-0	8-0	11,100	1938
6	Thos Green & Sons	0-4-4T	1893	200	The Muskerry	3'6"	2'0"	14'10"	6'0"	14x20	600	10½	500	20	140	25-0	8-0	11,100	1954
7	Brush Electrical Eng Co.	4-4-0T	1898	274	Peake	4'0"	2'3"	17'5"	6'0"	14x 22	646	10½	700	25	140	28-0	-	10,700	1935
8	Brush Electrical Eng Co.	4-4-0T	1904	307	Dripsey	4'0"	2'3"	17'5"	6'0"	12x18	646	10½	700	25	140	27-10	-	6,430	1935
4 (2)	Hunslet Engine Co.	4-4-0T	1919	1200	Blarney	3'6"	2'0"	15'6"	6'0"	13x20	467	8¼	600	20	160	28-0	10-10	10,900	1927

Notes
No. 1 – Originally 2-4-0T rebuilt as 4-4-0T 1890-4. Name removed, suffix K added 1924 by GSR.
No. 2 – Originally 2-4-0T rebuilt as 4-4-0T 1890-4. Name removed, suffix K added 1924 by GSR.
No. 3 – Originally 2-4-0T rebuilt as 4-4-0T 1890-4..
No. 5 – No 5K under GSR. Later trans to T&D (9T) but never worked.
No. 6 – Later Muskerry. No 6K under GSR. Later trans to S&SR 1938(6S).
No. 7 – No. 7K under GSR.
No. 8 – No. 8K under GSR.
No. 4 (2nd) – No. 4K under GSR.

Along Cork's Western Road locomotive No. 2K brings its train in towards the terminus on 10th June, 1932.   *H.C. Casserley, courtesy R.M. Casserley*

Cork & Muskerry Light Railway Rolling Stock

Carriages

No.	Type	Built	Maker	Length	Seats
1	Bogie third	1887	Falcon Engineering Co.	26'9"	26
2	Bogie third	1887	Falcon Engineering Co.	26'9"	26
3	Bogie third	1887	Falcon Engineering Co.	26'9"	26
4	Bogie third	1887	Falcon Engineering Co.	26'2"	26
5	Bogie first	1887	Falcon Engineering Co.	26'9"	26
6	bogie third	1887	Falcon Engineering Co.	26'9"	26
7	Bogie first/third composite	1888	Craven Brothers, Sheffield	29'0"	40
8	Bogie first/third composite	1888	Craven Brothers, Sheffield	29'0"	40
9	Bogie third	1890	Craven Brothers, Sheffield	29'0"	36
10	Bogie third	1890	Craven Brothers, Sheffield	29'0"	36
11	Bogie third	1890	Craven Brothers, Sheffield	29'0"	36
12	Bogie third	1890	Craven Brothers, Sheffield	29'0"	36
13	Bogie first	1890	Craven Brothers, Sheffield	29'0"	30
14	Bogie first	1890	Craven Brothers, Sheffield	29'0"	30
15	4 wheel brake composite	1890	Unknown	19'0"	18
16	Bogie third	1890	Unknown	30'0"	30
17	Bogie third	1890	Unknown	30'0"	30
18	Bogie third	1890	Unknown	30'0"	30
19	Bogie first/third composite	1890	Unknown	30'0"	40
20	Bogie third	1890	Unknown	29'0"	30
21	Bogie first	1890	Unknown	29'0"	30
22	Bogie first	1890	Unknown	29'0"	30

Wagons

Nos	Type	Capacity (t. cwt)
1-11	Ballast wagons 3-plank	4-0
13-24	Covered goods	4-0
27-31	Covered goods	6-0
32-35	Open goods	6-0
36-41	Covered goods	6-0
42-50	Open goods	6-0
52-54	Open goods	6-0
55-63	Covered goods	6-0
64-66	Open goods	6-0
67-72	Covered goods	6-0
80-83	Timber wagons	6-0
1, 2	16 ft brake	
3-6	12 ft brake	
7,8	16 ft brake	

In February 1889, a branch from the C&MLR at St Annes to Donoughmore was promoted by local ratepayers. A separate company, the Donoughmore Extension Light Railway (DELR), was formed, with baronially-guaranteed capital of £30,000, and an agreement reached with the C&MLR to work the extension. Approval was obtained in August 1891 and, after some delay, due to alterations to the original route, the extension opened on 6th May, 1893.

The company generally enjoyed healthy overall finances despite the early emergence of competition from road transport, when the city tramways extended their system along the Western Road. As the years went by, the company was to face heavy expenditure in the renewal of the permanent way and repairs to the buildings at Western Road but traffic returns continued to be good, that for 1913 being a record for the company. The war years were to see a rise in costs for coal and materials, together with an increase in staff pay, a consequence of Government control of Irish Railways which took effect on the 1st January, 1917. Moreover, in the motive power and permanent way departments, it was almost impossible to secure spare parts and sleepers, resulting in some curtailments of service.

The post-war years presented new difficulties with the passing into law of the eight-hour working day, continued high wages and increasing industrial unrest. A brief respite came in August 1921 with the passing of the Irish Railways (Settlement of Claims) Act, whereby railways could make claims for compensation for the effects of Government control and arrears of maintenance, the C&MLR benefiting to the tune of £8,446. However, the 'Troubles' following the creation of the Irish Free State were to lead to considerable damage to buildings and rolling stock, resulting in cessation of services in August 1922, the disruption resulting in more freight traffic being lost to road transport and the start of working losses.

In July 1924, the company was absorbed into the Great Southern Railways. Under its new owners, rolling stock had the suffix 'K' added to their numbers and engine names were deleted. For the next few years, the GSR attempted to maintain services but the growth of motor transport continued to take traffic from the railway and inevitable reductions in service were introduced. By 1934, the writing was on the wall and the GSR announced the railway would close at the end of the year, with services to be replaced with bus and lorry services. The last trains ran on Saturday 29th December, 1934, with No. 6K (formerly *Muskerry*) in steam, departing Western Road at 6.15 pm to the sound of detonating fog signals which had been laid on the track. When it returned some hours later, the C&MLR passed into history.

Chronology

12.12.1883	Cork, Coachford & Blarney Tramway incorporated under Tramways Act of 1883.
08.08.1887	Line opened to Blarney.
19.03.1888	Line opened to Coachford.
22.02.1889	Donoughmore Extension Light Railway formed.
06.05.1893	Donoughmore Branch opened to traffic.
01.01.1925	C&MLR became a part of Great Southern Railways.
29.12.1934	Line closed to all traffic.

Route

Distance	Station/Halt	Opened	Closed	Notes
0	Cork (Western Road)	1887	1934	
½	Gaol Cross	1887	1898	Urban boundary.
1	Victoria Cross	1887	1934	'Victoria' in timetables.
3½	Carrigrohane	1887	1934	Passing loop.
4	Leemount	1887	1934	Request stop.
4¾	Healy's Bridge	1887	1934	Request Stop. Tramway left road soon after station.
6¼	Coachford Junction	1887	1934	Originally known as 'Blarney Junction'.
6¾	Tower Bridge	1887	1934	Request stop.
7¼	St Anne's	1887	1934	Junction for Donoughmore.
8½	Blarney	1887	1934	
6¼	Coachford Junction	1888	1934	
7¾	Cloghroe	1888	1934	Also 'Inchbeg'.
9¼	Gurteen	1888	1934	
11¾	Dripsey	1888	1934	Passing loop.
12½	Kilmurry	1888	1934	
14¼	Peake	1888	1934	'for Aughabollogue'.
15½	Coachford	1888	1934	
7¼	St Anne's	1887	1934	Branch owned by separate company. (Donoughmore Extension LR).
8¼	Burnt Mill	1893	1934	Request stop.
10½	Gurth	?	?	In timetable early 1890s but not thereafter.
11¼	Fox's Bridge	1893	1934	
12¼	Knockane	?	1934	Request stop.
14¼	Firmount	1893	1934	
15¾	Donoughmore	1893	1934	

The, by then, disused station at Healy's Bridge on 4th September, 1938.

R.W. Kidner/Oakwood Collection

Chapter Twenty

Irish Narrow Gauge Today

Preservation came late to the Irish narrow gauge. Unlike their Welsh counterparts there were no bands of enthusiasts ready to take over while track and rolling stock were still intact. Many of the unique little vehicles of the systems that closed in the 1930s and 1940s were lost forever. The opening of the Belfast Transport Museum in 1956 saved a number of vehicles from lines surviving into the mid-1950s and these can still be seen today at the Ulster Folk and Transport Museum in Cultra, Hollywood, County Down.

On closure of the Cavan & Leitrim Railway in 1959, a C&L 4-4-0T, an ex-T&DR 2-6-2T and two ex-T&DR coaches were sold for preservation in the USA, with the 2-6-2T subsequently being repatriated and restored to working order for the reopening of a section of the T&DR from Tralee to Blennerville in May 1994.

Following closure of the CDRJC, a large amount of rolling stock was purchased by Dr Ralph Cox at auction in 1961 but prohibitive transport costs prevented planned shipment to the USA, and the stock remained in the open, suffering from the elements, vandals and scrap merchants. A 2-6-4T locomotive, two railcars and a coach survived in the stores at Stranorlar and these were rescued by the North West of Ireland Railway Society (NWIRS), formed in 1970, and moved to the old CDRJC Victoria Road site, with a view to opening a restored railway line. Their stay was short-lived, as the site was soon sold for development, but they found a refuge on the Shane's Castle Railway, a private railway operated by Lord O'Neil on his estate in Antrim. They returned to Derry in 1989 with the opening of the Foyle Valley Railway Museum, on the site of the old GNR(I) station on the city-side bank of the river. This was a joint venture between the NWIRS and Derry City Council. The NWIRS also rescued two 2-6-4T locomotives from Strabane in 1987, when the old station site was being bulldozed for a new road system.

In County Donegal itself, the South Donegal Railway Restoration Society (later County Donegal Railway Restoration Ltd, CDRRL) was founded in 1991 with the aim to return a running steam railway to the county. Donegal railway station was reopened as a museum with a collection of stock undergoing restoration. An offshoot of the SDRRS, Cumann Traenach na Gaeltachta Láir (CTGL), re-opened a stretch of the Glenties line at Fintown in 1995 - on the centenary of the opening of the Glenties branch line itself.

The former Cavan & Leitrim Railway station at Dromod was opened as a volunteer-run museum in 1993. The station house, engine shed and water tower have been restored and a short length of track has been laid. Among a collection of narrow gauge vehicles from a variety of sources is a restored 0-4-0 steam tank engine.

A group of local enthusiasts in West Clare secured Moyasta station, which has been restored, and have had track relayed with the main attraction being a restored to steam WCR 2-6-2T.

In 1988, on the centenary of the opening of the unique Listowel & Ballybunion Railway, sufficient interest was reawakened to result in the formation of a restoration committee, which reopened a short section of track in Listowel in 1995.

A section of the Giant's Causeway Tramway was reopened in 2002 as far as Bushmills, initially using some rolling stock from the Shane's Castle Railway.

Further information on some of these various projects can be obtained from the following websites (accessed February 2012):

CDRRL: http://www.donegalrailway.com
West Clare Railway: http://www.westclarerailway.ie
CTGL, Fintown: http://www.antraen.com
Ulster Folk and Transport Museum, Cultra: http://www.nmni.com/uftm
Lartigue Monorail (Listowel & Ballybunion):
    http://www.lartiguemonorail.com
Giant's Causeway & Bushmills Railway:
    http://giantscausewayrailway.webs.com
Foyle Valley Railway Museum:
    http://www.derrycity.gov.uk/Museums/Foyle-Valley-Railway-Museum
Cavan & Leitrim Railway: http://www.cavanandleitrim.com
Tralee & Dingle: No website – some information can occasionally be found on The Tralee Blog:
    http://blog.tralee.org/ and details on the Kerry Guide:
    http://www.kerryguide.com/kerry_places_to_see/steam-railway.html

The authors have donated their royalties from this book towards the restoration of CDR class '5' locomotive *Drumboe* back to full steaming condition. The work is underway at the Railway Preservation Society of Ireland depot, Whitehead, Co. Antrim.   *Steve Flanders*

Appendix One

Irish Narrow Gauge Mileage 1875-1961

End Year	*BR*	*BC&RB*	*B&LR*	*B&NT*	*C&VBT*	*C&LR*	*CVR*	*C&MLR*	*CB&PR*	*CDR*	*D&LST*	*GCT*	*L&BR*	*L&LSR*	*PT*	*S&SR*	*T&DR*	*WCR*	*Total*
1875		11¼																	11¾
1876		16½																	16½
1877		16½	11½																28
1878		16½	29																45½
1879		16½	29																45½
1880	16¼	16½	29																61¾
1881	16¼	16½	29								1¾								63½
1882	16¼	16½	29							13¾	1¾				1¾				77½
1883	16¼	16½	29							13¾	7	6¾		18½	1¾				111½
1884	16¼	16½	31		7					13¾	7	6¾		18½	1¾				118½
1885	16¼	16½	31	3	7					13¾	7	6¾		30¾	1¾				133¾
1886	16¼	16½	31	3	7					13¾	7	6¾		30¾	1¾	14½			148¼
1887	16¼	16½	31	3	7	33¾	37	8¾		13¾	7	9¼		30¾	1¾	14½		27	257¼
1888	16¼	16½	31	3	7	48½	37	18		13¾	7	9¼	9¾	30¾	1¾	14½		27	291
1889	16¼	16½	31	3	7	48½	37	18		18	9	9¼	9¾	30¾	1¾	14½		27	297¼
1890	16¼	16½	31	3	7	48½	37	18		18	9	9¼	9¾	30¾	1¾	14½		27	297¼
1891	16¼	16½	31	3	7	48½	37	18		18	9	9¼	9¾	30¾	1¾	14½	38¼	27	335½
1892	16¼	16½	31	3	7	48½	37	18		18	9	9¼	9¾	30¾	1¾	14½	38¼	53	361½
1893	16¼	16½	31	3	7	48½	37	26½		37	9	9¼	9¾	30¾	1¾	14½	38¼	53	389
1894	16¼	16½	31	3	7	48½	37	26½		50¾	9	9¼	9¾	30¾	1¾	14½	38¼	53	402¾
1895	16¼	16½	31	3	7	48½	37	26½		74¾	9	9¼	9¾	30¾	1¾	14½	38¼	53	426¾
1896	16¼	16½	31	3	7	48½	37	26½		74¾	7	9¼	9¾	30¾	1¾	14½	38¼	53	424¾
1897	16¼	16½	31	3	7	48½	37	26½		74¾	7	9¼	9¾	30¾	1¾	14½	38¼	53	424¾
1898	16¼	16½	31	3	7	48½	37	26½		74¾	7	9¼	9¾	30¾	1¾	14½	38¼	53	424¾
1899	16¼	16½	31	3	7	48½	37	26½		74¾	7	9¼	9¾	30¾	1¾	14½	38¼	53	424¾
1900	16¼	16½	31	3	7	48½	37	26½	6½	89¼	7	9¼	9¾	30¾	1¾	14½	38¼	53	445¾
1901	16¼	16½	31	3	7	48½	37	26½	6½	89¼	7	9¼	9¾	49	1¾	14½	38¼	53	464
1902	16¼	16½	31	3	7	48½	37	26½	8	89¼	7	9¼	9¾	49	1¾	14½	38¼	53	465½
1903	16¼	16½	31	3	7	48½	37	26½	11½	89¼	7	9¼	9¾	98¾	1¾	14½	38¼	53	518¾
1904	16¼	16½	31	3	7	48½	37	26½	16	89¼	7	9¼	9¾	98¾	1¾	14½	38¼	53	523¼
1905	16¼	16½	31	3	7	48½	37	26½	16	104¾	7	9¼	9¾	98¾	1¾	14½	38¼	53	538¾
1906	16¼	16½	31	3	7	48½	37	26½	16	104¾	7	9¼	9¾	98¾	1¾	14½	38¼	53	538¾
1907	16¼	16½	31	3	7	48½	37	26½	16	104¾	7	9¼	9¾	98¾	1¾	14½	38¼	53	538¾
1908	16¼	16½	31	3	7	48½	37	26½	16	104¾	7	9¼	9¾	98¾	1¾	14½	38¼	53	538¾
1909	16¼	16½	31	3	7	48½	37	26½	16	124½	7½	9¼	9¾	98¾	1¾	14½	38¼	53	559
1910	16¼	16½	31	3	7	48½	37	26½	16	124½	7½	9¼	9¾	98¾	1¾	14½	38¼	53	559
1911	16¼	16½	31	3	7	48½	37	26½	16	124½	7½	9¼	9¾	98¾	1¾	14½	38¼	53	559
1912	16¼	16½	31	3	7	48½	37	26½	16	124½	7½	9¼	9¾	98¾	1¾	14½	38¼	53	559

Year																			
1913	559	53	38¼	14½	1¾	98¾	9¾	9¼	7½	124½	16	26½	37	48½	7	3	31	16½	16¼
1914	559	53	38¼	14½	1¾	98¾	9¾	9¼	7½	124½	16	26½	37	48½	7	3	31	16½	16¼
1915	559	53	38¼	14½	1¾	98¾	9¾	9¼	7½	124½	16	26½	37	48½	7	3	31	16½	16¼
1916	559	53	38¼	14½	1¾	98¾	9¾	9¼	7½	124½	16	26½	37	48½	7	3	31	16½	16¼
1917	559	53	38¼	14½	1¾	98¾	9¾	9¼	7½	124½	16	26½	37	48½	7	3	31	16½	16¼
1918	559	53	38¼	14½	1¾	98¾	9¾	9¼	7½	124½	16	26½	37	48½	7	3	31	16½	16¼
1919	559	53	38¼	14½	1¾	98¾	9¾	9¼	7½	124½	16	26½	37	52	7	3	31	16½	16¼
1920	562½	53	38¼	14½	1¾	98¾	9¾	9¼	7½	124½	16	26½	37	52	7	3	31	16½	16¼
1921	562½	53	38¼	14½	1¾	98¾	9¾	9¼	7½	124½	16	26½	37	52	7	3	31	16½	16¼
1922	562½	53	38¼	14½	1¾	98¾	9¾	9¼	7½	124½	16	26½	37	52	7	3	31	16½	16¼
1923	562½	53	38¼	14½	1¾	98¾	9¾	9¼	7½	124½	16	26½	37	52	7	3	31	16½	16¼
1924	552¾	53	38¼	14½	0	98¾	0	9¼	0	124½	16	26½	37	52	7	3	31	16½	16¼
1925	544¼	53	38¼	14½		98¾		9¼		124½	16	26½	37	50¼	7	3	31	16½	16¼
1926	543½	53	38¼	14½		98¾		9¼		124½	16	26½	37	50¼	7	3	31	16½	16¼
1927	543½	53	38¼	14½		98¾		9¼		124½	16	26½	37	50¼	7	3	31	16½	16¼
1928	543½	53	38¼	14½		98¾		9¼		124½	16	26½	37	50¼	7	3	31	16½	16¼
1929	541¾	53	38¼	14½		98¾		9¼		124½	16	26½	37	50¼	7	3	31	16½	16¼
1930	525¾	53	38¼	14½		98¾		9¼		124½	16	26½	37	50¼	7	3	31	16½	16¼
1931	516¾	53	38¼	14½		98¾		9¼		124½	16	26½	37	50¼	7	3	31	16½	16¼
1932	490¼	53	38¼	14½		98¾		9¼		124½	16	26½	37	50¼	7	3	31	16½	16¼
1933	472	53	38¼	14½		98¾		9¼		124½	16	26½	37	50¼	7	3	31	16½	16¼
1934	472	53	38¼	14½		98¾		9¼		124½	0	26½	37	50¼	7	3	31	16½	16¼
1935	461½	53	38¼	14½		98¾		9¼		124½		0	37	50¼	0	3	31	16½	16¼
1936	455½	53	38¼	14½		98¾		9¼		124½			0	50¼		0	31	16½	16¼
1937	420¼	53	38¼	14½		98¾		9¼		124½				50¼			31	16½	16¼
1939	383¾	53	38¼	14½		98¾		9¼		124½				50¼			31	16½	16¼
1940	383¾	53	32¼	14½		80½		9¼		124½				50¼			29	16½	16¼
1941	383¾	53	32¼	14½		80½		9¼		124½				50¼			29	16½	16¼
1942	383¾	53	32¼	14½		80½		9¼		124½				50¼			29	16½	16¼
1943	383¾	53	32¼	14½		68¾		9¼		124½				50¼			11½	16½	16¼
1944	383¾	53	32¼	14½		68¾		9¼		124½				50¼			11½	16½	16¼
1945	306¾	53	32¼	14½		68¾		9¼		124½				50¼			11½	16½	16¼
1946	303¾	53	32¼	14½		68¾		9¼		124½				50¼			11½	16½	16¼
1947	294¾	53	32¼	14½		68¾		9¼		100½				50¼			11½	6	16¼
1948	266¾	53	32¼	14½		30¾		9¼		100½				50¼			11½	6	16¼
1949	266¾	53	32¼	14½		30¾		9¼		100½				50¼			11½	0	16¼
1950	266¾	53	32¼	14½		30¾		9¼		100½				50¼			0		0
1951	203¾	53	32¼	14½		30¾		9¼		100½				50¼					
1952	203¾	53	32¼	14½		30¾		9¼		100½				50¼					
1953	189¼	53	0	0		0		0		100½				50¼					
1954	189¼	53								86				50¼					
1955	189¼	53								86				50¼					
1956	189¼	53								86				50¼					
1957	189¼	53								86				50¼					
1958	53	53								0				0					
1959	53	53																	
1960	0	0																	
1961																			

Appendix Two

Railway Locomotives

Wheels	Railway	Rly Nos.	Name	Builder	Works. No.	Year built	Withdrawn/scrapped
0-4-0CT	D&LST	7		Thos Green	169	1892	1896
0-4-0T	C&VBT	1		Kitson	T106	1884	1904
0-4-0T	C&VBT	2		Kitson	T107	1884	1912
0-4-0T	C&VBT	3		Kitson	T257	1891	1928
0-4-0T	CVR	8		Atkinson-Walker	114	1928	1932
0-4-0T	D&LST	1		Kitson	T57	1882	1899
0-4-0T	D&LST	2		Kitson	T74	1883	1899
0-4-0T	D&LST	3		Kitson	T81	1883	1899
0-4-0T	D&LST	4		Kitson	T104	1884	1912
0-4-0T	D&LST	5		Kitson	T108	1884	1912
0-4-0T	D&LST	6		Kitson	T224	1887	1912
0-4-0T	GCT	1		Wilkinson	-	1883	1908
0-4-0T	GCT	2		Wilkinson	-	1883	1898
0-4-0T	GCT	3	Dunluce Castle	Wilkinson	-	1886	1931
0-4-0T	GCT	4	Brian Boroimhe	Wilkinson	-	1896	1931
0-4-0T	PT	1		Kitson	T56	1882	Preserved Hull
0-4-0T	PT	2		Kitson	T84	1883	Preserved Belfast Transport Museum
0-4-0T	PT	3		Kitson	T302	1901	1926
0-4-0T	S&SR	1	Marion	Dick, Kerr	A	1886	1906
0-4-0T	S&SR	2	Ida	Dick, Kerr .	B	1886	1926
0-4-0T	S&SR	3	Ilen	Dick, Kerr	C	1886	1914
0-4-2ST	BC&RBR	1		Black, Hawthorn	301	1874	1923
0-4-2ST	BC&RBR	2		Black, Hawthorn	302	1875	1923
0-4-2ST	BC&RBR	3		Black, Hawthorn	303	1875	1911
0-4-2T	CVR	1	Caledon	Sharp, Stewart	3369	1886	1934
0-4-2T	CVR	2	Errigal	Sharp, Stewart	3370	1886	1942
0-4-2T	CVR	3	Blackwater	Sharp, Stewart	3371	1887	1942
0-4-2T	CVR	4	Fury	Sharp, Stewart	3372	1887	1929
0-4-2T	CVR	5	Colebrooke	Sharp, Stewart	3373	1887	1936
0-4-2T	CVR	6	Erne	Sharp, Stewart	3374	1887	1942
0-4-2T	T&DLR	4		Hunslet Engine Co.	514	1890	1907
0-4-2WT	C&MLR	4	Blarney	Kitson	235	1888	1911
0-4-4T	C&MLR	5	Donoughmore	Thos Green	180	1892	1938
0-4-4T	C&MLR	6	The Muskerry	Thos Green	200	1893	1954
0-4-4T	C&VBT	5		Hudswell, Clarke	978	1912	1934
0-4-4T	CVR	7	Blessingbourne	Hudswell, Clarke	914	1910	1934
0-6-0ST	BR	3 (1st)	Lady Boyd	Black, Hawthorn	513	1877	1908
0-6-0ST	BR	1	Dalriada	Black, Hawthorn	554	1879	1924
0-6-0ST	BR	2	Countess of Antrim	Black, Hawthorn	555	1879	1924
0-6-0T	B&LR	2		Beyer, Peacock	1700	1877	1933
0-6-0T	B&LR	3		Beyer, Peacock	1701	1877	1931
0-6-0T	B&LR	6		Beyer, Peacock	2304	1883	1932
0-6-0T	L&LSR	4 (17)	Inishowen	Black, Hawthorn	834	1885	1940
0-6-0T	WCR	1		W.G. Bagnall	730	1886	1912
0-6-0T	WCR	2		W.G. Bagnall	738	1886	1900
0-6-0T	WCR	3	Clifden	W.G. Bagnall	792	1887	1915
0-6-0T	WCR	4	Besborough	W.G. Bagnall	793	1887	1901
0-6-2T	L&LSR	1	J.T. Macky	Black, Hawthorn	684	1882	1911
0-6-2T	L&LSR	2	Londonderry	Black, Hawthorn	742	1883	1912
0-6-2T	L&LSR	3	Donegal	Black, Hawthorn	743	1883	1913
0-6-2T	WCR	5	Slieve Callan	Dubs	2890	1892	Preserved Moyasta
0-6-2T	WCR	6	Saint Senan	Dubs	2891	1892	1956
0-6-2T	WCR	7	Lady Inchiquin	Dubs	2892	1892	1922
0-6-4T	C&LR	9	King Edward	R. Stephenson	3136	1904	1934

Wheels	Railway	Rly Nos.	Name	Builder	Works. No.	Year built	Withdrawn/scrapped
2-4-0T	B&LR	1		Beyer, Peacock	1687	1877	1920
2-4-0T	B&LR	4		Beyer, Peacock	1828	1878	1933 (on C&VBT)
2-4-0T	CDRJC	1	Alice	Sharp, Stewart	3023	1881	1926
2-4-0T	CDRJC	2	Blanche	Sharp, Stewart	3021	1881	1912
2-4-0T	CDRJC	3	Lydia	Sharp, Stewart	3022	1881	1912
2-4-0T	L&LSR	5 (5A)		R. Stephenson	2088	1873	1900
2-4-0T	L&LSR	6 (6A)		R. Stephenson	2089	1873	1900
2-4-2CT	B&LR	70 (S)		Beyer, Peacock	3464	1892	1954
2-4-2CT	B&LR	112 (S1)		York Road (NCC)	-	1908	1950
2-4-2CT	B&LR	113 (S1)		York Road (NCC)	-	1909	1954
2-4-2CT	B&LR	103 (S)		York Road (NCC)	-	1919	1938
2-4-2CT	B&LR	104 (S)		York Road (NCC)	-	1920	1954
2-4-2CT	BR	102		York Road (NCC)	-	1908	1954
2-4-2CT	BR	41		York Road (NCC)	-	1909	1954
2-4-2CT	BR	43		York Road (NCC)	-	1920	1954
2-4-2T	CB&PR	4		Neilson, Reid	5561	1899	1959 (on C&LR)
2-4-2T	CB&PR	5		Neilson, Reid	5562	1899	1939 (on C&LR)
2-4-2T	CB&PR	6		Neilson, Reid	5563	1899	1959 (on C&LR)
2-4-2T	CB&PR	7		Neilson, Reid	5564	1899	1954 (on C&LR)
2-4-2T	D&LST			Manlove, Alliott & Fryer	-	1881	1926
2-4-4CT	B&LR	69 (S2)		Beyer, Peacock	3463	1892	1946
2-6-0ST	B&LR	5		Beyer, Peacock	1947	1880	1934
2-6-0T	C&VBT	4		Hudswell, Clarke	698	1904	1942 (on CVR)
2-6-0T	T&DLR	1		Hunslet Engine Co.	477	1889	1955
2-6-0T	T&DLR	2		Hunslet Engine Co.	478	1889	1955
2-6-0T	T&DLR	3		Hunslet Engine Co.	479	1889	1959 (on C&LR)
2-6-0T	T&DLR	6		Hunslet Engine Co.	677	1898	1959 (on C&LR)
2-6-0T	T&DLR	7		Kerr, Stuart	800	1902	1928
2-6-0T	T&DLR	8 (4)		Kerr, Stuart	836	1903	1959 (on C&LR)
2-6-0T	T&DLR	8		Hunslet Engine Co.	1051	1910	1956 (on WCR)
2-6-2T	T&DLR	5		Hunslet Engine Co.	555	1890	Preserved Tralee
2-6-2T	WCR	8	Lisdoonvarna	Dubs	3169	1894	1925
2-6-2T	WCR	9	Fergus	Thos Green	229	1898	1954
2-6-2T	WCR	2	Ennis	Thos Green	234	1900	1955
2-6-2T	WCR	4	Liscannor	Thos Green	236	1901	1928
2-6-4T	CDRJC	16	Donegal	Nasmyth, Wilson	828	1907	Preserved Derry
2-6-4T	CDRJC	17	Glenties	Nasmyth, Wilson	829	1907	Preserved Donegal
2-6-4T	CDRJC	18	Killybegs	Nasmyth, Wilson	830	1907	Preserved Derry
2-6-4T	CDRJC	19	Letterkenny	Nasmyth, Wilson	831	1908	1940
2-6-4T	CDRJC	20	Raphoe	Nasmyth, Wilson	832	1908	1955
2-6-4T	CDRJC	21	Ballyshannon	Nasmyth, Wilson	958	1912	1961
2-6-4T	CDRJC	2A	Strabane	Nasmyth, Wilson	956	1912	Preserved Belfast Transport Museum
2-6-4T	CDRJC	3A	Stranorlar	Nasmyth, Wilson	957	1912	1961
4-4-0T	C&LR	1	Isabel	R. Stephenson	2612	1887	1959
4-4-0T	C&LR	2	Kathleen	R. Stephenson	2613	1887	Preserved Belfast Transport Museum
4-4-0T	C&LR	3	Lady Edith	R. Stephenson	2614	1887	Preserved USA
4-4-0T	C&LR	4	Violet	R. Stephenson	2615	1888	1959
4-4-0T	C&LR	5	Gertrude	R. Stephenson	2616	1888	1925
4-4-0T	C&LR	6	May	R. Stephenson	2617	1888	1927
4-4-0T	C&LR	7	Olive	R. Stephenson	2618	1888	1945
4-4-0T	C&LR	8	Queen Victoria	R. Stephenson	2619	1888	1959
4-4-0T	C&MLR	1	City of Cork	Falcon Engineering	137	1887	1934
4-4-0T	C&MLR	2	Coachford	Falcon Engineering	136	1887	1934
4-4-0T	C&MLR	3	St Annes	Falcon Engineering	138	1887	1924
4-4-0T	C&MLR	7	Peake	Brush Electrical Engineering	274	1898	1935
4-4-0T	C&MLR	8	Dripsey	Brush Electrical Engineering	307	1904	1935
4-4-0T	C&MLR	4 (2)	Blarney	Hunslet Engine Co.	1200	1919	1927

Wheels	Railway	Rly Nos.	Name	Builder	Works. No.	Year built	Withdrawn/scrapped
4-4-0T	S&SR	4	Erin	Nasmyth, Wilson	342	1888	1954
4-4-0T	S&SR	1	Gabriel	Peckett	1085	1906	1937
4-4-0T	S&SR	3	Kent	Peckett	-	1914	1954
4-4-2T	BR	3 (2nd)		Kitson	4665	1908	1946
4-4-2T	BR	4		Kitson	4666	1908	1946
4-4-4T	CDRJC	10	Sir James	Neilson, Reid	6103	1902	1933
4-4-4T	CDRJC	11	Hercules	Neilson, Reid	6104	1902	1933
4-6-0T	CDRJC	4	Meenglas	Neilson	4573	1893	1935
4-6-0T	CDRJC	5	Drumboe	Neilson	4574	1893	1931
4-6-0T	CDRJC	6	Inver	Neilson	4575	1893	1931
4-6-0T	CDRJC	7	Finn	Neilson	4576	1893	1931
4-6-0T	CDRJC	8	Foyle	Neilson	4577	1893	1937
4-6-0T	CDRJC	9	Columbkille	Neilson	4578	1893	1937
4-6-0T	L&LSR	1		Andrew Barclay	933	1902	1940
4-6-0T	L&LSR	2		Andrew Barclay	934	1902	1954
4-6-0T	L&LSR	3		Andrew Barclay	935	1902	1954
4-6-0T	L&LSR	4		Andrew Barclay	936	1902	1953
4-6-0T	WCR	10	Lahinch	Kerr, Stuart	818	1903	1952
4-6-0T	WCR	11	Kilkee	W.G. Bagnall	1881	1908	1953
4-6-0T	WCR	1	Kilrush	Hunslet Engine Co.	1098	1912	1953
4-6-0T	WCR	3	Ennistymon	Hunslet Engine Co.	1432	1922	1953
4-6-0T	WCR	7	Malbay	Hunslet Engine Co.	1433	1922	1956
4-6-2T	L&LSR	5 (15)		Hudswell, Clarke	518	1899	1954
4-6-2T	L&LSR	6 (16)		Hudswell, Clarke	519	1899	1953
4-6-2T	L&LSR	7	Edward VII	Hudswell, Clarke	577	1901	1940
4-6-2T	L&LSR	8		Hudswell, Clarke	562	1901	1954
4-6-2T	L&LSR	9	Aberfoyle	Kerr, Stuart	845	1904	1927
4-6-2T	L&LSR	10	Richmond	Kerr, Stuart	846	1904	1954
4-6-2T	L&LSR	13		Hawthorn, Leslie	2801	1910	1940
4-6-2T	L&LSR	14		Hawthorn, Leslie	2802	1910	1943
4-6-4T	CDRJC	12	Eske	Nasmyth, Wilson	697	1904	1954
4-6-4T	CDRJC	13	Owenea	Nasmyth, Wilson	698	1904	1952
4-6-4T	CDRJC	14	Erne	Nasmyth, Wilson	699	1904	1967
4-6-4T	CDRJC	15	Mourne	Nasmyth, Wilson	700	1904	1952
4-8-0	L&LSR	11		Hudswell, Clarke	746	1905	1933
4-8-0	L&LSR	12		Hudswell, Clarke	747	1905	1954
4-8-4T	L&LSR	5		Hudswell, Clarke	985	1912	1954
4-8-4T	L&LSR	6		Hudswell, Clarke	986	1912	1954

Key

B&LR	Ballymena & Larne Railway
BC&RBR	Ballymena, Cushendall & Red Bay Railway
BR	Ballycastle Railway
C&LR	Cavan & Leitrim Railway
C&MLR	Cork & Muskerry Light Railway
C&VBT	Castlederg & Victoria Bridge Tramway
CB&PR	Cork, Blackrock & Passage Railway
CDRJC	County Donegal Railways Joint Committee
CVR	Clogher Valley Railway
D&LST	Dublin & Lucan Steam Tramway
GCT	Giant's Causeway Tramway
L&LSR	Londonderry & Lough Swilly Railway
PT	Portstewart Tramway
S&SR	Schull & Skibbereen Railway
T&DLR	Tralee & Dingle Light Railway
WCR	West Clare Railway

Appendix Three

Narrow Gauge Coupling Heights

	ft	in.
Ballymena & Larne Railway	1	10 ½
Castlederg & Victoria Bridge Tramway	1	11
Ballymena, Cushendall & Red Bay Railway	2	0
Schull & Skibbereen Railway	2	0
Cavan & Leitrim Railway	2	2
Clogher Valley Railway	2	2
Cork & Muskerry Light Railway	2	2
West Clare Railway	2	3
Ballycastle Railway	2	3
Tralee & Dingle Railway	2	3
Londonderry & Lough Swilly Railway	2	7 ½
Cork, Blackrock & Passage Railway	2	9
County Donegal Railway	2	10 ½

Appendix Four

Rolling Stock Drawings

The following is a list of books cited in references for the individual railways (grouped according to year of publication). Railway journal references are individually cited.

Books

Narrow Gauge Railways of Ireland, Fayle, H., Greenlake Publications, London (1946) (republished by SR Publishers, Wakefield), ISBN 0-85409-627-2 1970.

Narrow Gauge Album, Whitehouse, P.B., Ian Allan, London (1957).

The County Donegal Railways, Patterson, E.M., David & Charles, Newton Abbot (first Ed. 1962), ISBN 0-7153-8167-9.

The Lough Swilly Railway, Patterson, E.M., David & Charles, Newton Abbot (first Edn 1964).

The Ballycastle Railway. Patterson, E.M., David & Charles Newton Abbot (first Edn 1965)/2nd Edn Colourpoint Books, Newtownards, ISBN 1-904242-49-9 (2006).

The Cavan & Leitrim Railway, Flanagan, Patrick J., David & Charles, Newton Abbot (1966), ISBN 0-7153-8167-9.

The Ballymena Lines, Patterson, E.M., David & Charles, Newton Abbot (first Edn 1968)/*The Mid-Antrim Narrow Gauge*, Colourpoint Books, Newtownards (2007) ISBN 1-904242-70-3)

The Clogher Valley Railway, Patterson, E.M., David & Charles, Newton Abbot (1972), ISBN 0-7153-5605-6.

The Tralee & Dingle Railway, Rowlands, D., Bradford & Barton (1977), ISBN 0-85153-267-5.

Narrow Gauge Railway Modelling, Boreham, D., Model & Allied Publications/Argus Books Ltd, Watford (2nd Edn 1978), ISBN 0-85242-611-9.

The Londonderry & Lough Swilly Railway, Boyd, J.I.C., Bradford & Barton, Truro, Cornwall (1980), ISBN 0-85153-447-3.

The Redlake Tramway and China Clay Works, Wade, E.A., Twelvehead Press, Truro (1982), ISBN 0-906294-09-6.

The Irish Narrow Gauge (*Narrow Lines Extra* No. 6), 7mm Narrow Gauge Association (1988), ISBN 0-95133000-0-4.

Modelling the Irish Narrow Gauge (A Railway Modeller Special), Lloyd, D. Peco Publications, Beer, Seaton, Devon (1989), ISBN 0-900586-15-X.

The Listowel & Ballybunion Railway, Newham, A.T., & Foster, M., Oakwood Press, Headington, Oxford, ISBN 0-85361-3761 (revised edition 1989).

The Cork & Muskerry Light Railway, Jenkins, S.C., Oakwood Press, Headington, Oxford, ISBN 0-85361-4075 (revised edition 1992).

The Cork, Blackrock & Passage Railway, Jenkins, S.C., Oakwood Press, Headington, Oxford, ISBN 0-85361-4059 (revised edition 1993).

The West Clare Railway, Taylor, Patrick, Plateway Press (1994), ISBN 1-871980-16X.

The Dingle Train, Rowlands, D., McGrath, W., & Francis, T., Plateway Press (1996), ISBN 1-871980-27-5.

The Castlederg & Victoria Bridge Tramway, Patterson, E.M., Colourpoint Books, Newtownards (1998), ISBN 1-898392-29-3.

The Last Years of the Wee Donegal, Botham, R., Colourpoint Books, Newtownards (1998), ISBN 1-898392-43-9.

The Schull & Skibbereen Railway, Boyd, J.I.C., Oakwood Press, Usk, Monmouthshire (1999), ISBN 0-85361-534-9.

The Wee Donegal Revisited, Botham, R., & Curran, J., Colourpoint Books, Newtownards (2002), ISBN 1-904242-02-2.

The County Donegal Railways Companion, Crombleholme, R., Midland Publishing Ltd, Leicester (2005), ISBN 1-85780-205-5.

Narrow Gauge Rolling Stock: An Irish Railway Pictorial, Coakham, D., Midland Publishing Ltd, Hinkley (2007), ISBN 0-71103-149-5.

General Journal Articles

Livesey, R.M., 'Rolling Stock on the principal Irish narrow gauge railways', *Engineering* 12th August, 1912; pp169-176. Reproduced in: *Narrow Gauge & Industrial Railway Modelling Review* No. 61, Jan. 2005; pp178-189 (contains a variety of line drawings and small scale drawings).

Carnes, T., 'Gazetteer of Irish Narrow Gauge Drawings', *Narrow Gauge & Industrial Railway Modelling Review* 1993; 7: pp226-231.

County Antrim Railways
(BR, B&LR, BC&RB, Glenarrif Iron Ore & Harbour Railway (GIOH), Giant's Causeway Tramway, Portstewart Tramway, B&NCR, NCC)

Locomotives
GIOH 2-4-0T (Stephenson & Co. 1873)
The Ballymena Lines, p126 (side elevation).
Journal of the Stephenson Locomotive Society, 1950;Vol. 26, pp108-110 (side and rear end).
BR 0-6-0ST No. 2 *Countess of Antrim* (Black, Hawthorn 1879)
Narrow Gauge Album, pp58 and 108 (3 mm scale).
Narrow Gauge Railways of Ireland, p22 (3 mm scale).
BR 4-4-2T (Nos. 3 / 4, Kitson 1908)
The Ballycastle Railway, p134, enlargement of Livesey sketch to just under 5 mm scale.
Narrow Gauge Album, pp86, 134 & 135 (as NCC No. 114).
Narrow Gauge Railways of Ireland, p20, 3 mm scale (as NCC No. 114).
B&LR 2-4-0T Nos. 1 / 4 (Beyer, Peacock 1878/1880)
Model Railways, April 1974, p194.
2-6-0ST No. 5 (Beyer, Peacock 1880):
Railways, December 1943, p190 (reproduced in *New Irish Lines* May 2009, p100).
B&LR Class 'S' 2-4-2T No. 70 (as NCC No. 111, Beyer, Peacock 1892)
Model Railway News, Aug. 1965, pp282/3 (7 mm scale).
Narrow Gauge Album, p120 (3 mm scale).
Narrow Gauge Railways of Ireland, p22 (3 mm scale).
NCC 2-4-4T No. 110 (Ex-B&LR 2-4-2T No. 69, Beyer, Peacock 1892 as rebuilt by NCC York Road Belfast 1931)
Narrow Gauge Railways of Ireland, p26 (3 mm scale).

Carriages
BR 4-wheel passenger brake van (Railway Carriage & Wagon Co. 1880)
Narrow Gauge Rolling Stock: An Irish Railway Pictorial, p34 (5 mm scale).
The Ballycastle Railway, (1st edn) p106 (3.3mm scale)/(2nd edn) p87 (4 mm scale).
BR 6-wheel Cleminson composite (Nos. 1-3, Railway Carriage & Wagon Co. 1880)
Narrow Gauge Rolling Stock: An Irish Railway Pictorial, p34 (5 mm scale).
The Ballycastle Railway, (1st edn) p106 (3.3mm scale)/(2nd edn) p87 (4 mm scale).

BR bogie brake third (Metropolitan Railway Carriage & Wagon Co. 1899)
The Ballycastle Railway, p114, enlargement of Livesey sketch to just under 4 mm scale.
B&LR 6-wheel Cleminson brake-composite (No. 315, Bristol Wagon Works 1877)
Narrow Gauge Rolling Stock: An Irish Railway Pictorial, p12 (4 mm scale).
The Ballymena Lines, p149 (c.3mm scale)/*The Mid-Antrim Narrow Gauge*, p114.
B&LR bogie third (No. 318, LMS/NCC)
Three Foot (Journal of the Isle of Man Railway & Tramway Preservation Society) February 1995, No. 1
  pp11-15 (4 mm scale) reproduced in *The Phoenix* (Journal of the County Donegal Railway
  Restoration Society) Summer 1995, No. 9 pp10-13.
B&LR bogie third saloon (Nos. 327/328, LMS/NCC)
Narrow Gauge Rolling Stock: An Irish Railway Pictorial, p12 (4 mm scale).
The Ballymena Lines, p149 (c.3mm scale)/*The Mid-Antrim Narrow Gauge*, p114.
BC&RB 8-wheel third (No. 2, B&NCR Belfast, later No 306)
Narrow Gauge Rolling Stock: An Irish Railway Pictorial, p12 (4 mm scale).
The Ballycastle Railway, 1st Edn, p126, 2nd Edn, p108 (4mm scale).
Model Railway News, December 1964, p 608/9.

Londonderry & Lough Swilly Railway

Locomotives
L&BER 4-6-0T (Andrew Barclay, Sons & Co. 1902)
Model Railway News, May 1962, p184 (4 mm scale).
L&LSR 0-6-0T No. 17 (formerly No. 4 *Inishowen* - Black, Hawthorn & Co. 1885)
The Londonderry & Lough Swilly Railway, p90, 6 mm scale.
L&LSR 4-8-4T (Hudswell, Clarke & Co. 1912)
The Londonderry & Lough Swilly Railway, p90, 5 mm scale.
The Narrow Gauge, No 51, July 1969, 7 mm scale.
The Irish Narrow Gauge, Drawing No. 1, 7 mm scale.
Railway Modeller, Dec. 1984, p489 (4 mm scale).
Modelling the Irish Narrow Gauge, p10 (4 mm scale).
L&LSR 4-6-2T No. 8 (Hudswell, Clarke & Co. 1901)
The Londonderry & Lough Swilly Railway, p87, 6 mm scale.
L&LSR 4-6-2T No. 10 *Richmond* (Kerr, Stuart 1904)
Narrow Gauge Railways of Ireland, p153, 3 mm scale.
The Londonderry & Lough Swilly Railway, p89, approx 5.5 mm scale.
Railway Modeller, Aug. 1985, p329 (4 mm scale).
The Irish Narrow Gauge (*Narrow Lines Extra* No. 6), 7 mm scale.
L&LSR 4-8-0 Nos. 11/12 (Hudswell, Clarke & Co. 1905)
The Londonderry & Lough Swilly Railway, pp84/5, 8 mm scale.
The Narrow Gauge, No 38, May 1965, p12.
L&BER 4-6-2T No. 13 (Hawthorn, Leslie 1910)
The Londonderry & Lough Swilly Railway, p88, 5.5 mm scale.

Carriages
L&LSR No. 10: 6-wheel third (Railway Carriage Co., Oldbury 1884)
The Londonderry & Lough Swilly Railway, p92 (4 mm scale).
L&LSR No. 25: bogie brake third, 2-compartment (Lancaster Railway Carriage & Wagon Co. 1901)
The Londonderry & Lough Swilly Railway, p91 (4 mm scale).
L&LSR No. 34: bogie brake third, 3-compartment (Lancaster Railway Carriage & Wagon Co. 1901)
The Londonderry & Lough Swilly Railway, p91 (4 mm scale).

L&BER Nos. 1B-5B: bogie 6-compartment third (Pickering 1903)
The Londonderry & Lough Swilly Railway, p92 (4 mm scale).
L&BER No 6-9: Bogie 3 compartment brake third Pickering 1904)
The Londonderry & Lough Swilly Railway, p91 (4 mm scale).
L&BER Nos. 10B-12B: bogie 6-compartment tricomposite (Pickering 1904)
The Londonderry & Lough Swilly Railway, p91 (4 mm scale).

Goods Vehicles
L&LSR No. 5: 4-wheel centre swing door goods brake van
The Londonderry & Lough Swilly Railway, p93 (4 mm scale).
L&LSR No. 24: 4-wheel centre swing doors goods van
The Londonderry & Lough Swilly Railway, p96. (4 mm scale).
L&LSR No. 35: 4-wheel, 3-plank drop side wagon
The Londonderry & Lough Swilly Railway, p94 (4.3 mm scale).
L&LSR No, 78: 4-wheel, centre swing doors, roofless cattle wagon
The Londonderry & Lough Swilly Railway, p95 (6.5 mm scale).
L&LSR No. 112: 4-wheel, 4-plank centre drop door open
The Londonderry & Lough Swilly Railway p94 (4.3 mm scale).
L&LSR No 148: 4-wheel Esso tank wagon
The Londonderry & Lough Swilly Railway, p96 (4 mm scale).

L&BER No. 7: bogie goods brake van - rebuilt from brake third (Pickering 1884)
The Londonderry & Lough Swilly Railway, p93 (4 mm scale).
L&BER No. 23: 4-wheel centre swing doors goods
The Londonderry & Lough Swilly Railway, p96 (4 mm scale).
L&BER No. 55: 4-wheel centre swing doors goods
The Londonderry & Lough Swilly Railway, p93 (4 mm scale).
L&BER No. 62: 4-wheel horse box
The Londonderry & Lough Swilly Railway, p94. (4.3 mm scale).
L&BER No. 89/90: Bogie twin sliding doors ventilated van)
The Narrow Gauge, No. 51 July 1969 (7 mm scale).
L&BER No. 205: 4-wheel centre swing doors cattle van
The Londonderry & Lough Swilly Railway, p95 (6.5 mm scale)

County Donegal Railways Joint Committee

Locomotives
Class '2' 4-6-0T (Neilson 1893)
Model Railway News, July 1963, p265/6 (4 mm scale).
Narrow Lines, April 1983, No. 20, p11. (7 mm scale).
The County Donegal Railways Companion, p17 - No. 8 *Foyle* (7 mm scale).
Class '3' 4-4-4T (Neilson Reid 1902)
The Irish Narrow Gauge, drawing No. 7 (7 mm scale).
Railway Modeller, July 1986, p282 (4 mm scale).
Modelling the Irish Narrow Gauge, p33 (4 mm scale).
The County Donegal Railways Companion, p19 (5.5 mm scale).
Class '4' 4-6-4T No. 11 *Erne* (Nasmyth Wilson 1904)
The County Donegal Railways Companion, p21 (7 mm scale).
Class '5a' 2-6-4T (Nasmyth Wilson 1912)
The Irish Narrow Gauge, drawing No. 2 (7 mm scale).
Railway Modeller, Dec. 1984, p489 (4 mm scale).
Modelling the Irish Narrow Gauge, p10 (4 mm scale).
The County Donegal Railways Companion, p24 - No. 3 *Lydia* (7 mm scale).
The Wee Donegal Revisited, p46 (6 mm scale); p47 (outline only - 4 mm scale).
Phœnix (Atkinson Walker 1928, ex-Clogher Valley Rly No, 8, acquired 1933)
The Redlake Tramway and China Clay Works, p78 (sister locomotive - 5 mm scale).
The County Donegal Railways Companion, p44 (7 mm scale).

Railcars / Trailers
Railcar No. 1 (Allday & Onions 1906)
Railway Times No. 20. Spring 1981, p31 (Side elevation - c.1920) and line drawing p32.
Railcar No. 2/3 (ex-Derwent Valley Light Rly)
Railway World, June 1961, p206 (as running on DVLR just under 3mm scale).
The County Donegal Railways Companion, p39 (4 mm scale).
Railcar Trailer No. 2 (2nd; ex-C&VBT)
The County Donegal Railways Companion, p29 (4 mm scale).
Railcar No. 3 (2nd; Baguley-Drewry 1926, ex-Dublin & Blessington Steam Tramway)
The Irish Narrow Gauge, drawing No. 12 (7 mm scale).
Railway Modeller, February 1987, p81 (4 mm scale).
Modelling the Irish Narrow Gauge, p35 (4 mm scale).
The County Donegal Railways Companion, p35 (4 mm scale).

Railcar No. 4 (GNRI/O'Doherty 1928)
The Irish Narrow Gauge, drawing No. 13 (7 mm scale).
Railway Modeller, September 1987, p386 (4 mm scale).
Modelling the Irish Narrow Gauge, p36 (4 mm scale).
The County Donegal Railways Companion, p29 (4 mm scale).
Railcar Trailer No. 5 (GNRI/O'Doherty 1929)
The County Donegal Railways Companion, p29 (4 mm scale).
The Wee Donegal Revisited, p56 (outline only - 4mm scale).
Railcar No. 6 (GNRI/O'Doherty 1930)
The County Donegal Railways Companion, p32 (4 mm scale).
Railcar No. 7/8 (GNRI/O'Doherty 1930/31)
Model Railway Constructor, July 1961, p164 (3 mm scale).
Railway Modeller, September 1987, p387 (4 mm scale).
The County Donegal Railways Companion, p35 (4 mm scale).
Railcar No. 10 (Walker Bros 1932; ex-Clogher Valley Rly No. 1, acquired 1942)
The Irish Narrow Gauge, drawing No. 14 (7 mm scale).
Railway Modeller, November 1987, p478 (4 mm scale).
Modelling the Irish Narrow Gauge, p40 (4 mm scale).
The County Donegal Railways Companion, p32 (4 mm scale).
Railcar No. 12, 15-18 (GNRI/Walker Bros 1934-40)
The Irish Narrow Gauge, drawing Nos. 15 & 16 (7 mm scale).
Railway Modeller, December 1987, pp526/7 (4 mm scale).
Modelling the Irish Narrow Gauge, pp41/2 (4 mm scale).
The County Donegal Railways Companion, p39 - No. 12 (4 mm scale).
Railcar No. 19/20 (GNRI/Walker Bros 1950/51)
The Irish Narrow Gauge, drawing No. 17 (7 mm scale).
Railway Modeller, January 1988, p35 (4 mm scale).
Modelling the Irish Narrow Gauge, pp43/4 (4 mm scale).
The Wee Donegal Revisited, p65 (4 mm scale).

Carriages
No. 1: 6-wheel Directors' saloon (Railway Carriage & Wagon Co. 1882)
The County Donegal Railways Companion, p49. (4 mm scale).
The Wee Donegal Revisited, p70 (outline only - 4mm scale).
No. 13: first/third composite (Oldbury Carriage & Wagon Co. 1893)
The County Donegal Railways Companion, p51 (4mm scale - as rebuilt in 1953 with central guard's
    compartment and 5 ft wheelbase bogies).
The Wee Donegal Revisited, p71 (outline only – 4mm scale).
Nos. 12 & 14-17: five-compartment composite (Oldbury Carriage & Wagon Co. 1893)
Engineering, August 1912, p170 (2 mm scale).
No. 16: five-compartment tri-composite (Oldbury Carriage & Wagon Co. 1893)
The County Donegal Railways Companion, p49 (4 mm scale).
No. 23-28: brake/third passenger coaches (Oldbury Carriage & Wagon Co. 1893)
Engineering, August 1912, p170 (2 mm scale).
No. 28: brake/third passenger coach (Oldbury Carriage & Wagon Co. 1893)
The County Donegal Railways Companion, p51. (4 mm scale)
No. 30: centre gangway third saloon (Oldbury Carriage & Wagon Co. 1901)
The Wee Donegal Revisited, p70 (outline only - 4mm scale).
Nos. 35-38: bogie lavatory composite first/third (Pickering 1905)
Model Railways, February 1979, pp116/7 (4+5 mm scale).
No. 47: brake/third (Oldbury Carriage & Wagon Co 1907 - S&LR)
The County Donegal Railways Companion, p51 (4 mm scale – as rebuilt 1944; originally 6-compartment
    third)
Nos. 52-54: brake/third (Oldbury Carriage & Wagon Co 1907 - S&LR)
The Wee Donegal Revisited, p71 (outline only – 4mm scale).
No. 58: ex-LMS/NCC No. 318
Three Foot (Journal of the Isle of Man Railway & Tramway Preservation Society) February 1995, No. 1
    pp11-15 (4 mm scale). Reproduced in *The Phoenix* (Journal of the County Donegal Railway
    Restoration Society) Summer 1995, No. 9 pp10-13.
The County Donegal Railways Companion, p55 (5.5 mm scale).
No 59: exLMS/NCC No 351
Model Railway Constructor, December 1951, No. 2, p54.

Goods Vehicles
Nos. 46-95: 4-wheel centre sliding door van (Oldbury Carriage & Wagon Co 1893)
Model Railways, May 1973, p244 (No. 48, 4 mm scale).
The County Donegal Railways Companion, p59 (No. 56, 4 mm scale).
The Wee Donegal Revisited, p95 (outline only - 4mm scale).
No. 108: 4-wheel, 4-plank centre drop door open (Oldbury Carriage & Wagon Co. 1893)
Model Railways, May 1973, p244 (4 mm scale).
No. 121-154: 4-wheel, 4-plank centre drop door open (Oldbury Carriage & Wagon Co. 1893)
The Wee Donegal Revisited, p95 (outline only - 4mm scale).
No. 159: bogie wagon (Oldbury Carriage & Wagon Co. 1900)
The County Donegal Railways Companion, p59 (4 mm scale - as rebuilt in 1923 with 2 ft 6 in. sides).
The Wee Donegal Revisited, p106 (outline only - 4mm scale).
No. 169-198: 4-wheel centre sliding door van (Metropolitan Carriage & Wagon Co. 1905)
The Wee Donegal Revisited, p95 (outline only - 4mm scale).
No. 228 (2nd): 4-wheel, 3-plank centre drop door open (Pickering 1912 - ex-C&VBT)
The County Donegal Railways Companion, p68 (7 mm scale).
No. 230: 4-wheel, 4-plank centre drop door open (Pickering 1907)
Model Railways, June 1973, p278 (4 mm scale), reproduced in *The County Donegal Railways Companion*,
    p62 (4 mm scale).
No. 243: 4-wheel centre swing doors, goods/cattle (Pickering 1907)
Model Railways, June 1973, p277 (4 mm scale), reproduced in *The County Donegal Railways Companion*,
    p62 (4 mm scale).
No. 265: 4-wheel centre swing doors goods (Hurst Nelson 1908)
Model Railways, June 1973, p278 (4 mm scale), reproduced in *The County Donegal Railways Companion*,
    p62 (4 mm scale).
The Wee Donegal Revisited, p106 (outline only - 4mm scale).
No. 299: 4-wheel, 4-plank centre drop door open 16 ft 6 in. (Hurst Nelson 1909)
Model Railways, June 1973, p278 (4 mm scale), reproduced in *The County Donegal Railways Companion*,
    p62 (4 mm scale).
No. 313: 6-wheel open wagon (1926 conversion of passenger van No. 10 - Railway Carriage &
    Wagon Co. 1882)
The County Donegal Railways Companion, p59 (4 mm scale).
No. 1539: Shell tank wagon (Midland Railway Carriage & Wagon Co. 1923)
The County Donegal Railways Companion, p65 (7 mm scale).
No. 3009: Pratts tank wagon (Midland Railway Carriage & Wagon Co. 1923)
The County Donegal Railways Companion, p65 (7 mm scale).
No. 3010: Esso tank wagon (Midland Railway Carriage & Wagon Co. 1923)
The County Donegal Railways Companion, p65 (7 mm scale).
Red Wagon No. 6: 4-wheel, 3-plank centre drop door open (Oldbury 1884 - ex-C&VBT)
The County Donegal Railways Companion, p68 (7 mm scale).

Castlederg & Victoria Bridge Tramway

Locomotives
0-4-0T No. 3 (Kitson 1891)
The Castlederg & Victoria Bridge Tramway, p79 (line drawing only, 4.8 mm scale).
2-6-0T No. 4 (Hudswell, Clarke 1904)
The Irish Narrow Gauge, drawing No. 4 (7 mm scale).
Railway Modeller, July 1985, p207 (5.5 mm scale).
Modelling the Irish Narrow Gauge, p14 (modification on CVR also included - 5.5 mm scale).
The Castlederg & Victoria Bridge Tramway, p79 (line drawing only, 4.8 mm scale).
0-4-4T No. 5 (Hudswell, Clarke 1912)
The Castlederg & Victoria Bridge Tramway, p80 (line drawing only, 4.8 mm scale).
2-4-0T No. 6 (ex-B&LR; Beyer, Peacock 1880)
The Castlederg & Victoria Bridge Tramway, p80 (line drawing only, 4.8 mm scale).

Railcar
Paraffin-engined railcar (Castlederg Works 1924)
The Castlederg & Victoria Bridge Tramway, p59 (line drawing only, 4.8 mm scale).

Carriages
Nos. 1/2: 4-wheel, end-platformed, first/third composite (Oldbury Carriage & Wagon Co. 1884)
The Castlederg & Victoria Bridge Tramway, p81 (line drawing only, 4.8 mm scale).
No. 3: 4-wheel, end-platformed, second (Oldbury Carriage & Wagon Co. 1884)
The Castlederg & Victoria Bridge Tramway, p82 (line drawing only, 4.8 mm scale).
Nos. 4: 4-wheel, end-platformed, first (Oldbury Carriage & Wagon Co. 1884)
The Castlederg & Victoria Bridge Tramway, p83 (line drawing only, 4.8 mm scale).
No. 5: bogie third (Oldbury Carriage & Wagon Co. 1887)
The Castlederg & Victoria Bridge Tramway, p84 (line drawing only, 4.8 mm scale).
Nos. 1/2: 4-wheel, brake (Oldbury Carriage & Wagon Co. 1884)
The Castlederg & Victoria Bridge Tramway, p85 (line drawing only, 4.8 mm scale).

Goods Vehicles
Nos 1-14: 4-wheel, centre door cattle/goods vans (Oldbury Carriage & Wagon Co. 1884)
The Castlederg & Victoria Bridge Tramway, p86 (line drawing only, 4.8 mm scale).
Nos. 15-20: 4-wheel, 5-plank centre drop door open (Oldbury Carriage & Wagon Co. 1884)
The Castlederg & Victoria Bridge Tramway. p87 (line drawing only, 4.8 mm scale).
Nos. 21-23: 4-wheel, centre door open cattle vans (Oldbury Carriage & Wagon Co. 1890)
The Castlederg & Victoria Bridge Tramway, p87 (line drawing only, 4.8 mm scale).
No. 24: bogie 5-plank double door open (Oldbury Carriage & Wagon Co 1896)
The Castlederg & Victoria Bridge Tramway, p 88 (line drawing only, 4.8 mm scale).
Nos. 25-27: 4-wheel, centre door covered cattle vans (Oldbury Carriage & Wagon Co. 1899)
The Castlederg & Victoria Bridge Tramway, p86 (line drawing only, 4.8 mm scale).
No. 28: 4-wheel, 5-plank open (Pickering 1912)
The Castlederg & Victoria Bridge Tramway, p89 (line drawing only, 4.8 mm scale).
No. 29: Bogie 5-plank double door open (Pickering 1912)
The Castlederg & Victoria Bridge Tramway, p89 (line drawing only, 4.8 mm scale).

Bessbrook & Newry Tramway

No known drawings.

Clogher Valley Railway

Locomotives
0-4-2T Nos. 1-6 (Sharp, Stewart & Co. 1886/7)
Model Railway Constructor, Oct. 1966, p258 (4 mm scale).
2-6-2T No. 4 (ex-C&VBT 2-6-0T No. 4, Hudswell, Clarke 1904)
The Irish Narrow Gauge, drawing No. 4 (as C&VBT 2-6-0T – 7 mm scale).
Railway Modeller, July 1985, p207 (modification on CVR also included – 5.5 mm scale).
Modelling the Irish Narrow Gauge, p 14 (modification on CVR also included – 5.5 mm scale).
The Modeller Book of the Narrow Gauge, p56 (side elevation, 3 mm scale).
0-4-0T No. 8 (Atkinson, Walker Class 'A3' Steam tractor 1928, Works No. 114)
The Redlake Tramway and China Clay Works, p78 (sister locomotive, 5 mm scale).
The County Donegal Railways Companion, p44 (as *Phœnix* on CDR, 7mm scale).

Railcar
Railcar No. 1 (Walker Bros 1932)
The Irish Narrow Gauge, drawing No. 14 (as CDR No. 10 – 7mm scale).
Railway Modeller, November 1987, p478 (as CDR No. 10 – 4 mm scale).
Modelling the Irish Narrow Gauge, p40 (as CDR No. 10 – 4 mm scale).

Carriages
Nos. 10/11: bogie end-platformed first/third clerestory composite (Metropolitan Railway Carriage & Wagon Co. 1886)
The Clogher Valley Railway, p230 (4 mm scale).
The Modeller Book of the Narrow Gauge, p56 (No. 10, side elevation – 3 mm scale).
No. 1: 4-wheel luggage, parcel & brake van (Metropolitan Railway Carriage & Wagon Co. 1886)
The Modeller Book of the Narrow Gauge, p57 (side elevation – 3 mm scale).

Cavan & Leitrim Railway

Locomotives
4-4-0T No. 2 (Robert Stephenson 1887/8)
The Irish Narrow Gauge, drawing No. 10 (7 mm scale).
Railway Modeller, May 1958, p110 (4 mm scale).
0-6-4T No. 9 *King Edward* (Robert Stephenson 1904)
Narrow Gauge Railways of Ireland, p144 (3mm scale).
Railway Modeller, May 1958, p110 (4 mm scale).
The Irish Narrow Gauge, drawing No. 11. (7 mm scale).
2-4-2T Nos. 10L-13L (*ex CB&PR*) (Neilson Reid 1899)
Narrow Gauge Railways of Ireland, p49 (No. 5 as on CB&PR. Side elevation, 3 mm scale).
Narrow Gauge Album, p100 (as No. 5 on CB&PR. Side elevation, 3 mm scale).
The Modeller Book of Narrow Gauge, p17 (4 mm scale).
The Irish Narrow Gauge, drawing No. 9 (7 mm scale).
Modelling the Irish Narrow Gauge, p18 (4 mm scale).
Railway Modeller, November 1958, p258 (4 mm scale).
The Cork, Blackrock & Passage Railway, p51 (No. 5. 4 mm scale).
Narrow Lines, April 1983, No. 20, p11 (7 mm scale).
2-6-0T No. 4T (*ex-T&DR, originally No. 8*) (Kerr, Stuart & Co. 1903)
The Dingle Train, p87 (7 mm scale).
2-6-2T No. 5T (*ex-T&DR*) (Hunslet Engine Co. 1890)
Railway Modeller, Aug 1958, p176 (4 mm scale – reproduced in *Railway Modeller* May 1962 p107).
The Tralee & Dingle Railway, p83 (6 mm scale).
The Dingle Train, p97 (7 mm scale).

Railcar
Inspection railcar (Ford/Baguley/T&DR 1922)
The Tralee & Dingle Railway, p84 (5 mm scale).
The Dingle Train, p96 (7 mm scale).

Carriages
Nos. 1L: bogie end-platform composite (Metropolitan Carriage & Wagon Co. 1887)
Model Railway News, Aug. 1953, pp166/167 (7 mm).
Railway Modeller, Sept 1958, p203 (4 mm scale. Nos. 5/6 as rebuilt by CIE).
Narrow Gauge Rolling Stock: An Irish Railway Pictorial, p53 (4 mm scale).
No. 13-18: 4-wheel, centre swing doors passenger brake van (Metropolitan Carriage & Wagon Co. 1887)
Model Railway News, Jan. 1955, pp8/9.
Railway Modeller, Sept. 1958, p203 (No. 18 as rebuilt by CIE, 4 mm scale).
No. 21: bogie saloon composite (Midland Carriage & Wagon Co. 1907) [Originally *T&DR* No. 18, later WCR No. 42]
Model Railway News, Jul. 1963, p268/9 (7 mm scale). Reproduced in *The Dingle Train*, p112 (7 mm scale).
No. 22: bogie passenger brake van (Bristol Carriage & Wagon Co. 1907)[Originally *T&DR* No. 5]
Model Railway News, Jul. 1963, p268/9 (7 mm scale).
Narrow Lines, Feb. 1983, No. 19 p6 (7 mm scale).
Narrow Gauge Rolling Stock: An Irish Railway Pictorial, p51 (4 mm scale).

Goods Vehicles
No. 15: 4-wheel, 4-plank centre drop door open (Metropolitan Carriage & Wagon Co. 1887)
Railway Modeller, May 1958, p110 (4 mm scale).
Nos. 51-60: 4-wheel, 4-plank end-of-sides drop door open (Pickering 1912)
Model Railway News, Feb. 1956, p29.
Railway Modeller, May 1958, p110 (4 mm scale).
Model Railways, Dec. 1971, p223 (4 mm scale).
Nos. 61-80: 4-wheel, centre swing doors semi-covered goods/cattle van
Model Railway News, Apr. 1957, pp94/5 (8 mm scale).
Railway Modeller, Aug. 1958, p176 (4 mm scale).
No. 189: 4-wheel, 3-plank centre drop door open (*ex-CB&PR*)
Model Railways, Dec. 1971, p224 (4 mm scale).
Narrow Gauge Rolling Stock: An Irish Railway Pictorial, p51 (4 mm scale).

Nos. 190/191: 4-wheel goods brake vans (*ex-CB&PR*)
Model Railways, Dec. 1971, p225. (4 mm scale).
Narrow Gauge Rolling Stock: An Irish Railway Pictorial, p50 (4 mm scale).
No. 2L 4-wheel milk van (C&LR Ballinamore 1900)
Narrow Gauge Rolling Stock: An Irish Railway Pictorial, p51 (4 mm scale).

West Clare Railway

Locomotives
0-6-0T Nos. 3 *Clifden* & 4 *Besborough* (Bagnall 1887)
The Narrow Gauge, Spring 1990, No. 126; p15 (5.4 mm scale).
The West Clare Railway, p76 (No. 4. 7 mm scale).
0-6-2T Nos. 5 *Slieve Callan*, 6 *St Senan* & 7 *Lady Inchiquin* (Dübs & Co. 1892)
Narrow Lines, October 1984, No. 29, pp 4/5 (7 mm scale).
The West Clare Railway, p94 (No. 5. 7 mm scale).
4-6-0T No. 10 *Lahinch* (Kerr, Stuart & Co. 1903)
The West Clare Railway, p82 (7 mm scale).
4-6-0T No. 11 *Kilkee* (Bagnall 1908):
The Narrow Gauge Spring 1990, No. 126; p16/7 (6 mm scale).
The West Clare Railway, p89 (7 mm scale).
2-6-2T Nos. 2 *Ennis*, 4 *Liscannor* & 9 *Fergus* (Thos Green & Sons 1900, 1901 and 1898)
The Irish Narrow Gauge (Narrow Lines Extra No 6), drawing No. 8 (7 mm scale).
Railway Modeller, Oct. 1986, p433 (4 mm scale).
Modelling the Irish Narrow Gauge, p34 (4 mm scale).
Model Railways, Feb. 1991, p97 (3.5 mm scale).
The Narrow Gauge Winter 1994, No. 141; p28 (7 mm scale).
4-6-0T No. 7 *Malbay* (Hunslet Engine Co. 1922)
The West Clare Railway, p105 (7 mm scale).
The Locomotive, 14th April, 1923, p94 (7 mm scale).
B-B 214 hp centre cab diesel locomotives Nos. F501-3 (Walker Bros 1954)
The Irish Narrow Gauge, drawing No. 18 (7 mm scale).
Railway Modeller, Jun. 1985, p 249 (4 mm scale).
The West Clare Railway, p119 (7 mm scale, reproduction of *Railway Modeller* drawing).
Modelling the Irish Narrow Gauge, p16 (4 mm scale).
Model Railways, Dec. 1974, pp 604/5 (7 mm scale).
Narrow Gauge Times, Winter 1978/9 No. 12; Supplement No. 12 (13 mm scale).

Railcars
Baguley-Drewry/Ford 4-w petrol inspection car (ex-*T&DR* 1922)
The Tralee & Dingle Railway, p84 (5 mm scale).
The Dingle Train, p96 (7 mm scale).
Diesel railcar Nos. 3386-89 (Walker Bros, Wigan 1952)
The West Clare Railway, pp116/7 (7 mm scale).

Carriages
No. 11: third class coach (Bristol Wagon & Carriage Works 1887)
The West Clare Railway, p124 (7 mm scale).
No. 19: composite coach (Bristol Wagon & Carriage Works 1894)
The West Clare Railway, p126 (7 mm scale).
No. 34: tourist saloon (WCR Ennis Works 1906)
The West Clare Railway, p129 (7 mm scale).

Goods Vehicles
No. 28c: 4-wheel 5T horse box 16'0" (Bristol Wagon & Carriage Works 1887)
The West Clare Railway, p144 (7 mm scale).
Narrow Gauge Rolling Stock: An Irish Railway Pictorial, p46 (4 mm scale).
No. 20c: 4-wheel 5T covered goods wagon (Bristol Wagon & Carriage Works 1887)
The West Clare Railway, p144 (7 mm scale).
Narrow Gauge Rolling Stock: An Irish Railway Pictorial, p46 (4 mm scale).
No. 166c: 4-wheel 5T covered cattle wagon (WCR Ennis Works 1913)
The West Clare Railway, p144 (7 mm scale).
Narrow Gauge Rolling Stock: An Irish Railway Pictorial, p48 (4 mm scale).

No. 134c: open wagon 4-wheel 5T ballast (WCR Ennis Works 1907)
The West Clare Railway, p145 (7 mm scale).
No. 47c: open wagon 4-wheel 5T goods (Bristol Wagon & Carriage Works 1887)
The West Clare Railway, p145 (7 mm scale).
Narrow Gauge Rolling Stock: An Irish Railway Pictorial, p46 (4 mm scale).
No. 65c: open wagon 4-wheel 5T ballast (Bristol Wagon & Carriage Works 1887)
The West Clare Railway, p145 (7 mm scale).
Narrow Gauge Rolling Stock: An Irish Railway Pictorial, p46 (4 mm scale).
No. 29c: 4-wheel 5T flat (Bristol Wagon & Carriage Works 1887)
The West Clare Railway, p145 (7 mm scale).
Narrow Gauge Rolling Stock: An Irish Railway Pictorial, p48 (4 mm scale).
All above goods stock drawings reproduced from Gardner, J., *Model Railways*, January 1972, pp278-
281 and February 1972, pp348-349 (4 mm scale).

Listowel & Ballybunion Railway

Locomotives
0-3-0 Nos. 1-3 (Hunslet Engine Co. 1889)
The Listowel & Ballybunion Railway, pp66/7 (works drawing); p68 (front / rear elevations).
0-3-0 'Coffee Pot' (Tubize, Belgium 1889)
The Listowel & Ballybunion Railway, p 48 (7 mm scale).

Carriages
B2: third/first/brake composite; A7: all-first; B1: third/brake/steps composite
All *The Listowel & Ballybunion Railway*, p72 (4 mm scale).
Parcels van; A8: first/third composite; A37: first/third composite; A5: all-third
All *The Listowel & Ballybunion Railway*, p75 (4 mm scale).

Tralee & Dingle Railway

Locomotives
2-6-0T No. 2T (Hunslet Engine Co. 1889)
The Tralee & Dingle Railway, p82 (approx. 6.3 mm scale).
The Dingle Train, p79 (7 mm scale).
0-4-2T No. 4 (Hunslet Engine Co. 1890)
The Dingle Train, p83 (approx 5.9 mm scale).
2-6-0T No. 4T (2nd - originally No. 8 - Kerr, Stuart & Co. 1903)
The Dingle Train, p87 (7 mm scale).
2-6-2T No. 5T (Hunslet Engine Co. 1890)
Railway Modeller, Aug. 1958, p176 (4 mm scale) and May 1962 p107.
The Tralee & Dingle Railway, p83 (approx 5.9 mm scale).
The Dingle Train, p97 (7 mm scale).

Railcar
Inspection railcar (Ford/Baguley/T&DR 1922)
The Tralee & Dingle Railway, p84 (5 mm scale).
The Dingle Train, p96 (7 mm scale).

Carriages
No. 3: bogie saloon third (Bristol Carriage & Wagon Co. 1890)
The Dingle Train, p108 (7 mm scale).
No. 5: brake third (Bristol Carriage & Wagon Co 1890)
Model Railway News, Jul. 1963, p268/9 (as C&L No. 22L, 7 mm scale).
Narrow Lines, Dec. 1982, p10 (7 mm scale).
No. 13: bogie saloon brake composite (Bristol Carriage & Wagon Co. 1898)
The Tralee & Dingle Railway, p84 (6.5 mm scale).
The Dingle Train, p110 (7 mm scale).
No. 18: bogie saloon composite (Midland Carriage & Wagon Co. 1907)
Model Railway News, Jul. 1963, p268/9 (as C&LR No. 21. 7 mm scale). Reproduced in *The Dingle Train*,
p112 (7 mm scale).

Goods Vehicles
No. 40T: bogie double swing doors covered goods van (Tubular Frame Wagon Co. 1892)
The Tralee & Dingle Railway, p85 (approx. 4.3 mm scale).
The Dingle Train, p117 (4 mm scale).
No. 42T: bogie centre doors covered goods van (T&DR Tralee 1904)
The Tralee & Dingle Railway, p85 (approx 4.3 mm scale).
The Dingle Train, p117 (4 mm scale).
No. 12T: centre door covered goods van (Bristol Carriage & Wagon Co. 1890)
The Dingle Train, p119 (4 mm scale).
No. 14T: centre door covered goods van (Bristol Carriage & Wagon Co. 1890, *as modified in 1940 with side drop vents to accommodate livestock*)
The Dingle Train, p119 (4 mm scale).
No. 56T: open cattle wagon (Pickering 1904)
The Tralee & Dingle Railway, p90 (7 mm scale).
The Dingle Train, p119 (4 mm scale).
No. 76T: Cattle Wagon (Midland Carriage & Wagon Co. 1907)
The Tralee & Dingle Railway, p90 (7 mm scale).
The Dingle Train, p119 (4 mm scale).

Schull & Skibbereen Railway

Locomotives
0-4-0T No. 3 *Ilen* (Dick, Kerr & Co. 1886)
The Schull & Skibbereen Railway, p168 (4 mm scale. Includes detail of 1902 rebuild).
4-4-0T No. 4 *Erin* (Nasmyth, Wilson 1888)
The Schull & Skibbereen Railway, p172 (4 mm scale) and p184 (CIÉ line drawing).
Modelling the Irish Narrow Gauge, p33 (4 mm scale).
The Irish Narrow Gauge, drawing No. 6 (7 mm scale).
Railway Modeller, Jan. 1986, p31 (4 mm scale).
4-4-0T No. 1 *Gabriel* (Peckett & Sons 1906)
The Schull & Skibbereen Railway, p172 (4 mm scale).
Model Railway News, July 1969, p328 (3 mm scale).
4-4-0T No. 3 *Kent* (Peckett & Sons 1914)
The Schull & Skibbereen Railway, p180 (4 mm scale).
0-4-4T No 6 *The Muskerry* (Thos Green & Sons, 1893)
The Schull & Skibbereen Railway, p186 (former C&MLR No. 6 *The Muskerry*).

Carriages
No. 2: 4-wheel, all-first (Dick, Kerr & Co. 1888)
The Schull & Skibbereen Railway, p192 (4 mm scale, as at opening of tramway); p193 (4 mm scale, as at Aug. 1946).
Model Railway Constructor, October 1968, p 310/11 (4 mm scale).
No. 4: 4-wheel, all-third (Dick, Kerr & Co. 1888)
Model Railway Constructor, October 1968, p 310/11 (4 mm scale).
No. 8: 4-wheel, all-third (Dick, Kerr & Co. 1912)
The Schull & Skibbereen Railway, p198 (4 mm scale).
No. 5: bogie composite first/third (Gloucester Railway Carriage & Wagon Co. 1890)
The Schull & Skibbereen Railway, p199 (4 mm scale, as rebuilt 1908).
No. 7: Bogie, end platform, saloon third (Gloucester Railway Carriage & Wagon Co. 1903)
The Schull & Skibbereen Railway, p203 (4 mm scale).
The Narrow Gauge, July 1970, No. 54; pp18/19 (7mm scale).

Goods Vehicles
The Schull & Skibbereen Railway, Boyd, J.I.C., Oakwood Press, Usk, Monmouthshire, 1999. ISBN 0-85361-534-9 (4 mm scale).
Nos. 1-5: 4-wheel, 4-plank centre drop door open (Dick, Kerr & Co. 1886)
The Schull & Skibbereen Railway, p206 (4 mm scale).
Nos. 6-9: 4-wheel timber bolster wagons (Dick, Kerr & Co. 1886)
The Schull & Skibbereen Railway, p207 (4 mm scale).
Nos. 10-35: 4-wheel cattle wagons (Dick, Kerr & Co. 1886)
The Schull & Skibbereen Railway, p208 (4 mm scale).

Nos. 36-45: 4-wheel covered wagons (Dick, Kerr & Co. 1886)
The Schull & Skibbereen Railway, p210 (4 mm scale).
No. 46: 4-wheel Goods Brake Van (Dick, Kerr & Co. 1886)
The Schull & Skibbereen Railway, p214 (4 mm scale).
Nos. 47-49: 4-wheel box vans (Dick, Kerr & Co. 1886)
The Schull & Skibbereen Railway, p215 (4 mm scale).
Nos. 50-51: 4-wheel open dropside ballast wagons (Skibbereen 1908)
The Schull & Skibbereen Railway, p216 (4 mm scale).
No. 52: 4-wheel large cattle van (Skibbereen 1909)
The Schull & Skibbereen Railway, p217 (4 mm scale).
Nos. 53-54: 4-wheel passenger brake van (Skibbereen 1909)
The Schull & Skibbereen Railway, p218 (4 mm scale).
Nos. 55-60: 4-wheel large fitted box van (Skibbereen 1909-12)
The Schull & Skibbereen Railway, p219 (4 mm scale).

Cork, Blackrock & Passage Railway

Locomotives
2-4-2T Nos, 4-7 (Neilson, Reid 1899, Works Nos. 5561-5564)
Narrow Gauge Railways of Ireland, p49 (No. 5 as on CB&PR. Side elevation, 3mm scale).
Narrow Gauge Album, p100 (as No. 5 on CB&PR. Side elevation, 3mm scale).
The Modeller Book of Narrow Gauge, p17 (4 mm scale).
The Irish Narrow Gauge, drawing No. 9 (7 mm scale).
Modelling the Irish Narrow Gauge, p18 (4 mm scale).
Railway Modeller, November 1958, p258 (4 mm scale).
The Cork, Blackrock & Passage Railway, p51 (No. 5. 4 mm scale).
Narrow Lines, April 1983, No. 20, p11 (7 mm scale).

Goods Vehicles
4-wheel goods brake vans (as Nos. 190L/191L on C&LR)
Model Railways, December 1971, p225 (4 mm scale).
4-wheel 3-plank centre drop door open (as No. 189L on C&LR)
Model Railways, December 1971, p224. (4 mm scale).

Cork & Muskerry Light Railway

Locomotives
4-4-0T No. 4 *Blarney* (Hunslet Engine Co. 1919, Works No. 1200)
Narrow Gauge Railways of Ireland, p11 (3 mm scale).
Railway Modeller, February 1985, p81 (7 mm scale).
The Irish Narrow Gauge, drawing No. 3 (7 mm scale).
Modelling the Irish Narrow Gauge, p12, D. Lloyd. (7 mm scale).
The Cork & Muskerry Light Railway, p73 (5.5 mm scale) (reproduced from *Railway Modeller* 1985).
0-4-4T No 6 *The Muskerry* (Thos Green & Sons, 1893; Works No. 200)
The Schull & Skibbereen Railway, p186 (as No. 6s on Schull & Skibbereen) and p185 (CIÉ line drawing).

Bibliography

General

Books
The Light Railway Handbook, Kidner, R.W., (collected edition including Light Railway Handbooks Nos. 1-6 and 8). Oakwood Press first edn Dec. 1938 (2nd revised edition 1950; 3rd revised edition 1958; 4th revised edition 1965; 5th edition reprinted, 1971).
Also published as individual handbooks:
Three-Foot Gauge Railways of Northern Ireland, Light Railway Handbooks No. 5.
Light and narrow gauge locomotives, Light Railway Handbooks No. 7.
The Light Railways of Eire, IOM and Channel Islands. Light Railway Handbooks No.6.
Narrow Gauge Railways of Ireland, H. Fayle, Greenlake Publications London. 1946 (republished by S.R. Publishers, Wakefield, 1970, ISBN 0-85409-627-2).
The ABC of Irish Locomotives, Clements, R.N., & Robbins, J.M., Ian Allan, London (1949).
Lines of Character, Rolt, L.T.C. & Whitehouse P.B, Constable & Co., London (first edn 1952).
Ulster Tramways and Light Railways, McNeill, D.B., Belfast Museum & Art Gallery (Publication No. 156).
Narrow Gauge Album, Whitehouse, P.B. & Allen, G.F., Ian Allan, London (1957).
ABC of Narrow Gauge Railways, Davies, W.J.K., Ian Allan, London (1961).
On The Narrow Gauge, Whitehouse, P.B., Thos Nelson & Sons Ltd (1964).
Irish Railway Album, Boocock, C.P., Ian Allan, London (1968), ISBN 0-71100-043-3.
Railway History in Pictures: Ireland Vol. 1., McCutcheon, A., David & Charles, Newton Abbot (1969), ISBN 0-6780-5548-3.
Railway History in Pictures: Ireland Vol 2., McCutcheon, A., David & Charles, Newton Abbot (1969). ISBN 0-7153-4998-8.
Irish Railways since 1916, Baker, M.H.C., Ian Allan, London (1972), ISBN 0-71100-0282-7.
Outline of Irish Railway History, Casserley, H.C., David & Charles, Newton Abbot (1974), ISBN 0-7153-6377-8.
Irish Railways in the Heyday of Steam, Casserley, H.C., Bradford Barton, Truro (1979), ISBN 0-85153-347-7.
Narrow Gauge Story, Hendry, R.P., Hillside Publishing Co. (1979), ISBN: 0-90509-331-1.
The Irish Narrow Gauge Railway, Prideaux, J.D.C.A., David & Charles, Newton Abbot (1981), ISBN 0-7153-8071-0.
Irish Steam, Nock, O.S., David & Charles, Newton Abbot (1982), ISBN 0-7153-7961-5.
Narrow Gauge Charm of Yesteryear, Peters, I., Oxford Publishing Co. (1976), ISBN 0-90288-865-X.
Narrow Gauge Railways of the British Isles, Whitehouse, P.B., & Snell J.B., Book Club Associates, London (reprint by arrangement with David & Charles Ltd, 1984), ISBN 0-7153-8523-2.
Britain's Light Railways, Burton, A., Scott-Morgan, J., Moorland Publishing (1985), ISBN 0-86190-146-0
Great Days of the Country Railway, Thomas, D. St J, & Whitehouse, P.B., David & Charles, Newton Abbot (1986), ISBN 0-71531-379-7.
The Modeller Book of the Narrow Gauge, Lloyd, D., Peco Publications, Beer, Seaton, Devon (1986), ISBN 0-900586-00-1.
The Irish Narrow Gauge (Narrow Lines Extra No. 6), 7mm Narrow Gauge Association (1988), ISBN 0-95133000-0-4. Modellers drawings (7 mm scale).
Modelling the Irish Narrow Gauge (A Railway Modeller Special), Lloyd, D., Peco Publications, Beer, Seaton, Devon (1989), ISBN 0-900586-15-X.
Encyclopaedia of Narrow Gauge Railways in Great Britain and Ireland, Middlemass, T., Guild Publishing, London (1991), 1-85260-270-8.
Irish Railways in Colour, Ferris, T., Midland Publishing Ltd, Hinkley (1992), ISBN 1-85780-000-1.
Irish Narrow Gauge Vol. 1: From Cork to Cavan, Ferris, T., Midland Publishing Ltd, Hinkley (1993), ISBN 1-85780-010-9.
Irish Narrow Gauge Vol. 2: The Ulster Lines, Ferris, T., Midland Publishing Ltd, Hinkley (1993), ISBN 1-85780-017-6.
Landscape with Figures, Rolt, L.T.C., Sutton Publishing Ltd (1995), ISBN 0-75090-593-X.
Irish Railways in Colour: a second glance, Ferris, T., Midland Publishing Ltd, Hinkley (1995), ISBN 1-85780-019-2.
Irish Railways Past & Present Vol 1., Baker, M.H.C., Past and Present Publishing, Peterborough (1995), ISBN 1-85895-046-5.
Off the Beaten Track, Irish Railway Walks, Cronin K., Appletree Press, Belfast (1996), ISBN 0-86281-563-0.
Johnson's Atlas & Gazetteer of the Railways of Ireland, Johnson, S.M., Midland Publishing Ltd, Hinkley (1997), ISBN 1-85780-044-3. Highly detailed route maps of all Irish Railways.

Irish Railways: 40 years of change 1956 – 1996, Boocock, C., Atlantic Publishers, Penryn, Cornwall (1997), ISBN 0-90689-975-3.
Irish Narrow Gauge Railways, A view from the past, Baker, M.H.C., Ian Allan (1999), ISBN 0-7110-2680-7.
The Narrow Gauge in Britain and Ireland, Thomas, C., Atlantic Publishers, Penryn, Cornwall (2002), ISBN: 1-90282-705-8.
The Irish Narrow Gauge in Colour, Johnston, N., Colourpoint Books, Newtownards (2003), ISBN 1-904242-13-8.
Modelling Irish Railways, Johnson, S.M., O'Rourke, A.J., Midland Publishing Ltd, Hinkley (2004), ISBN 1-85780-185-7.
Rails Around Cork and Kerry, Baker, M.H.C., Ian Allan (2005), ISBN 0-7110-3158-4.
Broken Rails, Crashes and Sabotages on Irish Railways, Mac Aongusa, B. Columba Press (2005), ISBN 1-85607-925-2.
Rails Around Cork and Kerry: An Irish Railway Pictorial, Baker, M.H.C., Ian Allan (2005), ISBN 0-7110-3158-0.
Saga by rail: Ireland, Boyd, J.I.C., Oakwood Press, (2006) ISBN 0 85361 651 5.
Railways in Ireland. Vol. 1 (Vols 2-4 to be published), Bairstow, M., Amadeus Press, Cleckheaton, W. Yorks (2006), ISBN: 1-87194-431-7.
Lost Lines, Ireland, Welbourn, N., Ian Allan (2006), ISBN 0-7110-3065-0.
Narrow Gauge Rolling Stock: An Irish Railway Pictorial, Coakham, D., Midland Publishing Ltd, Hinkley (2007), ISBN 0-71103-149-5.

Journal Articles

Anon, 'Narrow Gauge Railways in Ireland', *Railway Magazine*, May 1904, Vol. 14, No. 84; pp 508-514.
Livesey, R.M., 'Rolling Stock on the principal Irish narrow gauge railways', *Engineering*, 12th August, 1912; pp 169-176. Reproduced in *Narrow Gauge & Industrial Railway Modelling Review* No. 61, Jan. 2005; pp 178-189.
'Barum', 'Notes on the Railways of Cork', *Railway Magazine*, May 1936, Vol. 80, No. 467; pp 338-343.
Nock, O.S., 'Irish Railway Jottings', *Railway Magazine*, May 1939, Vol. 84, No. 503; pp 313-318.
MacCartney Robbins, J., 'A Railway Tour of Ireland', *Railway Magazine*. May & June 1948, Vol. 94, No. 575; pp 150-152 & 187.
Reynolds, S.B., 'A Round Trip into Eire', *Railways*, April 1949, pp 58-60.
Mace, Revd A.W.V., 'An Irish Journey - I', *Railway Magazine*, May 1955, pp 297-304 & 317.
Mace, Revd A.W.V., 'An Irish Journey - II', *Railway Magazine*, June 1955, pp 389-394.
Casserley, H.C., 'A Trip to Ireland' (10 parts), *Railway World* 1956, Vol. 17 [Part I: Jan, No. 188; pp 9-12. Part II: Feb, No. 189; pp 36-38. Part III: Mar, No. 190; pp 61-63. Part IV: Apr, No. 191; pp 93-95. Part V: May, No. 192; pp 102-106. Part VI: June, No. 193; pp 165-167. Part VII: July, No 194; pp 178-180. Part VIII: Aug, No. 195; pp 209-212. Part IX: Oct, No. 197; pp 264-268. Part X: Nov, No. 198; pp 287-290].
Fry, C.L., 'Irish International Railway and Tramway System', *Railway Modeller* 1956 [Part 1: April, pp 74-78. Part 2: May, pp 108-111. Part 3: June, pp 131-133].
Lee, C.E., 'Railway Gauges and Mileages in Ireland', *Railway Magazine*. May 1958; pp 320-321.
Patterson, E.M., 'The Narrow Gauge in Ireland: Its growth and decay – 1', *Railway Magazine*. Feb. 1961, pp 75-83 & 96.
Patterson, E.M., 'The Narrow Gauge in Ireland: Its growth and decay – 2', *Railway Magazine*, Mar. 1961, pp 169-175.
Lloyd, D.E., 'Railway of the Month: Augher Valley', *Railway Modeller* Apr. 1964; Vol. 15, No. 162; pp 86-91.
Marshal, G., 'Last days on Ulster's Light Railways', *Railway World*, November 1979, pp 568-571.
Dougherty, H., 'Making Narrow Gauge Tracks', *Railway Magazine*, May 1987; pp 292-293.
Carnes, T., 'Gazetteer of Irish Narrow Gauge Drawings, *Narrow Gauge & Industrial Railway Modelling Review* 1993; 7: pp226-231
Coakham, D., 'Narrow Gauge Rolling Stock – an infinite variety', *Railway Bylines*, Feb. 2006; Vol. 11, No. 3; pp 140-143.
Hirsch, S., 'Irish Railcars 1907-2007', *Journal of the Irish Railway Record Society*, No. 164, October 2007.
Moriarty, T., 'History of Railway Legislation 5: Irish Tramway and Light Railway Law, Part 1', *Journal of the Irish Railway Record Society*, No. 164, October 2007.
Moriarty, T., 'History of Railway Legislation 6: Irish Tramway and Light Railway Law, Part 2', *Journal of the Irish Railway Record Society*, No. 165, February 2008.

Antrim NG Lines (Balleymena Cushendall & Red Bay Railway, Ballymena & Larne Railway, Ballycastle Railway, Giant's Causeway, The Portstewart Tramway)

Books
The Giant's Causeway Tramway, McGuigan, J.H., Oakwood Press, Surrey (1964, 2nd edn 1985), ISBN 0-85361-294-3.
The Ballycastle Railway, E.M. Patterson, David & Charles, Newton Abbot (first Edn 1965) ISBN 0-7153-4183-9. Updated edition (with additional material by Norman Johnston) Colourpoint Books, Newtownards (2006), ISBN 1-904242-49-9.
The Ballymena Lines, E.M. Patterson, David & Charles Newton Abbot (first Edn 1968). Updated edition: *The Mid-Antrim Narrow Gauge* (with additional material by Norman Johnston), Colourpoint Books, Newtownards (2007), ISBN 1-904242-70-3.
The Portstewart Tramway (Locomotion Papers No. 41). Currie, J.R.L., Oakwood Press (1968).
Northern Counties Railway, Volume 1 1845-1903, Currie, J.R.L., David & Charles, Newton Abbot (1973), ISBN 0-7153-5934-7.
Northern Counties Railway, Volume 2 1903-1972, Currie, J.R.L., David & Charles, Newton Abbot (1973), ISBN 0-7153-6530-4.
Giant's Causeway, Portrush & Bush Valley Railway & Tramway Co Ltd, McGuigan, J., Ulster Folk & Transport Museum, Belfast (1983), ISBN 0-902588-10-9.
Lost Railways of Co. Antrim, Johnson, S., Stenlake Publishing, Ayrshire (2002), ISBN 1-84033-193-3.
Irish Railways in pictures: No. 4 Giant's Causeway Tramway. Pollard, M., London: Irish Railway Record Society, ISBN 0-902564-07-2.
Locomotives of the LMS NCC and its predecessors, Scott, W., Colourpoint Books, Newtownards (2008) ISBN 1-904242-84-0).

Journal Articles
Anon, 'The Ballycastle Railway', *Locomotive Magazine*. 1903, Vol. 8; p 64.
Anon, '4-4-2 side tank locomotives, Ballycastle Railway', *Locomotive Magazine*, 1909; Vol. 15 (201); p 97.
Lee, C.E., 'The Giant's Causeway Electric Line', *Railway Magazine*, May 1936, Vol. 78, No. 467; pp 355-363.
Parkhill, H.C., 'Some Notable Ulster Tramways', *Railway Magazine*, May 1937, Vol. 80, No. 479; pp 313-314. .
Nock, O.S., .The locomotives of the LMSR, NCC section', *Railway Magazine*, August 1937; p 119.
Bruce, R.H.W., 'The LMSR in Northern Ireland – I. *Railway Magazine'*, May & June 1944, Vol. 90, No. 551; pp 145-150.
Bruce, R.H.W., 'The LMSR in Northern Ireland – II', *Railway Magazine*, July & Aug. 1944, Vol. 90, No. 552; pp 203-205.
Anon, 'The Two-Cylinder Compounds of the Northern Counties Railway', *Railway Magazine*, May & June 1949, Vol. 95, No. 581; pp 159-160.
Brown, H.T., McNeill, D.B., 'The Railways at Red Bay', *Journal of the Stephenson Locomotive Society*, 1950; Vol. 26, pp 108-110.
Fry, C.L., 'The Giant's Causeway Tramway', *Meccano Magazine*, 1950; pp 164-166.
Whitehouse, P.B., 'A Northern Ireland Miscellany', *Railway Magazine*, May 1950, Vol. 96, No. 589; pp 340-342.
Boyd, J.I.C., 'Glimpses of the Narrow Gauge: The Ballymena, Cushendall & Red Bay Railway', *Railways*, Vol. 11, No. 128, December 1950; p 219.
Patterson, E.M., 'County Antrim's last narrow gauge line', *Meccano Magazine* July 1951, Vol. 36, No. 7; p 310.
Boyd, J.I.C., 'The Ballycastle Railway', *Railway Magazine*, May 1952; pp 338-343.
Boyd, J.I.C., 'Glimpses of the Narrow Gauge: The Portstewart Tramway', *The Railway World*, Mar. 1953; Vol. 14, No. 3; p 158.
Boyd, J.I.C., 'Glimpses of the Narrow Gauge: Ballycastle Railway 4-4-2T engines', *Railway World*, July 1954; Vol. 15, No. 7; p 158.
Newham, A.T., 'The Portstewart Tramway', *Journal of the Irish Railway Record Society*, Autumn 1963; pp 288-295.
Coakham, D.G., 'LMS (NCC) Narrow-Gauge coaches', *Model Railway News* 1964, Vol. 40; p 608.

Londonderry & Lough Swilly Railway

Books

The Lough Swilly Railway, Patterson, E.M., David & Charles, Newton Abbot (first Edn 1964).

The Londonderry & Lough Swilly Railway, Boyd, J.I.C., Bradford & Barton, Truro, Cornwall (1981) ISBN 0-85153-447-3.

The Londonderry & Lough Swilly Railway (Donegal's Railway Heritage Guide No. 2). County Donegal Railway Restoration Society (1996), ISBN 1-874518-02-5.

The Londonderry & Lough Swilly Railway: an Irish Railway Pictorial, Flanders S., Midland Publishing Ltd, Hinkley (1996), ISBN 1-85780-074-5.

Lost Railways of Co. Derry, Johnson S., Stenlake Publishing, Ayrshire (2002), ISBN 1-84033-199-2.

That Old Sinner, The Letterkenny & Burtonport Extension Railway, Sweeney, F., Irish History Press (2006), ISBN 0-9553-184-0-8.

The Swilly and the Wee Donegal, Burges, A., Colourpoint Books, Newtownards (2006), ISBN 1-904242-63-5.

Journal Articles

Anon, 'Lough Swilly Railway 4-6-2T', *Engineering*, 1900, 23rd February. Reproduced in *Narrow Gauge & Industrial Railway Modelling Review* No. 63, Jul 2005; pp 298-299.

Anon, 'The Londonderry & Lough Swilly Ry and its connections', *The Locomotive Magazine*, July 1903; pp 8-10.

Anon, 'Heavy locomotives for the Londonderry & Lough Swilly Ry', *The Locomotive*, October 1912; pp 207-208.

Anon, 'Londonderry & Lough Swilly Railway', *Railway Magazine*, February 1919; pp 72-84.

Jackson, W.N., 'Replacing a Railway: The Londonderry & Lough Swilly Railway', *Railway Magazine*, May 1936, Vol. 787, No. 467; pp 313-318.

Casserley, H.C., 'The Londonderry & Lough Swilly Railway', *Railway Magazine*, May 1938, Vol. 84; pp 376-377.

Baillie Reynolds, S., 'A round trip into Eire', *Railways*, April 1949; pp 58-60.

Longbottom, K., 'By Goods Train to Gweedore', *Railway Magazine*, Nov. & Dec. 1949; pp 353-356 & 363.

Simmons, S.A., 'The County Donegal Light Railways', *Railways* February 1950; pp 23-24.

Prosser, O.H., 'The Londonderry & Lough Swilly Railway', *Trains Illustrated*, December 1951; Vol. IV, No. 12; pp 416-418.

Patterson, E.M., 'Exit … The Londonderry & Lough Swilly Railway', *Railway World*, Mar. 1953; Vol. 14, No. 3; pp 61-63.

Boyd, J.I.C., 'Glimpses of the Narrow Gauge: The Letterkenny & Burtonport Extension Railway', *Railway World*, July 1953; Vol. 14, No. 7; pp 162-163.

Casserley, H.C., 'Closure of the Londonderry & Lough Swilly Railway', *Railway Magazine*, October 1953; pp 701-705 & 708.

Patterson, E.M., 'The Londonderry & Lough Swilly Railway', *Trains Illustrated*, December 1953; pp 469-471.

Patterson, E.M., 'The Donegal derailments', *Railway World* July 1962; pp 222-226.

Patterson, E.M., 'The Other James Bond. A tale of a stationmaster', *Railway Magazine*, Dec. 1966; pp 690-692.

Patterson, E.M., 'Looking Back at a Vanished Railway: The Carndonagh Extension of the Londonderry & Lough Swilly Railway', *Railway Magazine*, March 1971; pp 124-127.

Dougherty, H., 'Swilly Survival Ensured', *Railway Magazine*, Sept. 1977; p 431.

Halton, P S., 'Lough Swilly Memories', *The Narrow Gauge*, No. 83, Spring 1979; pp 1-7.

Tucker, G.D., 'West Donegal Congested? Government built railways in Co Donegal', *The Narrow Gauge*, No. 120, Autumn 1988; pp 1-7.

Redman, R.N., 'The Pacific tank locomotives of the Londonderry & Lough Swilly Railway', *The Narrow Gauge*, No. 142, Spring 1994; pp 3-7.

County Donegal Railways Joint Committee

Books

The County Donegal Railways, Patterson, E.M., David & Charles, Newton Abbot (first Edn 1962; 2nd Edn 1969; 3rd Edn 1982), ISBN 0-7153-8167-9.

The County Donegal Railways, Patterson, E.M., Pan Books, London (1972), ISBN 0-330-02941-X. (Paperback version of above.)

The Bus Services of the County Donegal Railways 1960-1971, Dougherty, H., Transport Research
   Associates, Dublin (1973).
Through the Hills of Donegal, Carroll, J., South Donegal Railway Restoration Society, Donegal, 1992.
Railway days in Strabane, Strabane WEA Railway Reminiscence Group, WEA Peoples History series,
   Strabane (1994).
The County Donegal Railway: an Irish Railway Pictorial, Flanders, S., Midland Publishing Ltd, Hinkley
   (1996) ISBN 1-85780-054-0.
The Last Days of the 'Wee Donegal', Robotham, R., Colourpoint Books, Newtownards (1998), ISBN 1-
   898392-43-9.
The County Donegal Railway, A Visitor's Guide, County Donegal Railway Restoration Society (1999),
   ISBN 1-874518-04-1.
Call us back to Donegal, Piercy, J., Author (2000), ISBN 0-9514715-9-7.
The 'Wee Donegal' revisited, Robotham, R., & Curran, J., Colourpoint Books, Newtownards (2002),
   ISBN 1-904242-02-2.
Lost Railways of Co. Derry., Johnson, S., Stenlake Publishing, Ayrshire (2002), ISBN 1-84033-199-2.
The County Donegal Railways Companion, Crombleholme, R., Midland Publishing Ltd, Leicester (2005),
   ISBN 1-85780-205-5.
The Swilly and the Wee Donegal, Burges, A., Colourpoint Books, Newtownards (2006), ISBN 1-904242-63-5.
Lost Railways of Co. Donegal, Johnson, S., Stenlake Publishing, Ayrshire (2008), ISBN 1-84033-427-2.

Journal Articles
Anon, 'Six-coupled bogie tank locomotive, Donegal Railway', *The Locomotive Magazine* 1899; p 136.
Walker, J.F., 'The Donegal Railway', *Railway Magazine*, March 1900; pp 240-246.
Anon, 'Double bogie tank locomotive, Donegal Railway', *The Locomotive Magazine* 16th October, 1905;
   p 171.
Anon, 'New Passenger stock, Donegal Railway', *The Locomotive Magazine* 16th October, 1905; p 181.
Sekon, G.A., 'The Strabane & Letterkeny Railway', *Railway Magazine*, 1909; p 360.
Anon, 'County Donegal Railways Joint Committee, Superheater Tank Locomotive', *The Locomotive*,
   15th July, 1912; pp 141-142.
Anon, 'The County Donegal Railways Joint Committee', *Railway Magazine*, August 1912; pp 129-138.
Anon, 'The Railways and locomotives of the County Donegal Joint Committee (part I)', *The
   Locomotive* 15th May, 1919; pp 66-68.
Anon, 'The Railways and locomotives of the County Donegal Joint Committee (part II)', *The
   Locomotive* 14th June, 1919; pp 87-90.
Salter, R.W.A., 'The County Donegal Railways', *The Railway Magazine*, February 1931; pp 125-130.
Gordon-Stuart, C.R., Narrow Gauge lines in Northern Ireland, *The Railway Magazine*, November
   1933; p 375.
Anon, 'Diesel Traction in Ireland', *The Railway Gazette*, 1st December, 1933; pp 836-838.
Anon, 'Locomotive No 1. The Irish Railways, CDR', *Railway Magazine* June 1936; pp 436-437.
Reynolds, S.B., 'A round trip into Eire', *Railways*, April 1949; pp 58-60.
Simmons, S.A., 'The County Donegal Light Railways', *Railways*, Vol. 11, No. 18, February 1950; pp 23-24.
Carse, S.J., 'The County Donegal Railways', *Railways*, October 1951; pp 262-264.
Anon, 'The County Donegal Railways', *The Meccano Magazine* 1950; pp 484-487 & 524.
Carse, S.J., 'The County Donegal Railways', *Journal of the Irish Railway Record Society*, No. 10, Spring
   1952; pp 288-295.
Anon, 'Veteran Irish railcar preserved', *Railway Gazette*, 16th December, 1955; p 703.
Boyd, J.I.C., 'Donegal revisited', *Railway World*, December 1956; pp 315-320.
Smith, W.A.C., 'The County Donegal Railways', *Railway Magazine*, May 1957; pp 297-303 & 350.
Hanan, G.R., 'Railway of the Month: County Donegal', *Railway Modeller* July 1959; Vol. 10, No. 105;
   pp 150-153.
Curran, B.L., 'Steam and Diesel in Donegal', *Railway Roundabout*, 1960 pp 60-63.
Lynch, P.J., 'Recalling the heyday of the Donegal line', *The Meccano Magazine* February 1960; pp 271-
   272 & 318.
Newcombe, N.W., 'The end of the Donegal Railway', *Railway World* June 1960; pp166-170.
Thompson, G.R., 'The last days of the County Donegal', *Trains Illustrated*, Summer Annual 1960; pp 41-49.
Fry, C., 'History on the Narrow Gauge, Part one, County Donegal Railbus', *Model Railway
   Constructor*, July 1961, No. 28; pp 163-164.
Davies, W.J.K., 'Light Railway Notes (Killybegs)', *Railway World*, August 1961, Vol. 22, No. 255; pp
   277-278.
Patterson, E.M., 'The Ford railbuses of the DVLR and where they went', *Railway World*, January 1962;
   pp 17-18.

Patterson, E.M., 'The Donegal derailments', *Railway World*, July 1962; pp 222-226.
Hanan, G.R., 'County Donegal (Killybegs)', *Railway Modeller*, March 1963; pp 50-53.
Anon, 'County Donegal Remains', *Railway Magazine*, February 1969; pp 104-105.
Gardner, J.A., 'County Donegal Railway Wagons (part I)', *Model Railways*, May 1973; pp 243-244.
Gardner, J.A., County Donegal Railway Wagons (part II), *Model Railways*, June 1973; pp 277-278.
Anon, 'County Donegal Railcar Preserved', *Railway Magazine*, November 1974.
Anon, 'Donegal Locomotive at Londonderry', *Railway Magazine*, March 1975.
Anon, 'A Strabane & Letterkenny Railway Working Timetable of 1955', *Narrow Gauge Times*, No. 2 Spring 1976; pp 35.
Carse, S.J., 'Co. Donegal Railway Wagons 1906-1959', *Journal of the Irish Railway Record Society*, 1976, No. 72; pp 234-240.
Lloyd, D.J., 'The County Donegal Revival', *Narrow Gauge Times*, No. 5 Winter 1976-7; pp 6-9.
Ellis, C. Hamilton, 'Strabane in 1947', *Railway Magazine* ,April 1977, p 191.
Dougherty, H., 'Glenties', *Railway Modeller*, May 1978; pp 145-146.
Dougherty, H., 'Last railway in County Donegal', *Railway Magazine*, December 1978; pp 588-589.
Carse, S.J., 'A new coach for the Donegal Railway', *Model Railways*, February 1979; pp 116-117.
Dougherty, H., 'Glenties Mark II', *Railway Modeller*, March 1980; pp 90-91.
Carse, S.J., 'CDRJC Coaching Stock', *Journal of the Irish Railway Record Society* No. 83, October 1980; pp 129-134.
Anon, 'The Railcars of the County Donegal Joint Committee', *Railway Times*, No. 20, Spring 1980; pp 30-31.
Stretch, E.K., 'Donegal in a day', *The Narrow Gauge*, No. 97, Autumn 1982; pp 4-7.
Lloyd, D., 'Irish Giants, Irish Narrow Gauge - part 1', *Railway Modeller*. Dec. 1984; pp 488-489.
Lloyd, D., 'Irish Narrow Gauge - 7, Donegal Greyhounds', *Railway Modeller*, July 1986; p 282.
Lloyd, D., 'Irish Narrow Gauge - 9, CDR Drewry Railcar, *Railway Modeller*, February 1987; p 81.
Lloyd, D., Irish Narrow Gauge - 10, CDR Early Railcars', *Railway Modeller*, September 1987; p 386-387.
Carse, S.J., 'Motive Power of the CDR - 1', *Journal of the Irish Railway Record Society*, No. 104, October 1987; pp 288-295.
Lloyd, D., 'Irish Narrow Gauge - 11, Pioneer Railcar', *Railway Modeller*, November 1987 p 478.
Lloyd, D., 'Irish Narrow Gauge - 12, CDR Intermediate Railcars', *Railway Modeller*, December 1987; p 526/7.
Lloyd, D., 'Irish Narrow Gauge - 13, CDR modern railcars', *Railway Modeller*, January 1988; p 35.
Carse, S.J., Motive Power of the CDR - 2', *Journal of the Irish Railway Record Society*, No. 105, February 1988; pp 333-339.
Tucker, G.D., 'West Donegal Congested? Government built railways in Co. Donegal', *The Narrow Gauge*, No. 120, Autumn 1988; pp 1-7.
Wilkinson, B., 'Twilight of the County Donegal', *Railway World*, 1989; pp 18-20.
Taylorson, K., 'From Donegal to darkest Africa', *The Narrow Gauge*, No. 129, Winter 1990; pp 3-8.
Tawse, J.G., 'Goodbye to the County Donegal', *Steam Days*, Vol. 1, No. 32, April 1992; pp 193-200.
Tawse, J.G., 'Goodbye to the County Donegal', *Steam Days*, Vol. 2, No. 33, May 1992.
Porter, T., 'The "Little Railways" of old Ireland', *Railway Magazine*, October 1992; pp 53-56.
Langford, J., 'Railcar stopping places', *Journal of the Irish Railway Record Society*, No. 119, October 1992; pp 132-137.
'Donemana 1913', *Journal of the Irish Railway Record Society*, No. 120, February 1993; p 163.
Fitzgerald, J.D., 'Forbes on the L&LSR, 1928', *Journal of the Irish Railway Record Society*, No. 120, February 1993; pp 184-197.
Fitzgerald, J.D., 'County Donegal Railways 1921-23', *Journal of the Irish Railway Record Society*, No. 121, June 1993; pp 210-226.
Hyson, D., 'Return to Donegal', *Back Track* Vol. 8, No. 2, March-April 1994; pp 81-83.
Stott, W.T., 'Irish Baltic Tanks', *Back Track* Vol. 8, No. 2, March-April 1994; pp 98-100.
Bradley, V., 'Go forth - for soon it is too late'. *The Narrow Gauge*, No. 150, Winter/Spring 1996; pp 10-13.
Begley, J., 'The County Donegal Railway Restoration Society. Bringing back the "Wee Donegal".' *Narrow Lines*, No 99, June 1996; pp 14-15.
Begley J., '"Bringing back the Wee Donegal". The County Donegal Railway and its Restoration', *Industrial Heritage*, Spring 1999; pp 2-4.
Robotham, R., 'The story of the "Wee Donegal"', *Narrow Gauge World*, Vol. 1, No. 2, June 1999; pp 7-12.
Robotham, R., 'The story of the "Wee Donegal"', *Narrow Gauge World*, Vol. 1, No. 3, July 1999.
Seward, J., 'Inver, CDRJC. Irish Narrow Gauge portrayed in 7mm scale', *Railway Modeller*, August 1999; pp 370-375.
Seward, J., 'Inver, CDRJC. Irish Narrow Gauge in 7mm scale, Part 2', *Railway Modeller*, September 1999; pp 448-451.

Coakham, D., 'The "County Donegal" – its further extremities', *Railway Bylines*, Vol. 7, No. 8, July 2002; pp 372-379.
Robinson, D., 'Donegal Farewell', *Narrow Gauge World*, Vol. 2, No. 27, July 2003; pp 5-40.
Robinson, D., 'Donegal Farewell', *Narrow Gauge World*, Vol. 2, No. 28, August/September 2003; pp 37-41.
Gee, G.A., 'Donegal. Part 1 – first step in Irish Narrow Gauge modelling', *Railway Modeller*, September 2006; pp546-550.
Gee, G.A., 'Donegal, Part 2 – structures, stock and road vehicles', *Railway Modeller*, October 2006; pp 642-647.
Gee, G.A., 'The Last Baltic Tank, Class 4 No. 11 *Erne*', *Railway Modeller*, October 2007; pp 684-686.

Castlederg & Victoria Bridge Tramway

Books
The Castlederg & Victoria Bridge Tramway, Patterson, E.M., Colourpoint Books, Newtownards (1998), ISBN 1-898392-29-3.
Lost Railways of Co. Tyrone & Fermanagh, Johnson, S., Stenlake Publishing, Ayrshire (2002), ISBN 1-184033-200-X.

Journal Articles
Parkhill, H.C., 'Some Notable Ulster Tramways', *Railway Magazine*, May 1936, Vol. 80, No. 479; pp 313-314.

Bessbrook & Newry Tramway

Books
The Bessbrook & Newry Tramway (Locomotion Papers No. 115), Newham, A.T., Oakwood Press, 1979.
Lost Railways of Co. Down and Co. Armagh, Johnson, S., Stenlake Publishing, Ayrshire (2002), ISBN 1-84033-176-3.

Journal Articles
Fayle, H., 'The Bessbrook & Newry Tramway', *Railway Magazine*, May 1940, Vol. 86, No. 515; pp 285-292.
Beaumont, H., 'The Bessbrook & Newry Tramway', *Journal of the Irish Railway Record Society*, No. 165, February 2008.

Clogher Valley Railway

Books
The Clogher Valley Railway, Patterson, E.M., David & Charles, Newton Abbot (1972), ISBN 0-7153-5605-6. Updated edition: (with additional material by Norman Johnston) Colourpoint Books, Newtownards (2007), ISBN 1-904242-15-4.
In the Days of the Clogher Valley, (Photographs of the Clogher Valley and its railway 1887-1942), Jack Johnston, Friars Bush Press (1987, reprint 1991), ISBN 0-946872-08-2.
Lost Railways of Co. Tyrone & Fermanagh, Johnson, S., Stenlake Publishing, Ayrshire (2002), ISBN 1-184033-200-X.

Journal Articles
Hurst, E., 'The Clogher Valley (Light) Railway', *Railway Magazine*, October 1900; pp 315-320.
Anon, 'Diesel Locomotive, Clogher Valley Railway', *The Locomotive*. January 1934; p 8.
Anon, 'Pertinent Paragraphs: The Clogher Valley Railway', *Railway Magazine*, May 1937; Vol. 80, No. 479; pp 374-5.
'Voyageur', 'The Clogher Valley Railway', *Railway Magazine*, May 1941; Vol. 87, No. 527; pp 193-195 & 212.
Anon, 'Clogher Valley Railway: Further sale', *Railway Magazine*, July & August 1944; p 246 (Notes & News).
McDevitte, T.P., 'The Clogher Valley Railway', *Trains Illustrated:Railway Heritage*, No. 57 Jan.-Mar. 1986; pp 35-37.
Boyd, J.I.C., 'Glimpses of the Narrow Gauge: The Clogher Valley Railway', *Railway World*, Jan. 1956, Vol. 17, No. 188; p 24.
Anon, 'Dismantling the Clogher Valley Railway', *Railway Gazette*, March 1960; p 369.

Cavan & Leitrim Railway

Books
The Cavan & Leitrim Railway, Flanagan, Patrick J., David & Charles, Newton Abbot (1966), ISBN 0-
    7153-8167-9.
The Cavan & Leitrim Railway, Flanagan, Patrick J., Pan Books (1972 paperback, reproduction of
    above) ISBN 0-330-02942-8.
The Cavan & Leitrim Railway - the last decade. An Irish Railway Pictorial. Ferris, Tom, & Flanagan,
    Patrick J., Midland Publishing Ltd, Hinkley (1997) ISBN 1-85780-073-7.
Smoke Amidst the Drumlins, Burges, A., Colourpoint Books, Newtownards (2006), ISBN 1-904242-62-6.

Journal Articles
Kirkland, R.K., 'The Cavan & Leitrim Railway', *Railway Magazine*, May 1951, Vol. 97, No. 601; pp
    339-345.
Powell, A.J., 'Cavan & Leitrim Railway: Narrow Gauge Composite Coach', *Model Railway News*,
    August 1953; pp 166-167.
Powell, A.J., 'Cavan & Leitrim Railway: Narrow Gauge 4-wheeled Passenger Brake Van', *Model
    Railway News*. January 1955; Vol. 31, No. 361; pp 8-9.
Boyd, J.I.C., 'Glimpses of the Narrow Gauge: The Cavan & Leitrim Railway', *Railway World*, Nov.
    1955; Vol. 16, No. 11; pp 257-258.
Powell, A.J., 'Cavan & Leitrim Railway: Narrow Gauge Open Wagons', *Model Railway News*,
    February 1956; pp 28-29.
Casserley, H.C., 'A Trip to Ireland, Part VIII', *Railway World*, Aug. 1956, Vol. 17 No. 195; pp 209-212.
Powell, A.J., 'Cavan & Leitrim Railway: Standard covered goods vans', *Model Railway News*, April
    1957; pp 94-95.
Emslie, J.A.N., 'For Narrow Gaugers', *Railway Modeller*, May 1958; Vol. 9, No. 91; pp 110.
Lynch, P.J., 'The Cavan & Leitrim Railway', *The Meccano Magazine*, April 1961, Vol. XLVI, No. 5; pp
    88-89.
Coakham, D,G., 'Narrow Gauge Miscellany', *Model Railway News*, July 1963; pp 267-269.
Gardner, J.A., 'The Cavan & Leitrim Section of CIE (Wagon Page), *Model Railways*. December 1971;
    pp 223-225.
Bradley, V., 'Go forth - for soon it is too late', *The Narrow Gauge* No. 150, Winter/Spring 1996; pp 10-13.
Coakham, D., 'The Cavan & Leitrim Railway', *Railway Bylines*, November 1999; pp 540-547.

West Clare Railway

Books
In the Tracks of the West Clare Railway, Linehan, E., The Mercier Press (1990) ISBN 0-85342-909-X.
    Description of a walking journey over the remains of the line almost 30 years after closure.
The West Clare Railway, Taylor, P., Plateway Press (1994) ISBN 1-871980-16X.
The West Clare Railway, An Irish Railway Pictorial, Taylor, J., Midland Publishing Ltd, Hinkley (2002)
    ISBN 1-85780-073-7.

Journal Articles
Anon, 'Locomotives of the West and South Clare Rys', *The Locomotive Magazine*, April 1901; Vol. 6
    (64): pp 64-65.
Anon, 'Locomotives of the West and South Clare Rys. Part 2', *The Locomotive Magazine*, May 1901;
    Vol. 6 (65); pp 82-83.
Anon, 'Six-coupled bogie locomotive, West Clare Ry', *The Locomotive Magazine*, November 1903; p 301.
Anon, '4-6-0 Tank Locomotives, West Clare Railway, Ireland', *The Locomotive*, April 1923; pp 94-95.
Anon, 'Drewry Railcars, Great Southern Railways of Ireland', *The Locomotive*, October 1928; pp 315-316.
Fayle, H., 'The West Clare Railway', *Railway Magazine*, May 1939, Vol. 84, No. 503; pp 339-345.
Boyd, J.I.C., 'Once daily and Once Monthly', *Railways*, Mar. 1951, Vol. 12, No. 131; pp 50-52.
Whitehouse, P.B., 'The West Clare Railway', *Railway Magazine*, May 1951, Vol. 97, No. 601; pp 296-
    298, 345.
Hyland, L., 'The West Clare Railway', *Journal of the Irish Railway Record Society*, Aug. 1954, No. 15; pp
    248-262.
Patterson, E.M, 'Farewell to the Irish Narrow Gauge', *The Meccano Magazine*, April 1961, Vol. XLVI,
    No. 5; pp 142, 148.
Boyd, J.I.C., 'The West Clare Railway', *Railway World*, August 1961, Vol. 22, No. 255; pp 272-276.

Anon, 'Working to Rule, A Christmas Story with illustrations by courtesy of the West Clare Railway Company', *Railway World*, January 1962; pp31-33.
Gardner, J.A., 'The West Clare Section of CIE (Wagon Page) *Model Railways*, January 1972; pp 278-281.
Gardner, J.A., 'The West Clare Section of CIE (Wagon Page). Part 2', *Model Railways*, February 1972; pp 348-349.
Carter, R.S, West Clare Railway (EIRE) 3 ft gauge diesel-mechanical locomotive', *Model Railways*, Dec. 1974; pp 604-605.
Smyth, W.A., 'My Service on Irish Railways', *Journal of the Irish Railway Record Society*, No. 83, October 1980; pp 117-128.
Lloyd, D., 'Modern Image, West Clare style', *Railway Modeller*, June 1985; p 249.
Lloyd, D., 'West Clare 2-6-2T', *Railway Modeller*, October 1986; p 433.
Baker, A.C., 'Brave little Bagnalls in County Clare', *The Narrow Gauge*, No. 125, Winter 1989/90; pp 3-9.
Baker, A.C., 'Brave little Bagnalls in County Clare', *The Narrow Gauge*, No. 126, Spring 1990; pp 11-19.
Windle, P., 'West Clare 2-6-2T locomotive', *The Narrow Gauge*. No. 141, Winter 1994; pp 27-28.
Taylor, P., 'The West Clare Railway during the troubles', *The Narrow Gauge*, No. 143, Summer 1994; pp 16-25.
Bradley, V., 'Go forth - for soon it is too late', *The Narrow Gauge*, No. 150, Winter/Spring 1996; pp 10-13.

Listowel & Ballybunnion Railway

Books
The Listowel & Ballybunion Railway, (Locomotion Papers No. 33), Newham, A.T., Oakwood Press (1967, 2nd edn 1989), ISBN 0-85361-376-1.
The Lartigue; Listowel and Ballybunion Railway, Guerin, M., Lartigue Centenary Committee, Listowel (1989), ISBN 0-95135-491-4.

Journal Articles
Sekon, G.A., 'The Listowel & Ballybunion Railway', *Railway Magazine*, November 1924, Vol. 55, No. 329; pp 353-359.
Anon, 'The Listowel & Ballybunion Railway', *Railway Magazine*, November 1950, Vol. 96, No. 589; pp 337-338.
Dougherty, H., 'Centenary of "The Lartigue"', *Railway Magazine*, Nov. 1988; p 705.
Neale, A., 'Listowel & Ballybunion Railway Nos. 1-3', *Narrow Gauge & Industrial Railway Modelling Review*, No. 71; July 2007: pp 286-89.

Tralee & Dingle Railway

Books
The Tralee & Dingle Railway, Whitehouse, P.B., Locomotive Publishing Co. Ltd (1958).
The Tralee & Dingle Railway, Rowlands, D., Bradford & Barton (1977), ISBN 0-85153-267-5.
Thro' Rare West Kerry (facsimile copy/reprint in aid of 5T restoration), AnCO Industrial Training Centre, Tralee (1987).
The Dingle Train, Rowlands, D., McGrath, W., & Francis, T., Plateway Press (1996), ISBN 1-871980-27-5.

Journal Articles
Mytton-Davies, C., 'The Tralee & Dingle Railway', *Railway Magazine*, May 1939, Vol. 84, No. 503; pp 319-322 & 337.
Boyd, J.I.C., 'Once daily and once monthly', *Railways*, May 1951, Vol. 12, No. 133; pp 90-22.
Swift, F.N., 'Adventure on the Tralee & Dingle', *Trains Illustrated* (1952); pp 174-176.
Vale, WL., 'The Tralee and Dingle Railway', *Railway Magazine*, May 1955, pp 347-349.
Boyd, J.I.C., 'Glimpses of the Narrow Gauge: T&D 2-6-2T', *Railway World*, Mar 1956, Vol. 17, No. 3; pp 81-82.
Chapman, W,G., 'Three Foot in Four M, The construction of a OOn3 Tralee and Dingle 2-6-2 tank', *Railway Modeller*, May 1962; pp 107-108.
Rowlands, D., 'Bearings and Buckets', *Narrow Gauge Times*, No. 5 Winter 1976-7; pp 4-6.
Dougherty, H., 'Tralee and Dingle in OOn3', *Railway Modeller*, March 1979; pp 90-91, 96.
Griffin, J., 'Tralee & Dingle back on the rails', *Railway World*, Vol. 54, No. 637, May 1993; pp 41-43.
Foster, D., 'Thro' rare West Kerry', *Ireland of the Welcomes*, Vol. 42, No. 3, May-Jun. 1993.
Rowlands, D.G., 'Roadside rails to the West', *Trains and Railways*, Vol. 3, No. 3; pp 61-64.
Wilkinson, R., 'Relics of the Irish Narrow Gauge in Cork and Kerry', *The Narrow Gauge*, No. 150, Winter/Spring 1996; pp 14-21.

Schull & Skibbereen Railway

Books

The Schull & Skibbereen Tramway, (Locomotion Papers No. 24), Newham, A.T., Oakwood Press, 1964.
The Schull & Skibbereen Railway, Boyd, J.I.C., Oakwood Press, Usk, Monmouthshire (1999), ISBN 0-85361-534-9.
Irish Railways in Pictures, No 3 – The Railways of Cork, Irish Railway Record Society, London (1997), ISBN 0-902564-064.
Lost Railways of Co. Cork, Johnson, S., Stenlake Publishing, Ayrshire (2005), ISBN 1-84033-331-6.

Journal Articles

Fayle, H, & Camwell, W.A., 'Round Roaring Water Bay: The Schull & Skibbereen Light Railway', *Railway Magazine*, May 1940, No. 515; pp 257-262, 273.
Fry, C.L., 'The Schull and Skibbereen Railway', *The Meccano Magazine*. Jan. 1952; pp 44-46.
Boyd, J.I.C., 'Glimpses of the Narrow Gauge: The Schull & Skibbereen Railway', *Railway World*, Dec. 1953; Vol. 14, No. 12; pp 286-287.
Thompson, G.R., 'Schull & Skibbereen RIP', *The Narrow Gauge* July 1970, No. 54; pp 17-20.
McGrath, W., 'Schull & Skibbereen Centenary – a poser on the last train', *The Narrow Gauge*, No. 115, 1987; pp 1-3.
Tucker, G., 'The Schull & Skibbereen Railway', source unknown, *The Narrow Gauge* (c. 1988); pp 41-47.
Gunston, H., 'Which Body at the Wake, A Schull & Skibbereen Mystery, *source unknown, The Narrow Gauge (c.* 1989).
Lloyd, D., '*Erin* (Schull & Skibbereen 4-4-0T No. 4)', *Railway Modeller,* January 1986, p 31.

Cork, Blackrock & Passage Railway

Books

The Cork, Blackrock & Passage Railway (Locomotion Papers No. 49), Newham, A.T., Oakwood Press, 1970.
Cork City Railway Stations [1849-1985], An Illustrated History, Creedon, J.C., Quality Print Cork (1985. 2nd edn 1986).
The Cork, Blackrock & Passage Railway and River Steamers, 1850-1932, An Illustrated History, Creedon, J.C., Cork Quality Print (1992).
The Cork, Blackrock & Passage Railway (Locomotion Papers No. 49), Jenkins, S.C., (incorporating material by Newham, A.T.), Oakwood Press, Headington, Oxford (1993), ISBN 0-85361-4059.
Irish Railways in Pictures No. 3 – The Railways of Cork, Irish Railway Record Society, London (1997), ISBN 0-902564-064.
Lost Railways of Co. Cork, Johnson, S., Stenlake Publishing, Ayrshire (2005), ISBN 1-84033-331-6.

Journal Articles

'Barum', 'Notes on the Railways of Cork', *Railway Magazine,* May 1936, Vol. 80, No. 467; pp 338-343.
Wilkinson, R., 'Relics of the Irish Narrow Gauge in Cork and Kerry', *The Narrow Gauge* No. 150, Winter/Spring 1996; pp 14-21.

Cork & Muskerry Light Railway

Books

The Cork & Muskerry Light Railway (Locomotion Papers No. 39), Newham, A.T., Oakwood Press (1968).
Cork City Railway Stations [1849-1985]: An Illustrated History, Creedon, J.C., Quality Print Cork (1985).
The Cork & Muskerry Light Railway (Locomotion Papers No. 39), Newham, A.T., (revised and expanded by Jenkins, S.C.), Oakwood Press, Headington, Oxford (1992), ISBN 0-85361-4075 .
Irish Railways in Pictures, No 3 – The Railways of Cork, Irish Railway Record Society, London (1997), ISBN 0-902564-064.
Lost Railways of Co. Cork, Johnson, S., Stenlake Publishing, Ayrshire (2005), ISBN 1-84033-331-6.

Journal Articles

'Barum', 'Notes on the Railways of Cork', *Railway Magazine,* May 1936, Vol. 80, No. 467; pp 338-343.
Wilkinson, R., 'Relics of the Irish Narrow Gauge in Cork and Kerry', *The Narrow Gauge* No. 150, Winter/Spring 1996; pp 14-21.